ESSAYS IN
ETHICAL THEORY

ESSAYS IN
ETHICAL THEORY

R. M. Hare

CLARENDON PRESS · OXFORD
1989

Oxford University Press, Walton Street, Oxford OX2 6DP

Oxford New York Toronto
Delhi Bombay Calcutta Madras Karachi
Petaling Jaya Singapore Hong Kong Tokyo
Nairobi Dar es Salaam Cape Town
Melbourne Auckland

and associated companies in
Berlin Ibadan

Oxford is a trade mark of Oxford University Press

Published in the United States
by Oxford University Press, New York

British Library Cataloguing in Publication Data

Hare, R.M. (Richard Mervyn), 1919–
Essays in ethical theory.
1. Ethics
I. Title
170
ISBN 0-19-824439-8

Library of Congress Cataloging in Publication Data
Data available

Set by Oxford Text Systems
Printed in Great Britain by
Biddles Ltd., Guildford and Kings' Lynn

PREFACE

This is the first of several volumes into which I am collecting essays of mine, some already published and some not. I have been sparing in revision, seeking only a certain uniformity of style, mainly by the removal of colloquialisms from those pieces which were originally given as lectures. I have also adopted a simpler and more compact system of references, made possible by the inclusion of a bibliography. In so doing I have left out some references, and also added a few to later works where they may be useful to readers—especially to my book *Moral Thinking*, which gives a conspectus of my views about moral reasoning. Occasionally, as in 'Relevance', I have altered the text where it was unclear or even wrong, or added footnotes. But to nearly all of the papers I can still subscribe, and have therefore not attempted to rewrite them.

As always with such volumes, it has not been possible to avoid some repetition of points that need to be made in the context of each paper. Though I have sometimes substituted cross-references for repeated arguments, to have done so always would have made things difficult for readers. My intention was, rather, that those who did not wish to read all the papers need not; I have therefore left the papers as self-contained as they were, but have tried to arrange them so that related ones are adjacent. A reader unfamiliar with my ideas might do well to start with the first paper, and then, for a bare and simple summary of my views, go on to the eleventh. Papers 1–9 deal mainly with the basics of moral reasoning in the logic of moral language, and with how it enables us to avoid sterile disputes about the so called 'objectivity' or 'subjectivity' of moral judgements. Papers 10–15 are intended to show how, if we avoid these disputes and the errors they lead to, we can found a viable theory of moral reasoning on this basis.

I am grateful to the original publishers for giving permission to reprint where necessary. The place of first publicaton is given at the foot of the first page of each paper. I am also enormously grateful to Angela Blackburn of the Oxford University Press for putting up with the mess inseparable from the compilation of a volume from many disparate sources. I am planning to collect, in other similar volumes, examples of the application of these ideas to reasoning about political morality, religion and education, and bioethics.

R. M. H.

Gainesville
March 1988

CONTENTS

1. Why Do Applied Ethics?   1
2. Some Confusions about Subjectivity   14
3. What Makes Choices Rational?   33
4. Principles   49
5. Supervenience   66
6. Ontology in Ethics   82
7. How to Decide Moral Quesions Rationally   99
8. A *Reductio ad Absurdum* of Descriptivism   113
9. The Promising Game   131
10. Rawls's Theory of Justice   145
11. The Structure of Ethics and Morals   175
12. Relevance   191
13. Ethical Theory and Utilitarianism   212
14. Utilitarianism and the Vicarious Affects   231
15. Some Reasoning about Preferences   245
References and Bibliography   251
Index   257

I

Why Do Applied Ethics?

IT is becoming quite common nowadays to see writers, whether popular or academic, speaking of a happy period which has just dawned, in which philosophers actually try to say something relevant to practical issues. This rather patronizing pat on the back is not really intended as a compliment to our profession. It is intended, rather, as a rebuke to those in the recent past who, allegedly, did *not* say anything relevant to practice. As one who came into philosophy in the Forties with the dominant motive of doing something to help us resolve practical moral problems, I may perhaps be forgiven for finding this a little irritating. My first published philosophical contribution to a practical issue (that of what the duties of citizens are when their governments are acting immorally) was delivered in the Fifties, first in Germany, then on the BBC Third Programme (H 1955*b*); and since then I have published many papers on practical topics. I do not think that I am alone in this among moral philosophers. It is true that some of them have confined their attention to ethical theory; but their theoretical contributions, none the less, may have been valuable indirectly in helping those of us who *were* applying theory to practice to improve the theory. On the other hand, they may not have been valuable, if the theoretical work was poor, as it may have been for reasons I shall be discussing. But what the writers I am complaining about fail to say is that there can be no helpful intervention of philosophers, as philosophers, in practical issues unless the philosophy has been well done. It is not easy to make any useful application of theory to practice unless one has a viable theory, or at least a firm and coherent grasp of the theoretical moves.

Why do people, and why do I, do applied ethics? One

From *New Directions in Ethics*, ed. R. M. Fox and J. P. de Marco (Routledge, 1986).

reason they do it is to make themselves more popular. They are in receipt of public money, and they think they will incur the public's displeasure if it can see no obvious helpful results from their researches. A better reason is that we want to find answers to moral questions and think that philosophy might help. I have found, since I first took up moral philosophy in the hope of tackling some acute moral problems that had confronted me during the Second World War, that it does help. It helps first of all by yielding clarifications on minor points of detail which, nevertheless, can generate major confusions. More importantly, it helps, if one does it well, by the clarification of-moral language in general—its meaning, its uses, and its logic. This is what I meant when I spoke of a viable ethical theory. I think I have one. Other theorists, I am sure, think the same of their own theories. The practical applications of these different theories are what make the theoretical disputes between us of practical importance. There are other theorists who are unlikely to say much that is of practical help. This can be for at least two different reasons. The first is that their theories are of an intuitionist sort which makes appeal to common moral convictions or consensus. These theories will be of little help because on any issue that is in the least contentious there are no common convictions and no consensus to appeal to. Try appealing to common intuitions about the abortion controversy, for example. I do not believe that even prolonged reflection on these intuitions will yield an equilibrium; what we need are firmly established rules of argument based on an understanding of the words we are using when we ask moral questions.

The second handicap which afflicts some moral philosophers can have the same consequence and worse. They may think that there is just no hope of finding an ethical theory—that is an account of the logic of the moral concepts—which will yield rules of reasoning. In default of that, all we can do is exchange intuitions from our pluralist armoury; but then there is no reason why, failing any way of testing the intuitions in argument, the exchange should ever stop. When there are conflicting intuitions battling for control of the conduct even of a single thinker, these philosophers can offer him no comfort or help beyond the armchair comment that such tragedies are one of the facts of life. Philosophers really would deserve a pat on the back if they succeeded instead, as they can if their theory is sound, in showing people how to sort out these conflicts.

There are, then, ways in which philosophers can help resolve practical issues by applying theory to them. But the benefit is mutual. Having taken part in a great many discussions, in working parties and seminars, with people from other professions who face moral problems (doctors and psychiatrists, for example) I have been struck by the way in which, in trying to apply theory to these problems, one gains confidence in certain parts of the theory but sees the need for improvements in others.

It often happens in such discussions that I am not the only philosopher present. There may be, for example, somebody also who is, not a non-descriptivist Kantian utilitarian like me, but a descriptivist intuitionist deontologist, perhaps pretending to be a Kantian. These theoretical differences are largely, though not wholly, independent of any differences on the practical issues. Before we start arguing, our unphilosophical opinions may or may not coincide. But when we do start arguing, it is likely to turn out that I am able to give Kantian utilitarian reasons for my opinions, and the other philosopher is not able to give any reasons at all. He just appeals to the consensus of those present, which, unless the working party has been stacked, may not be forthcoming. When he does produce reasons which seem to have any force with those who did not initially share his opinions, they turn out to be utilitarian reasons—appeals for example to the bad consequences of some policy.

A splendid example of this kind of thing occurring in a more august body is to be found in the report of the British Home Office working party on Obscenity and Film Censorship, chaired by Bernard Williams (1979). In his philosophical capacity, he is well known for the single-minded integrity (in his eccentric sense of the word) of his persecution of utilitarians, which rivals St Paul's of the Christians before his conversion. But the arguments of the Williams Report are utilitarian from start to finish, as has been pointed out by Ronald Dworkin (1981) in a review of the report, and by myself (H 1984*b*).

The key chapter in the report is called 'Harms?', and is a masterly cost-benefit analysis of various proposed legislative measures for the control or decontrol of pornography. Whether this presages any Damascus-road conversion of Williams to utilitarianism I doubt; but it illustrates my point that when anti-utilitarians produce arguments on practical issues they are usually utilitarian ones. The Williams Report is a really excellent piece of work, and it is a pity that, being a bit in advance of public opinion, it has not been acted on.

I could not honestly say the same for the report of another British working party headed by a philosopher, the Warnock Report on Human Fertilization and Embryology (Warnock 1984), which recommends new legislation for the regulation of *in vitro* fertilization and the treatment of embryos. My impression is that Mary Warnock and her working party, unlike Bernard Williams and his, did not set out to find solid arguments leading to conclusions that could be rationally defended. Rather, they looked around among the conflicting opinions that were current in the working party and outside, and tried to find recommendations which would arouse the least dissent. That, no doubt, is why Warnock had so much better a press than Williams, and is likely to be acted on by the legislature. But if one looks at the actual report, one finds again and again, in almost every paragraph, judgements which are mere affirmation without any argument. Many of these have struck the public, and have struck me, as perfectly sensible. But if one asks why they are sensible, one gets no answer from the report. It is significant that on the issues on which the report has been seriously challenged—that is, the issues which are most controversial and on which help would be most valuable—the disputes that have followed the publication of the report have been left unresolved by anything in it. This illustrates very well what I said about intuitionists. The issues I am referring to are those concerning the legalization of surrogate motherhood and the time-period after which embryos should be given legal protection (see H 1987*a*, *b*).

It might be claimed in favour of the Warnock approach that, if philosophers want to influence public opinion, it is more likely to be successful than that of Williams. I am reminded here of what Plato says in the *Republic* (496a ff.) about the difficulties philosophers face in politics. And no doubt Mary Warnock did her usual marvellous job as a practical adviser to government. And she has shown elsewhere (for example in her writings on education) that she is capable of giving reasons (most of them broadly utilitarian) for her views. But she seems not to have made all the *philosophical* contributions to the report that she could have, although such help is badly needed in this area.

Williams, on the other hand, has not yet had much influence; but if anybody now or in the future wants to understand the issues on the control of pornography and make up his mind rationally what should be done about them, Williams has provided a wealth of genuinely philosophical assistance. I would say that his time will come. The only trouble is that events and technology do move on, and may require new discussions and measures; for example, 'video nasties' have come on general sale on the black market in Britain since the Williams Report was published.

I am sure that there will be some philosophers (perhaps the majority) who will claim that they fall into neither of the two classes I have mentioned: the Kantian utilitarians like me, and the intuitionists who cannot provide any reasons for their opinions. All I can say in reply is that in my reading of the philosophical literature on practical issues (although I have not read enough of it to speak with authority) I have found that nearly all writers appeal to moral intuitions to a degree which quite destroys their claim to rational assent; and that where reasons are given, they are either covertly utilitarian reasons, or are invalid (e.g. because of suppressed premisses), or else rest on foundations for which themselves no reasons are given. I could also, if space permitted, give my justification for discarding the prevalent dogma, emanating from recent *soi-disants* 'Kantians', and bottle-fed to nearly all beginner students, that Kant and the utilitarians are at opposite poles of moral philosophy and cannot mix. I have shown elsewhere how they can be synthesized (pp. 108, 187; H 1989*a s.f.*).

So, then, one of the main benefits that ethical theory can get from a dose of real practical controversy in the company of practitioners of other disciplines is that we are brought to see the poverty of intuitionism and the appeal to conviction and consensus. Some philosophers, however, react to this experience, not by trying to find a viable theory which *will* yield arguments that can be defended, but by doubting the practical value of theory altogether. They join the pluralist anti-philosophers that I mentioned earlier. This is even more likely to happen in the case of someone who has not had much serious down-to-earth contact with practical issues, but whose education in applied philosophy has been limited to the classroom. It is perfectly true that discussion of practical issues with students may be inconclusive. It may even be corrupting, if badly handled by a philosopher who does not know the theoretical moves well enough to guide students through them to conclusions which they can rationally accept. The students may come to think that absolutely *any* moral opinion can find *some* ethical theory to buttress it. That, to my mind, is not an argument for abandoning theory, but for seeking the best theory, which involves serious discussion of the theoretical issues with one's students. It might also be thought (wrongly) to be an illustration of what Aristotle says (1095^a2), that the young are not a suitable audience for such lectures, because they lack practical experience. Certainly one does not find this happening with an audience of experienced practitioners, unless they have become too exasperated by the antics of bad philosophers. But nor, *pace* Aristotle, does one with the young either, if they are made acquainted in a serious way with the problems.

I may mention lastly another and even more pernicious kind of anti-philosopher, consisting of those whose motives for engaging in these discussions are not really philosophical at all. They have some deep unquestioned conviction, usually religious or political in origin, about, say, contraception or social justice, and, having learnt some philosophy, are prepared to make any eristical move they can think up, not to test the conviction, but to shore it up. To adapt the famous aphorism about politicians and statistics, they use logic as a drunkard uses a lamp post, not for illumination but for support. Some of these are good philosophers who have done excellent work in other fields; but when they come to applied ethics they are not prepared to expose to scrutiny opinions which they are certain are correct.

It might be thought from what I have said so far that my recommendation to philosophers engaged in practical discussion would be the following: discard all appeals to antecedent moral convictions; ascertain the facts from the practitioners; devise, by the theoretical methods available to the moral philosopher (essentially the methods of philosophical logic or conceptual analysis) a viable ethical theory yielding rules of sound reasoning on moral questions; and then reason from the facts in accordance with the rules and try to get the practitioners to follow the reasoning and accept its conclusions. This might be a possible approach to start with, but it suffers from certain disadvantages and is not what I am going to recommend. From experience I have come to see that a much more dialectical approach, in almost the true Platonic sense, is likely to be more fecund.

To begin with, the practitioners do not like to be given a theoretical lecture on moral philosophy, especially if they think you are trying to prove practical conclusions about which they have antecedent doubts. This difficulty will be increased if they are made aware, as they should be, that there are rival theories in moral philosophy which might not yield the same conclusions. But the biggest disadvantage of this procedure is that it cuts the philosopher off from a very important source of useful information. This is information about the moral opinions of those with experience of the issues. To paraphrase what Aristotle said about virtue (1098^b9), we have to examine it not merely in a logical way, but on the basis of what people say about it.

It might be supposed that I would never think that important, after what I have said about the futility of appeals to convictions. But what I am now going to recommend is not an *appeal* to convictions, but rather a study of them in the hope that we might learn something about the concepts, including the moral concepts, that the practitioners are using. It was J. L. Austin above all from whom we learnt that those doing conceptual analysis will make fewer mistakes if they study the words whose use they are investigating in their proper habitat. I am sure that Wittgenstein would have said the same about the study of words *in use*. I have come to see that this is especially true in moral philosophy, but that in moral philosophy there is a peculiar hazard to be avoided. That is the hazard I was warning against when I said that we cannot usefully *appeal* to moral convictions however widespread, especially on issues which are controversial. The 'moral majority' does not have the last word.

What I am recommending is not that we should produce arguments of the following form, as many do: Everybody but a few cranks and Buddhists thinks that meat-eating is all right, so it must be all right. I am recommending something quite different. That is that we should look at the opinions of people, and ask whether, if our theory about the uses of words and the rules of reasoning which they determine were correct, these are the opinions we could expect them to hold. The method is essentially that of Popper (1959): it tests an ethical theory by seeing whether it yields predictions which are false. The predictions are about what moral opinions people will hold; and the basis of them is a series of assumptions about their preferences, their factual beliefs, including beliefs about other people's preferences, the meaning and thus the logic of the moral words they are using, and the correctness and clarity with which they follow this logic. People come to their moral opinions as a result of a number of factors, not all of them rational, and they may be led astray. But one of the factors is the meaning and use of the moral words they are employing; and these generate the rules of reasoning which, if they understand the words, they will follow, perhaps without articulating them.

There is a difficulty here which is common to all such hypothetico-deductive procedures. We are basing our pre- diction on a number of assumptions; and we can test only one of these assumptions at a time, by taking the others as given. In the present case what we are trying to do is to test the assumption about the meaning and logic of the moral words as people use them. We therefore have to take as given the other assumptions just listed. But in fact we may have other evidence for the truth of these, so this is not a fatal objection to the method. We may have evidence, that is, that the people we are examining have certain factual beliefs and preferences, and are to some degree clear-headed and logical.

Given these other assumptions, we can test the single hypothesis that their use of the moral words is as we have assumed. Thus, on the basis of purely anthropological facts and assumptions about the people we are examining, we can test a hypothesis in ethical theory, though not, of course, any substantial moral hypothesis.

There is, however, a possible objection to this procedure which we must now consider. We have been assuming that substantial moral opinions are one thing, and logical theses about the uses of moral words another. Ethical naturalists deny this, but I shall not concern myself with them here (see p. 102). A more serious difficulty is posed by those who challenge us to say how we would discriminate between theses which people hold as a matter of logic (hold as analytically true) and their substantial moral opinions.

If we were not able to make this distinction, then there would be a loophole in the procedure I have been describing. Given information on their moral opinions about particular matters, and the other assumptions I mentioned, we might be able to test hypotheses about (to put it vaguely at first) their ways of moral thinking. But which of these ways were logically imposed, and which of them were substantial moral theses or rules, we should not be able to say.

I propose to leave this difficulty for another occasion (see p. 176 and H 1987*c*), remarking merely that even if we could not perform the required discrimination, as I think we can, we should still be able to make considerable progress in ethical theory by the method advocated. For, on the basis of information about people's opinions on particular matters, and the other assumptions mentioned, we should be able to test hypotheses to the effect that our subjects held some combination of rather high-level moral principles and rules for the use of words or the meaning of concepts. It would remain to sort out these two things from each other (which can be done). But at least we should have tested hypotheses in a combination of moral anthropology and conceptual analysis—hypotheses capable of shedding considerable light in ethical theory. What we should not have tested, let alone proved, would be any substantial *moral* theses. This is what differentiates the proposed method from any form of intuitionism (see *MT* 10 ff.).

We might give the following as an example of the application of the method. Suppose we are trying to test the thesis of universalizability (part of ethical theory). We find that people (for example King David when reproached by the prophet Nathan) do apply to themselves moral judgements which they have just been making about other cases they think similar in the relevant particulars (2 Sam. 12). From the fact that they make these moral judgements, in conjunction with assumptions of the sort mentioned above, we infer that the thesis of universalizability (that is, the thesis that, as people use words like 'wrong', they hold it inconsistent to make varying moral judgements about relevantly similar cases) is compatible with the observed facts of usage.

If other instances are produced with which it is claimed that the thesis is incompatible, then the thesis will have to be tested again on those cases, and its defender will have to show that the cases are in fact not incompatible with it. This, in all the cases I have seen produced, can be done; the cases are only thought to be incompatible with the thesis because those who produce them are confused (MacIntyre 1957; see Frankena 1958). But I am not here defending the thesis— only illustrating the method.

So the moral opinions of people are not a test of *moral* truth; they are, rather, a test of what I called a viable ethical (i.e. *metaethical*) theory. If we find people holding moral opinions different from what the rules of reasoning generated by the theory would justify, this does not in itself refute the theory. But it does raise the question of what *other* factor in their thinking could have led them to those opinions. As I said, the factor need not be a rational nor even a respectable one. They may simply have got their facts wrong, in which case, we hope, they will alter their opinions when they get them right. But it may be that they have deeply ingrained prejudices which are not amenable to reason, like some of the philosophers I mentioned earlier. I am sure that this is true both of some of the opponents of legalized abortion and of some of its defenders. Or it may be that they just have not thought very clearly and so have got into a muddle. All these factors, ignorance, prejudice, and muddled thinking, can reinforce one another.

However, I am not so pessimistic as to think that people, especially educated people, will always fall into these traps. Of such people, the 'moral majority' is not actually a majority, even now. Let me give an example of how public opinion, by sound reasoning, albeit inarticulate, can come to reject a moral opinion that it rationally ought to reject. It is by no means the only example I could give. Before the First World War, the ruling classes of all the major European powers were swayed by a kind of nationalism (misnamed 'patriotism') whose outcome in action led directly to the war. The public, having seen the appalling sufferings caused, came to the conclusion that any set of moral principles that allowed such policies must have something wrong with it. On the question of *what* was wrong, and what principles should take the place of those rejected, the public has not yet made up its mind. Some think they should be pacifists; others, like myself, think that there is a kind of patriotism which we can recommend to the citizens of all countries, not just our own (universalizing our prescriptions), and which will permit the use of force in resisting aggression, but not for national self-aggrandizement (see H 1985). That question is still being argued, as is the related question of what difference it makes that nuclear weapons are now available.

Nevertheless this is, so far as it goes, an example of how the public can, in the course of a generation, reach new moral convictions, or at least reject old ones, on rational grounds. And the grounds are ones which, when fully set out, are completely in accord with my own utilitarian ethical theory. I think that the application of the same style of reasoning could sort out the questions that remain, given more certainty about the facts than we yet possess. But for now all I want to claim is that this is an illustration of the mutual benefit that comes to theory and practice by their interaction. The conclusion (the rejection of nationalism) is one that we should expect people to come to, given their understanding of the moral concepts as set out in the theory, and given also their knowledge of the facts, a reasonable freedom from muddle and prejudice, and their ordinary non-moral preferences, such as the preference not to undergo the kind of sufferings that the two world wars entailed. So the theory has to that extent been tested. That is the benefit for theory. The benefit for practice is that, having provisionally, in Popperian style, tested the theory, we can go on using it in trying to solve the problems that remain.

So then the approach that I favour when discussing moral questions with the practitioners of other disciplines is not the somewhat condescending one that I described earlier, but rather something like this. First of all, find out from the practitioners as much as they know about the facts which generate the moral problems. Then discuss the moral problems with them in a perfectly open way, trying to find out what they think, and the reasons they give. It is my experience that one learns a lot by doing this. The practitioners may not be moral philosophers; but they have had in the course of their work to grapple with the problems; they do understand how to use the moral words, though they may not be able to give a philosophical account of their use that will stand up. So they can be expected to have thought rationally about the problems to the extent that they were free of prejudice and muddle (it would be implausible to accuse them of ignorance, because it is their own field and they have their noses in the problems). The doctors, for example, that I have met on working parties measure up very well to these expectations, unlike many people outside their disciplines who pontificate publicly about such questions. Admittedly, one occasionally meets very prejudiced irrational people; but I have not met them in the working parties I have served on.

Having elicited the opinions of our colleagues and the reasons they give for them, we can then ask to what extent a sound process of reasoning, based on the logic of the concepts that they are using, would yield those opinions. If opinions differ, as they will, then we can go further, and ask which of the opinions would be supported, and which rejected, by such a reasoning process. By the time the argument has reached this stage, it should be possible to explain one's reasoning to the non-philosophers, because they will have learnt something about philosophy in the process, just as the philosopher will have learnt something about medicine. Ideally, opinions will at this point start to converge as the reasons for them become clear, and you may even be able to present a unanimous report.

To sum up then, the chief benefits that ethical theory can get from an immersion in practical issues are two: first, the exposure of the pretensions of intuitionists (whether they call themselves that or not), who think that appeals to convictions or to consensus can carry any weight; and secondly, the testing of ethical theories about the meanings of moral words and the rules of moral argument which they generate, by seeing whether people's actual conclusions, when they are reasoning in favourable conditions, free from ignorance, muddle, and prejudice, tally with what sound argument, in accordance with these rules, would justify. In this way we can hope to establish, at least provisionally, a theory which can then be applied to new problems. Since the testing of the theory will have involved no appeal to any substantial moral convictions, but only to the empirical, non-moral (if you like anthropological) fact that people hold them, we can retain the hope that the same kind of application to new problems, in addition to shedding light on the problems and so helping with practice, will also further test the theory. It is a virtuous spiral.

2
Some Confusions about Subjectivity

THERE is a certain interrelated batch of confusions connected with the expressions 'objective' and 'subjective' as used in ethical theory, and with the words 'objectivism', 'subjectivism', and also 'relativism', used to describe types of ethical theory—confusions which I myself saw to be confusions quite near the beginning of my career as a moral philosopher, and thought I could put behind me. I saw that they were confusions, not by any original thought on my part, but because, as it seemed to me, *everybody* who had thought about the matter had seen that they were confusions. I did not devote more than a few desultory remarks in my own writings to showing that they were confusions, because I thought it unnecessary—instead, I tried to present my views in such a way that the confusions would be avoided. I hoped (naïvely as it turned out) that they would not continue to muddle moral philosophers in the future as they had in the past.

I was sadly disappointed—perhaps because I had not tried hard enough. It is no exaggeration to say that I constantly find these confusions being committed, not only by laymen or beginner students, but by well-established professional philosophers of good reputation. Worse than this, they are frequently made in relation to my own views, and I find myself either called a 'subjectivist', or assailed with arguments which are indeed cogent against theories which are subjectivist in what I think is the most natural sense of that word, but which my own theory was specifically designed to avoid, and does avoid. Perhaps I am not entirely blameless. It is difficult, even though one is oneself clear about a distinction, to avoid using phrases which those who are not clear about it will misinterpret. This is especially true where, in order to link up one's thought with the history of the subject, one uses

From *Freedom and Morality*, ed. J. Bricke (Lindley Lectures, U. of Kansas, 1976).

expressions which have been used by other people (including sometimes people, all of whose views one would not be prepared to endorse). Thus in *LM* 69, 78 I spoke of justifying or verifying moral judgements by reference to a standard or set of principles which itself has to be accepted by a decision; I did not mean that *the fact that* this decision had been made guaranteed, automatically, those moral judgements as correct, but only that it is no use thinking we can be sure about particular moral questions until we have made up our own minds on the moral principles according to which they are to be answered. *How* we are to make up our minds was a question that I left until later, though there are hints about the answer on *LM* 69.

On *LM* 77 I unwisely borrowed from intuitionist writers a rather loose use of the term 'subjectivist', which may have misled some readers into thinking that I am a subjectivist in the strict sense which I shall be using in this paper. And on *LM* 70 I said 'To ask whether I ought to do *A* in these circumstances is (to borrow Kantian language with a small though important modification) to ask whether or not I will that doing *A* in such circumstances should become a universal law.' Kant was hardly a subjectivist, and I did not think that by using his wording with this modification I was expressing a subjectivist view. I had already said on *LM* 6 that ' "I want you to shut the door" is not a statement about my mind but a polite way of saying the imperative "Shut the door" '; and similarly, when we ask what we will should become a universal law, we are not asking a question of psychological fact to be settled by introspection, but trying to make a decision, or, as I say in the next sentence on *LM* 70, asking 'What attitude shall I adopt and recommend?' (*not* 'What attitude do I or will I as a matter of fact have?'). I say also that 'attitude', if it means anything, means a principle of action. The late Professor H. J. Paton was the first person I heard assimilate Stevenson to Kant in this way. The question of *how* we decide what attitude to adopt was, again, left for later.

We have to distinguish between the view that to say that an action is morally right is to accept something, and the view that to say that an action is morally right is to say that, as a matter of fact, you do accept something (or are prepared to accept it, or find it acceptable). We have, in general, to distinguish between the following statements about the illocutionary force of utterances:

   (1) To say '*p*' is to *s*

(where '*s*' stands for some speech-act verb), and

   (2) To say '*p*' is to say that as a matter of fact you *s*, or are *s*-ing.

Thus, we have to distinguish between

   (1¹) To say 'Please pass me the butter' is to make a request,

and

   (2¹) To say 'Please pass me the butter' is to say that you are, as a matter of fact, making a request;

and likewise between

   (1¹¹) To say 'The tide is high' is to state that the tide is high,

and

   (2¹¹) To say 'The tide is high' is to say that as a matter of fact you are stating that the tide is high,

and between other similar pairs. In all these cases, it is a confusion to identify a speech act with that other speech act which consists in the statement that the first speech act is as a matter of fact performed. If, as in (1¹) and (2¹), the first speech act is a request and the second is a statement of fact, they obviously cannot be identical; and even when, as in (1¹¹) and (2¹¹), both are statements, it is perhaps not too hard to see that they are *different* statements, one about the tide and the other about the activities of the speaker. A more sophisticated example of the same sort of confusion is to be found in Foot 1961 (see H 1963*b*: § vi).

It will be noticed that I have myself put this point in terms of speech acts, because I find that it comes out much clearer that way. Mrs Foot and others speak in terms of states of mind or of dispositions to action. But they commit essentially the same confusion in failing to distinguish the statement that somebody has a certain state of mind or disposition from the statement, moral judgement, or whatever it is, which is the expression of that state of mind or disposition. Thus it is one thing to say that I as a matter of fact have a wish for a certain thing, and another to say 'Give me that thing'; one thing to say that I have a disposition to choose objects of a certain sort, and another to say (expressing that disposition) that objects of that sort are good ones.

A possible source of the confusion is my use, a good many times in *FR*, of expressions of the following sort:

> The real difficulty of making a moral decision is, as I have said before, that of finding some action to which one is prepared to commit oneself, and which at the same time one is prepared to accept as exemplifying a principle of action binding on anyone in like circumstances. (*FR* 73)

and:

> What we are doing in moral reasoning is to look for moral judgements and moral principles which, when we have considered their logical consequences and the facts of the case, we can still accept. (*FR* 88)

As I say in my review of Professor Rawls's *Theory of Justice*, however:

> The element of subjectivism enters only when a philosopher claims that he can 'check' his theory against his and other people's views, so that a disagreement between the theory and the views tells against the theory.

The paragraph should be read as a whole (p. 147 of this volume). Mr Urmson (1975: 112) quotes the beginning of it, ignores the rest, and, having misinterpreted it in the usual way, uses it to support arguments for what he calls 'intuitionism' (using the word in Rawls's misleading sense for 'pluralism'); but the view he is arguing for is one I would strongly repudiate, since it is subjectivist in the above sense, and does make the truth of moral views depend on agreement with his own opinions.

I have found such confusions irritating enough to make me look around (though not very systematically) for books or papers in which the distinctions that are necessary are clearly made; and I have not found any, though I am sure that they must exist (I am the world's worst bibliographer). So I thought it would be a useful exercise to set out some distinctions which, I am sure, must be familiar to any competent moral philosopher, but which, apparently, some moral philosophers find it extremely hard to grasp.

Perhaps the best way to approach the necessary distinctions is by distinguishing between two divisions which exist between types of ethical theory. There is first of all the division between what are sometimes called cognitivist and non-cognitivist theories, but which I prefer to call descriptivist and non-descriptivist theories (see p. 97). The pairs of terms do not mean precisely the same: ethical cognitivism is, presumably, if we are to rely on etymology, the view that moral judgements can be *known* to be true; ethical descriptivism is, rather, the view that their logical character is similar to that of other descriptive statements or judgements. I have attempted at some length to define the expression 'descriptive judgement' in *FR* ch. 2; here I shall only say (too summarily) that a statement or judgement is descriptive if its meaning (including its reference) determines uniquely its truth-conditions, and vice versa. Although 'cognitivism' and 'descriptivism' do not mean the same thing, I think that for most people they serve to pick out the same sort of theory; so I shall not pursue the distinction between them.

The second division that I wish to note is the division *within* descriptivist or cognitivist theories between those which are subjectivist and those which are objectivist. I repeat, with all the emphasis I can muster, that this is a division *within* descriptivist theories. It is not the same as the division *between* descriptivist and non-descriptivist theories. This is so obvious a point that to elaborate it might seem tedious; but, taught by bitter experience, I will elaborate it. A descriptivist theory holds that moral judgements are descriptive. To forestall another confusion, I must point out that this means that they are *purely* descriptive, i.e. that the meaning which is determined by their truth-conditions *is* their meaning—there is no other element in their meaning which can remain the same although this descriptive meaning changes, as I have maintained is the case with evaluative statements. I have also maintained that evaluative statements *have* a descriptive element in their meaning; in virtue of this it is perfectly proper to call them true or false. But I mention this point now only to prevent it confusing us; it is not strictly needed at this place in my argument, and we shall return to it later.

To revert, then: a descriptivist theory holds that moral judgements are purely descriptive; but it remains to be said what, according to the theory in question, they are descriptive of. According to a *subjectivist* descriptivist theory, they are descriptive of states of mind, dispositions, etc., of people (usually those who make them); whereas an *objectivist* descriptivist theory holds that moral judgements are descriptive of states of affairs other than states of mind, dispositions, etc., of people. To put this another way: according to an objectivist descriptivist theory, a moral statement is true if and only if some state of affairs obtains other than a state of mind or disposition of some person; according to a subjectivist descriptivist theory; a moral statement is true if and only if some state of mind or disposition of some person obtains.

From this it should be immediately clear that the division between objectivist descriptivist theories and subjectivist descriptivist theories is not the *same* division as that between descriptivist theories *in general* and non-descriptivist theories *in general*. Non-descriptivists must in consistency dissent (and with all the emphasis I can muster I *do* dissent) from the view that moral judgements are true if and only if some state of mind or some disposition of some person obtains. It is not true of any non-descriptivist theory (other than a thoroughly muddled one) that it makes the truth of moral statements depend on what somebody thinks or feels or how he is disposed towards something or other. In so far as a non-descriptivist ethical theory allows that a moral statement can be true or false (and I shall revert later to the sense in which it can allow this) it will hold that its truth or falsity will depend on whether states of affairs obtain *other* than states of mind etc. of people.

I must apologize for rubbing in this point at such tedious length; but the apology is not entirely sincere, because if it were sincere I would desist. I am, however, not going to desist, because it really seems to be necessary, surprisingly, to reiterate this obvious point. I am indeed going to rub it in further by illustrating it in terms of a particular non-descriptivist theory of a very simple sort. This is not a theory which I myself have ever held, though I have often enough been accused of holding it; but I choose it because, being very simple, it illustrates my point very clearly. In particular it avoids complications about the sense in which moral statements can be called true or false, because it holds that they *cannot* be called true or false (unlike my own theory). The theory which I am going to discuss I call *imperativism*. It is the theory that moral judgements are equivalent in meaning to ordinary imperatives. I repeat that I have never held this theory. According to this theory, for example, 'Jones ought to do *A*' is equivalent to the ordinary third person imperative 'Let Jones do *A*' (in Latin '*Jonesius A facito*').

Let us ask whether on such a theory the truth of a moral statement depends on whether some state of mind of some person obtains. It obviously does not, because on such a theory the moral statement 'Jones ought to do *A*' does not have a truth-value at all, being equivalent to an imperative. But this may seem too short a way with the people whose muddles I am attacking. So I am going to put the matter in slightly different terms. I am going to substitute the notions of assent and dissent for the notions of truth and falsity, in the following way. The gravamen of the objection which most of us feel to subjectivist theories of ethics is that they force a person who has assented to the statement that another person is in a certain state of mind to assent, in consistency, to the moral statement that that person is making. For example: if someone says to me 'Jones ought to do *A*', then according to one kind of subjectivism this is equivalent to 'I (the speaker) approve of Jones doing *A*'. According to this kind of subjectivism, therefore, if I assent to the psychological statement that the speaker approves of Jones doing *A*, I am committed in consistency to assenting to the moral statement that Jones ought to do *A*. I forbear to detail the well-known (dare I assume that they are well known?) objections to this absurd descriptivist theory, because my sole purpose is to *distinguish* it from the (equally absurd but different) non-descriptivist theory which I have called imperativism.

The unease that people seem to feel about imperativism,

which gets transferred to more defensible forms of prescriptivism, might be expressed in these new terms as follows. They
think that if imperativism were true, then if somebody said to
me 'Jones ought to do *A*', he would somehow make it
impossible for me to dissent from his statement, provided I
agreed that he had made it. As before, I am putting the
matter in terms of what he *said*, rather than of what he *thought*,
because we can thus more clearly illuminate what is essentially
the same problem. Let us for a moment consider a type of
subjectivist theory which might, if confused with imperativism,
make imperativism appear to have this absurd consequence.
I mean a theory which holds that 'Jones ought to do *A*' is
equivalent, not to the imperative 'Let Jones do *A*' but to the
indicative statement of fact 'I (the speaker) am issuing the
command that Jones do *A*'. Note that this latter sentence has
to be carefully distinguished from the performative 'I *hereby*
issue the command that Jones do *A*'. This explicit performative
(in Austin's terminology) probably *is* equivalent, at least
roughly, to the primary performative, the imperative 'Let
Jones do *A*'. But the factual statement 'I am issuing the
command that Jones do *A*' is not so equivalent. A report that
a command is being issued is not equivalent to the command
itself. Anyone who has any inclination to doubt this should
consider the example of a man who is writing something on
a piece of paper and says 'I am telling the frontier police to
let you through' when in fact what he is writing on the piece
of paper is an instruction to the frontier police *not* to let the
recipient through but to send him to Siberia. Here the spoken
utterance is false; but neither the message actually being
written nor that which it is falsely stated is being written is
either true or false.

In general, utterances are not equivalent to, or even entailed
by, reports that they are being made; and there is no cause
at all (except muddle) to suppose that what is in general false
is true of commands or imperatives. To take an indicative
example: if somebody is writing 'Buffalo is in Canada' and at
the same time says 'I am telling them that Buffalo is in
Canada', what he says with his mouth is true, but what he
says he is saying on paper is false; so how can they be
equivalent? It is true that there are well-known problems

about what is sometimes called 'pragmatic implication'. If I
say, with my mouth, 'I am not saying anything', then what
I do makes what I say false; and, similarly, if I say with my
mouth 'I am saying something', what I do makes what I say
true. In somewhat the same way, if I say 'Let Jones do A',
what I do makes true the statement, which I am not actually
making (though I suppose I might be simultaneously writing
it) 'I am issuing the command that Jones do A'. So there is
this much of a non-logical connection between the command,
and the statement that it is being issued: the issuing of the
command makes the statement true. In the same way, because
of a Gricean 'conversational implicature' that we are sincere
in saying what we say, there is a non-logical inconsistency in
saying 'p but I don't believe that p' or 'Do A but I don't want
you to do A'. But these complications have very little bearing
upon the present argument except that they might muddle
someone. What would have a bearing (a very awkward one)
upon the argument would be if assent to the statement that
the command is issued committed the assenter to assenting
also to the command itself. But there is no reason to suppose
this. I can agree that someone has issued or is issuing a
command, without being thereby committed to assenting to
the command. If someone says 'Let Jones do A', I can, without
any inconsistency, say 'He has said "Let Jones do A"', but let
Jones not do A'. The fact that all these phenomena are
paralleled in the indicative mood shows that they cannot be
relevant to the present discussion.

I therefore take it as established that I can assent to the
statement that a command has been issued without thereby
being committed to assenting to the command itself. It follows
that it would be a complete misunderstanding of even so
wrong-headed a doctrine as imperativism to accuse it of having
the consequence that by merely saying or thinking that Jones
ought to do A, I make it the case that Jones ought to do A.
This consequence, however, might seem to be entailed by
imperativism, if imperativism were confused with the even
more absurd theory which I mentioned just now: the theory
that 'Jones ought to do A' is equivalent to the factual report
'I am issuing the command that Jones do A'.

It is always a little difficult—a little speculative—trying to identify the particular muddles which muddle-headed people are making when they draw conclusions from a theory which it by no means entails. But here is one attempt to say how people can come to think (as undoubtedly some people do think) that imperativists are committed to holding that if I say 'Jones ought to do *A*' everybody has to agree with me (which is the revised version of the earlier doctrine, put in terms of truth and falsity, that according to imperativism one makes moral judgements true simply by uttering them). Suppose that someone says 'Jones ought to do *A*'. Call the person who says this 'X'. I suppose that someone who was not very particular about the opacity of intentional contexts might think that, if I agree that *X* said that Jones ought to do *A*, then I am, according to imperativism, committed to agreeing that *X* issued the command that Jones do *A*. This step in the argument depends on the thesis of imperativism itself, namely that 'Jones ought to do *A*' is equivalent to 'Let Jones do *A*'.

Now according to the *other* theory that I mentioned, and *distinguished* from imperativism, the factual report 'I am issuing the command that Jones do *A*' is equivalent to the moral judgement 'Jones ought to do *A*'. So, if we now switch, confusedly, to this *other* theory and away from imperativism proper, we can take the second step in this muddled argument (waiving, indulgently, the difference between '*X* issued' and 'I am issuing'): having by the first step got by the thesis of imperativism proper from '*X* said that Jones ought to do *A*' to '*X* issued the command that Jones do *A*' we can now, by this *other* thesis, get from the latter (from '*X* issued the command that Jones do *A*') to 'Jones ought to do *A*'. So, by this train of confusions, it can be made out that the imperativist is committed to the view that if we agree to the statement that someone has said 'Jones ought to do *A*', we cannot consistently dissent from the statement that Jones ought to do *A*.

I dare say some other train of confusions would do. It may be thought tedious of me to go on so long distinguishing between two ethical theories which nobody in his right mind would hold once he was clear about what they were saying, and establishing that one of them, imperativism, does not have a consequence which some people have thought it had. The point of doing this has been that many people *also* think that the same absurd consequence can be drawn from my own variety of prescriptivism. They do this, either because they confuse my variety of prescriptivism with imperativism (a confusion which is extremely common, in spite of several explicit statements of mine to the contrary, starting with *LM* 2); or because, although they do not make this confusion, they think, rightly, that my theory resembles imperativism in the important respect that according to both theories moral judgements are typically prescriptive, and this resemblance, so to speak, tars my theory with the imperativist brush, and makes it legitimate to draw from it the absurd consequence that you can make moral judgements true, or make it impossible for other people to dissent from them, just by uttering them—a consequence which, by the series of muddles I have just exposed, they think can be drawn from imperativism itself. And that is why I have thought it necessary to go into the muddles at such boring length.

Now let us turn to something a bit less boring and consider another argument which is probably valid against old-style subjectivism (i.e. against the variety of descriptivism which holds that moral statements are really statements about the states of mind of people), but is constantly being raked up in order to attack non-descriptivism, which is quite immune to it. This argument concerns the use of the words 'right' and 'wrong' with reference to moral statements. Now I agree readily that these words are used of moral statements that people have made. We say, for example, that somebody was right in thinking that Jones ought to have done *A*. Those who attack non-descriptivism often try to base an argument on this admitted fact. It is said that, if two people disagree about a moral question, one of them must be wrong. Let us take a particular example. *X* says 'It was wrong to take the money'. *Y* says 'No, it was not wrong'. One of these parties, says the argument, must be wrong; and with this we must agree. But to agree with this is not to admit nearly so much as is sometimes claimed. 'One of the parties must be wrong.'

This, if expanded, means 'Either it is wrong to say that it was wrong to take the money, or it is wrong to say that it was not wrong to take the money'. Let us abbreviate the proposition 'It was wrong to take the money' as '*p*', and the proposition 'It was not wrong to take the money' as 'Not *p*'. What is being maintained, then, and what we have agreed to, is that either it is wrong to say that *p*, or it is wrong to say that not *p*.

Let us see how much an opponent of non-descriptivism can legitimately argue on the basis of this admission. First of all, it can be argued that it follows that the law of the excluded middle applies to some moral statements. For if it is either wrong to say that *p* or wrong to say that not *p*, then (ignoring some obvious complications for a moment) the following proposition must be true: 'Either not *p* or not not *p*'; and by elimination of the double negation and reversing the order we get 'Either *p* or not *p*'. There are some pitfalls here. It has first to be assumed that '*p*' and 'not *p*' are contradictories where '*p*' stands for 'It was wrong to take the money'. Now of course it is notorious that in the case of some moral statements we do not get the contradictory of a given statement by adding 'not' injudiciously to it: for example, 'You ought not to' is not the contradictory of 'You ought to'. I have, however, been careful to choose an example in which this difficulty does not arise. For 'It was not wrong to take the money' *is* the contradictory of 'It was wrong to take the money'. And I have been careful to say that this argument only shows that the law of the excluded middle applies to *some* moral statements. Actually it applies to them all; but only when we are careful about what is, and what is not, the contradictory of a given moral statement. However, this complication need not concern us, because it does not affect the main point I wish to make, which is that this argument, so far, is not going to help the opponent of non-descriptivism in the least, because he has done nothing to show that the law of the excluded middle does not apply equally to imperatives, and therefore has not, by this argument, shown even that moral statements are not equivalent to imperatives. I think myself that the law of the excluded middle *does* apply to imperatives, but this is hardly the place to argue the matter (I have already done it in H 1954 and H 1967).

In order to use this argument to refute non-descriptivism, our opponents will have to extract more from it than the bare fact that the law of the excluded middle applies to moral statements. What more can they extract? One further thing is that we can use the words 'right' and 'wrong' when speaking of moral statements that people have made. Some opponents of non-descriptivism have made a great deal of play with this fact, as they have with the similar fact that we also use the words 'true' and 'false', in certain contexts, of moral statements. But there is no reason why a non-descriptivist should not readily admit that these words are used in speaking of moral statements, provided at any rate that he is prepared, as most non-descriptivists have been since Stevenson, to allow that moral statements do have, as *one* element in their meaning, what is usually called 'descriptive meaning' (see p. *LM* 117). For it may be this element to which we are adverting when we call a moral statement true or false; and this does not prevent there being other, non-descriptive elements in its meaning, which are sufficient to make it altogether misleading to call it a descriptive statement *tout court*. Thus, if I have been saying that a man is a good man because I think he spends all his weekends working as a scoutmaster, but then discover that that was another man of the same name—*this* man spends all his weekends seducing other men's wives—having discovered that he does not in fact possess the characteristics which, according to the standards which I and my listeners share, are the criteria for being called a good man, I may well say, adverting to the descriptive meaning of the term, that what I had been saying was false, or not true. But there is nothing in this which need disturb a judicious non-descriptivist.

What I have just said about 'true' and 'false' might, I think, be said about 'right' and 'wrong' in some of their uses. It may be that in some contexts when we say that the moral statement that somebody has made was right, or that he was right in making it, all we mean is that the subject of the statement does have the characteristics ascribed to it by his statement, if that is taken in its accepted descriptive meaning, or even with some other descriptive meaning, provided that it is obvious from the context what we are taking this to be. Thus, if somebody has said 'Jones is a bad man', I may say 'That's right' or 'You are right', meaning no more than that Jones does indeed have those characteristics (for example a habit of seducing other people's wives at weekends) which are commonly regarded, or regarded by us the parties to the conversation, as sufficient criteria of badness in men.

Although, however, I think that this may be the whole story with the word 'true', I cannot believe that it is with the word 'right'. For we do sometimes seem to use the words 'right' and 'wrong' of moral statements when we are not adverting to the descriptive meanings of the words used in the statements—and even when it is their descriptive meanings themselves which are in dispute. For example, suppose that a pacifist is arguing with a militarist, and says 'You are not right to say that it is glorious to mow down the enemy in swathes with a machine-gun'; it need not be the case that the two parties are in agreement about the descriptive meaning of the word 'glorious' (about the necessary and sufficient criteria for the application of the word), and are disputing merely about whether the act of mowing down the enemy in swathes does have the characteristics specified. It is much more likely that they are in fundamental disagreement about what characteristics acts have to have before one is entitled to call them glorious.

A move that might be tried, and which I was at one time inclined to make, is the following: we might say that sometimes the function of the word 'right' is simply to express agreement with what has been said, and similarly that of the word 'wrong' to express disagreement. So if someone has said 'Shut the door', I can express agreement by saying 'That's right'; and this is as if I had repeated the same words 'Shut the door'. Similarly if I had said 'That's wrong', this would be tantamount to repeating the words with the word 'not' inserted: 'Shut not the door', or, in modern idiom, 'Don't shut the door'. So, at any rate, it might be claimed; and the claim would receive support from the usage, now very common, by which 'Right' is used almost as the equivalent of 'Yes'. The usage is, unfortunately, misleading as to the logical properties of 'Right' in most of its other uses. If this move were admissible, we could say that the fact that we can use the words 'right' and 'wrong' of something that somebody has said tells us very little indeed about the logical character of what he has said; the fact, for example, that when a man has uttered a moral statement we can say that he was right or wrong does not even show that moral statements are not equivalent to plain commands; for we can agree with or disagree with, associate ourselves with or dissociate ourselves from, even plain commands, and use the words 'right' and 'wrong' for expressing this agreement or disagreement, as this example shows.

But this move will not quite do, for a reason which it will be interesting to examine. It is connected with the 'universalizability' of statements containing the words 'right' and 'wrong'. The thesis is now familiar and generally accepted that in moral and other evaluative contexts the words 'right' and 'wrong', like other value-words, give to the statements in which they occur a covertly universal character. When I say that a man acted rightly I imply that there is some universal moral principle according to which his act was right. I will not now go into the complications and confusions which easily arise in connection with this thesis, because I have tried to sort them out in *FR* ch. 3 (see also pp. 66 ff.). I merely want to point out that we have here a particular case of universalizability.

When I say, of something that somebody has said, that it was right, or that *he* was right, I am not merely expressing my agreement with him, or associating myself with what he has said—as I would be if I repeated his words after him. I am implying that his utterance conforms to some principle or standard, which I am invoking. What sort of principle this is will vary with the type of utterance in question; but in all cases to cite it would be to give the reason why the utterance was called right—and unless we are prepared to admit the propriety of the demand for such a reason, we cannot (except in the somewhat degenerate usage mentioned earlier) properly use the word 'right'. This is not so with the word 'Yes', used to express agreement, or with a mere repetition of the utterance. If somebody says 'Shut the door', and I then say 'Yes, shut the door', I may have no reason at all for saying this—though of course I normally will have; but if instead I say 'That's right, shut the door', I am doing more than merely associating myself with the command or request; I am implying that the command to shut the door conforms to some principle or standard. I could properly be asked 'Why is it right?'; and, if asked, I could not properly reply 'No reason at all'. The reason might be, that doors should be shut when there is a draught, or when privacy is lacking; these are both principles, and are universal. I think that (apart from the 'degenerate' usage mentioned earlier) 'right' and 'wrong' are not normally used unless there is some such reason or principle in the background.

However, it still will not be the case that we can learn very much about the logical character of moral judgements by observing that we can use 'right' and 'wrong' of them. Perhaps we can learn a little. We noticed earlier that, when two people make mutually self-contradictory moral statements, one of them must be wrong. The question at issue is, How much does this prove about the logical character of moral statements? It proves, I think, that they are not equivalent to simple singular imperatives. For if one man says 'Shut the door' and another says (to the same person) 'Do not shut the door', it is not logically necessary that one or the other of them should be *wrong*. It is, indeed, logically impossible consistently to *agree* with both of them (or, for that matter, to *disagree* with both of them). A man who agreed with both would be saying what would be equivalent to 'Both shut the door and do not shut the door', and would be contradicting himself; a man who disagreed with both would be saying what would be equivalent to 'Neither shut the door nor do not shut the door', and would likewise be contradicting himself. It is on such grounds that I have maintained that 'Shut the door' and 'Do not shut the door' are contradictories, and that the law of the excluded middle applies to them. But it might be the case that the two people who said 'Shut the door' and 'Do not shut the door' were just voicing mutually self-contradictory whims; or it might be that they were two serjeants trying an experiment on a recruit to see which of them he would obey; and in such cases it would be inappropriate to say that either of them was wrong (or for that matter right). But if one said 'You ought to shut the door' and the other said 'You ought not to shut the door', it would be appropriate to say either of these two things.

The reason for this is that, as I have repeatedly maintained, 'ought' is universalizable whereas the simple imperative is not. It is because an 'ought'-statement (owing to the universalizability of 'ought') already has to have a reason, that we can say of it that it is right or wrong; and so, naturally, to say these things of it commits us, in turn, to admitting the propriety of the question, What is *our* reason for agreeing or disagreeing with the moral statement? In short, the fact that we can say that one of the two parties to a moral disagreement must be wrong, shows us that moral judgements are universalizable. It does not, as some descriptivists have maintained, show that they are descriptive—in the sense of having descriptive meaning but no other.

This point is obscure, so I must explain it a bit more fully. If moral statements were descriptive (in this narrow sense) then the *meaning of the words* used would by itself determine the rightness or wrongness of the statement, given the situation about which the judgement was made. If we understood the meaning of the words used, and correctly observed the situation, we could no longer be in any doubt about the rightness or wrongness of the statement. This, I think, is what descriptivists want to prove to be the case; and it is to this end that they use the premiss that of two parties to a moral disagreement, one must be wrong. But the premiss does not justify so strong a conclusion. For suppose that we have two people who utter contradictory moral statements. I cannot, first, without self-contradiction, repeat their two moral statements after them with 'and' in between. But this a non-descriptivist can admit. Secondly, I cannot consistently agree with, or associate myself with, both of them. But this too need not trouble the non-descriptivist. Thirdly, I must admit that one or other of them is wrong. But from this it does not follow that there was some *pre-existing*, pre-determined principle or rule (whether a meaning-rule or some other sort of rule does not matter) which determines *which* of the two is wrong. I might think for a long time, and then decide that one, and not the other, was wrong. When I had done this, I should have necessarily taken up or adopted some principle or standard—and my use of the word 'wrong' would be improper unless I had done this.

But the point to notice is that it did not have to be the case that *what* principle I adopted was already fixed for me by the meanings of the words in the original two statements. That is what would have to be the case if descriptivism were correct. I cannot say that neither of the two parties is wrong, for they are in disagreement with each other, and they are therefore each implying that the other is wrong—and, moreover, wrong in accordance with some principle or other, which may be different in their two cases; for they are making moral statements, and these have, because of universalizability, to be in accordance with principles. Since the principles in question result, in this case, in divergent moral statements (given that the facts are agreed) one of the principles has to be rejected, by me or by anybody else who considers the matter. But *which* of the two principles I shall reject, and on *what* principle I shall base my rejection, is not determined in advance of my moral thought about the matter. And in particular it is not determined, as descriptivists would have it, by the meanings of the words the two parties used, and the situation of which they were speaking.

So, though I am bound to say that one of the two parties is wrong, and though, in saying which of them is wrong, I am bound to commit myself to a principle of judgement in accordance with which I say it, it is not predetermined for me what this principle is to be. Therefore this long and involved argument results, not in a victory for descriptivism, but only in a conclusion which I have always embraced, namely that moral statements are universalizable, and therefore have descriptive meaning among other kinds of meaning (see further pp. 70, 116).

There are in all parts of the world a great many philosophers who believe that they have not done their duty unless they have established the objectivity of moral statements. There are also a great many (the majority of American students, in my experience) who are convinced of their subjectivity. I am a very rare bird: one who is neither an objectivist nor a subjectivist, but believes that both these schools of thought are vitiated by the same error, namely descriptivism, and are thought to exhaust the field only because of muddles, some of which I have been trying to expose. It is high time that these muddles ceased to waste the time of moral philosophers, and divert them from what should be their proper task, that of asking how we can validly *reason* about what we ought to do—a task to which descriptivists have, *qua* descriptivists, contributed little that is durable.

3
What Makes Choices Rational?

My aim in writing this paper is to ask help in the laying of a pair of ghosts who continue to haunt moral philosophy. Their names are 'objectivism' and 'subjectivism'; but the second sometimes assumes the name of 'relativism'. I have long been convinced that the supposed battles between these two have no real substance; but for all that, they go on confusing many moral philosophers. It would be a great benefit to our profession if somebody could put an end to the confusion once for all; but it has proved harder than might have been hoped, and that is my excuse for trying again.

The confusion nearly always arises when moral philosophers discuss either what they term the 'objectivity' or what they term the 'rationality' of moral judgements. The first of these words would be best abandoned altogether, because the introduction of either it or its supposed opposite 'subjectivity' into ethical discussion seldom does anything except spread darkness. These two words 'objective' and 'subjective' are properly applied to different sorts of fact: objective facts are facts which hold independently of the states of mind etc. of subjects (e.g. of a perceiver or the maker of a moral judgement); subjective facts are facts about the state of mind of such a person, including facts about the relation (e.g. a causal one) in which some object stands to that state of mind. There was a time when moral philosophers disputed whether moral judgements were statements of objective fact or whether they were statements of subjective fact. The terms had a use in this dispute.

However, the dispute shifted some time ago to a different arena. Once the question had been raised (initially by the emotivists; latterly by other non-descriptivists like myself) whether the central function of moral judgements is to state

From *Review of Metaphysics* 32 (1979).

facts at all, or whether, rather, the central part of their meaning or use is a different one (e.g. that of prescribing what is to be or ought to be done or something of this general kind), the terms became wholly inapposite to the new arena of dispute. This may easily be seen if we imagine ourselves asking a prescriptivist whether he thinks that moral judgements state objective or subjective facts—in short, whether he is himself an ethical objectivist or an ethical subjectivist. He will of course answer that they do neither and that he therefore rejects both names for his view.

Attempts have indeed been made to convert the old name 'subjectivist' to new uses. In theory there would be no harm in this move if the new use of the term were carefully defined and distinguished from the old, as some of these writers (but only some) try to do (Ewing 1959: ch. 1, Mackie 1977: 17). But in practice there are quite enough people around who do not avoid the confusion between subjectivism (old style) and, say, non-descriptivism (two quite different views) for the confusion to remain widespread and chronic. The best course is therefore to retain the term 'subjectivist' for those who think that moral judgements state facts about the states of mind etc. of people, and use some new term ('non-descriptivist' is the most perspicuous) for those who do not think that their central function is to state facts at all. Then we should not be troubled so often by people who, because of the confusion I have mentioned, think that the arguments which were perfectly valid against subjectivism (old style) can be trotted out against non-descriptivists, whose views are quite immune to them— e.g. the argument that non-descriptivists make the truth of moral judgements depend on the state of mind of some person (perhaps the maker of them).

However, even if this source of the confusion were removed, there would remain another, connected with the word 'rational', which is not so easy to remove, and which is the subject of this paper. I do not aim to provide a once-for-all definition of the word—it could have many different ones—but only to locate and allay the unease that moral philosophers often express by saying that making moral judgements ought to be a rational activity, whereas some ethical theories prevent it being such. If I can succeed in separating the question of whether moral judgements state objective facts from the question of whether making them is a rational activity, that is the limit of my ambition. I need to do this, because it is my view, defended in many places, that, although there is a central element in the meaning of moral judgements (the prescriptive element) which stops us saying that they are just statements of fact, nevertheless the making of them is a rational activity.

The central issue is, Does the distinction between rational and irrational apply to prescriptions (e.g., if I tell or advise somebody to do something, could this prescription or advice be condemned as irrational)? The best approach to this question will be by taking examples of activities which are clearly not the statings of facts, and yet can be classified as rational or irrational. This may enable us to see that rationality is by no means tied to the stating of facts (indeed it is hard to explain why anybody should have thought that it was).

The best examples to take will be choices and decisions; for these are clearly not the statings of facts, and equally clearly can be classified as rational or irrational. I am going to start with extremely simple examples, and then go on to more complex ones. I shall begin with the choice that I make when somebody offers me a cup of coffee. He says, 'Shall I pour you a cup of coffee?' and I express the decision that I then make by saying the imperative 'Yes, pour me a cup of coffee (please)'. I shall go on to a question (simplified for the purposes of this argument) which the citizens of Scotland have been asked in the recent referendum: 'Shall there be a separate elected assembly for Scotland?' Having dealt with these non-moral choices or decisions, and suggested features which would make us call them rational or irrational, I shall go on to consider the decisions that we make when we adopt or embrace *moral* principles or norms. I hope to show that the fact, if it be a fact, that moral principles or norms are in part prescriptive does not stop us calling the adoption of them rational or irrational for the same reasons as we would apply these terms to the simpler decisions or prescriptions already discussed, and that no other reasons are needed. The difference between these simple prescriptions and moral prescriptions is indeed great; but in spite of this difference the criteria of rationality remain essentially the same.

Moral judgements are not, indeed, *pure* prescriptions, but contain a descriptive element in their meaning. To this I shall briefly allude at the end of this paper, though its bearing on the present argument is marginal. I am not wishing to claim that moral judgements are *wholly* different from ordinary factual statements. They seem to me to share *some* of the logical characteristics of these, but to have in addition *another* logical property (prescriptivity) which ordinary statements of fact do not have. The matter will be understood only when we have done justice to *both* sets of properties, as I have tried to do in my writings (e.g. *LM* ch. 7; *FR* ch. 2); and the attempt to emphasize one of them at the expense of the other has been responsible for most of the wasted breath in recent ethical disputes. The burden of this paper will be that even if moral judgements were pure prescriptions we could still call the adoption of them rational or irrational. It is therefore not necessary for my present purposes to say anything about the descriptive element in their meaning; but I will say something all the same, to show how it leads people on to a false trail.

Suppose, then, that somebody says to me, 'Shall I pour you a cup of coffee?' and I reply, 'Yes, please do', which is equivalent to 'Yes, pour me a cup of coffee (please)'. Even in this simple case there is a difference between various degrees of rationality or irrationality in my procedure. It might be that the question was asked in a language that I knew only imperfectly, and that therefore I did not know *what* offer I was accepting when I said, 'Yes, please do'—perhaps I thought I was going to get whisky. Secondly, it might be that, although I knew the language and therefore knew I would get coffee, I did not know the properties of the coffee I was being offered. I might not know what *sort* of coffee it would be; for example, perhaps we are in Egypt and the coffee is Turkish, which I have never had and shall much dislike when I taste it. Or perhaps it is coffee out of one of those machines that we have in England, which produce either tea or coffee and it is hard to tell which is which. Or perhaps I am unaware that coffee of the strength which I am being offered will stimulate my heart so much that I shall have a heart attack and die.

We should call irrational a man who, when asked this question, made no attempt to ascertain what the words meant but just said light-heartedly, 'Yes, please do'; and we should also call him irrational, though perhaps to a less degree, if he knew what the words meant, but made no attempt to ascertain the nature of the coffee that he was being offered or its consequences for his health or his pleasure. Even in this simple example we see two very important elements in the rationality of choices and prescriptions. The first is to understand what the prescription which expresses the choice *means* in the strict sense of understanding what the *words* mean, or what the speaker means by his words. The second (which is also sometimes confusingly expressed by asking what the choice *means*) is to find out what, concretely, the different answers to the question, the different choices, *involve* by way of actual differences in the future history of the world. To find this out, we have to make certain *factual* predictions about the consequences of carrying out the prescription 'Yes, please do', and of carrying out the negation of this prescription, 'No, thank you'.

It is my belief that if a person has satisfied both these criteria of rationality—if, that is to say, he both understands what he is being asked and is fully cognizant of what, concretely, he is prescribing, he has satisfied the main criteria of rationality in choices. It is to be noted, therefore, that logic (in the shape of understanding what the words mean and therefore understanding their logical properties) and facts (in the shape of the predicted consequences of the choice) do play an important part in making the choice rational. This may explain and indeed substantiate the relevance of logic and factual inquiry to the rationality of decisions and choices. I hope, therefore, that I shall not be accused of ignoring this relevance—as if I thought that there is no difference between a rational choice to decline the coffee on the ground that coffee is likely to kill one, and a completely irrational request for coffee regardless of the consequences, or of what we mean by saying, 'Yes, please do'.

Some complications arise here which have been much discussed, but which I shall just mention without discussion. I do this because the problem I wish to discuss is a different one and has not been discussed enough. First, a man might make a rational choice in partial ignorance. It is possible to make the best of the information one has. We are seldom fully informed, even about the relevant facts (and what those are is a further question—see pp. 191 ff.); but this does not stop us acting rationally. What is irrational is to ignore relevant facts which are available, or to fail to seek information which would be relevant and could be readily obtained. To go into this would require, to begin with, an excursus into the theory of probability. It is held that rational choice needs to be based on a rational estimate of the probabilities of outcomes. I have myself, following Professor Smart, called actions 'morally rational' if they are most likely to be morally right (though even this is inaccurate, as Smart and I allow—Smart 1973: 46 ff.; see p. 63). This sense of 'rational', however, is not in point here; it relates simply to the rational estimation of probable outcomes, whereas what concerns us here is the rationality which a choice itself has, not the rationality of the predictions on which it is based.

There is also an extensive literature in both philosophy and law about the failure to obtain relevant information, which can lead to a charge of negligence, or in extreme cases to one of irrationality; and I am not seeking to add to it. Nor do I wish to deny that it is sometimes rational to deprive oneself of information; the best-known example is that of the examiner who, in order to avoid partiality, takes steps to remain ignorant of the identity of the candidates. All this is well-trodden ground, and I wish merely to stake out, within the conditions for rationality, that area which is to be occupied by the requirement to obtain or seek to obtain the facts necessary for an informed choice, or probable estimates of them.

However, it might be alleged that there is a further necessary ingredient in rationality. Suppose that a man is asked the question 'Shall I pour you a cup of coffee?' and knows what the question means, and also knows that, because he has a very weak heart, the coffee will probably kill him, but is in a state of extreme depression, and therefore does not mind being killed, or even thinks of it as a happy release. So he says, 'Yes, please do', gulps down the strong coffee, and in a few minutes has a heart attack and expires. Is he not being irrational, even though he has a full understanding of what he is being asked, and a full knowledge of the likely consequences of answering the question in the way he does?

I feel inclined to answer that the case has been wrongly put. Such a man *is*, perhaps, choosing irrationally; but if he is, it is because, in spite of what has been posited, he is not fully cognizant of the relevant facts. For the relevant facts include facts about what will be his state of mind if he does not die, recovers from the depression (as we may suppose is probable), and lives thereafter a long and happy life. If he is not fully aware of this possibility, to the extent of giving weight to his possible future happiness and to his present temporary unhappiness in proportion to their intensity and duration, then he is not choosing rationally. This is because he is choosing in disregard of relevant facts.

Contrast the case of a man who has been arrested by an oppressive regime, and is about to be tortured to death; the torturers, in the mistaken opinion that coffee will, by heightening his sensibilities, increase his torment, offer him some; but he, knowing that he has a weak heart and that the coffee will kill him, accepts it and so dies without much pain. He chooses rationally. It has not been shown that there is here any element in rationality besides rational estimation of the facts and understanding of the question.

A common mistake at this point is to suppose that there is some *further* fact, over and above facts about outcomes, which has to be taken into account for a choice to be rational, namely the fact that a choice will or will not be in the chooser's *interest*. It may be thought by those who make this mistake that the rational, i.e. prudent, choice is made by first *finding out* what is in the chooser's interest, and then choosing accordingly. It is crucial to recognize, both in this prudential and, as we shall later see, in the moral case, that there is *no* such further fact. In both the two contrasting cases just described, *if* the choosers are or become aware of the outcomes, including future affective states of themselves, what they then choose will show what they think to be in their interest. And if they are not mistaken about the outcomes, they cannot be mistaken about which outcome is in their interest. The relation of this discussion to Plato's in his *Protagoras* will be obvious.

That they cannot be mistaken will become clear if we revert to the simple case in which the only outcome to be considered is the immediate experience, pleasant or unpleasant, of drinking the coffee. Someone might be mistaken about whether he is going to like the coffee, and how much. But let us suppose that he is not mistaken about this. What other mistake could there be which could lead to a choice that was not in his interest? If he chooses an alternative whose immediate outcome (the only outcome that has to be considered) is not going to be to his liking, that shows that he does not fully realize that it will not be to his liking. For what else could lead to such a choice?

Knowing the affective states of oneself in the future, or for that matter of another person, involves *sharing* those affective states in a strong enough sense to make a difference to one's own present dispositions. I have argued this for other people's affective states elsewhere (pp. 184, 200; *MT* ch. 5); but it is even more obvious in the case of one's own future affective states. To put it beyond doubt, let us start with our own *present* affective states. I cannot know that I am suffering, without suffering, or suffer, without knowing that I am; and I do not really know that I am, unless I become disposed to try to avoid the suffering, *ceteris paribus*[1] (though of course there may be other conflicting considerations which make me endure it all the same—see p. 245). But in the same way I cannot know that (and how) I am *going* to suffer if I make a certain choice, unless I become, *ceteris paribus*, disposed not to make it. Suppose that I am a prospective Christian martyr: what is it really to know what it would be like to be eaten by a lion? Unless I am vividly imagining what it would be like, I do not know what it would be like. But to imagine an

---

[1] I am not here retracting what I said about pain in H 1964. As I said there, 'pain' *can* be the non-evaluative, non-prescriptive name of a recognizable sensation, which is usually but not always, *pro tanto*, shunned; but suffering is always, analytically, the object of aversion, *pro tanto*.

affect vividly we have to *have* it in the imagination. We have in the imagination to suffer—to feel the lion tearing us apart. Those who know *to some extent* what it would be like, shudder; those who fully know, do not make the choice which would lead to it, unless their devotion to the faith, or their expectation of future bliss, is very strong indeed.

If, therefore, in our simplest example, it is the case that the chooser will like to have coffee more than not to have coffee, and he is fully aware of this, and there are no other considerations, then to have coffee is in his interest, and he will show that he thinks, and indeed knows, this by choosing to have coffee. So there is no further fact, *its being in his interest*, that he needs to know in order to make him choose coffee, and choose it rationally, if his knowledge of the outcomes is in order. Knowing that he will like it most, and knowing that it is most in his interest to choose it, are the same piece of knowledge, and, if he has this piece of knowledge, he will express it by choosing coffee. If we can grasp this in the simplest case, we may be able to see that the same holds for the more complex cases.

A similar point can be put in terms of the relation between present and future preferences of the same person, and that between preferences of different people. In recent years there has been a discernible shift among utilitarians (of whom I count myself as one) from a formulation of their doctrine in terms of states of mind (pleasure, happiness, and the like) to a formulation in terms of the satisfaction or fulfilment of desires or preferences (Griffin 1982). This is probably an improvement. It may be helpful, therefore, to point out that, if what I have just been maintaining is right, we cannot fully know the extent of our own future, or of somebody else's, preference for something over something else (e.g. for not being eaten by a lion over being eaten) unless we in the imagination experience the preference just as it will be or now is; and we cannot do this without ourselves preferring that the preferred thing should happen, were it we that were in that situation. What we thus prefer for our own future is the same thing as what we think in our interest. If we are fully apprised of our future preferences, we are rational in thinking this; our present preferences are then rational. Similarly, if we are fully apprised of the rational preferences of others (which involves sharing them in the imagination), then we shall rationally prefer that those same preferences should be realized were we in their situation and had them. But to explore this area fully would take us away from our present topic. I therefore merely indicate lines of argument which will have to be deployed at greater length elsewhere (*MT* ch. 5).

Let us now look at the choice offered to the Scots in the referendum. Each individual Scot has a choice as to what to put on the voting paper. For simplicity, let us suppose that the question asked is 'Shall there be a separate elected assembly for Scotland? Yes or no?' If the voter puts a cross against 'Yes', he is in effect saying, 'Let there be a separate elected assembly for Scotland'. The choice presented is here much more complex. To begin with, there will be a Scottish assembly only if the required majority of voters put crosses against 'Yes'. The individual voter is not deciding the question all by himself. Indeed, some might claim that his single vote has no actual effect if, as is overwhelmingly probable, the issue is not so evenly balanced as to depend on his single vote. His vote then has the merely hypothetical effect that *if* others had voted otherwise than they did, the result would have been affected by his vote. I shall spare the reader these complications. Secondly, the vote affects many others besides the individual voter—not only other Scots but the inhabitants of England and Wales and perhaps other countries too. And the consequences for these affected parties are extremely wide-ranging. Thus the meaning of the question he is asked, and the consequences of answering it one way or the other, determine very narrowly what is involved in answering it. In other words, *what* the voter is deciding is determined by these conditions; his choice is restricted to the consequences, as things are, of putting a cross against 'Yes' and putting a cross against 'No'.

The voter may be completely self-interested, i.e. concerned only with how his vote will affect his own interest and advantage. Or he may be to some extent public-spirited and think about the effect of his vote, and of the result of the referendum, on the interests of all the others concerned. But in either case he is being rational, as in the previous example, if he makes his decision in the light of the actual facts, so far as he can ascertain them, and of the meaning of the question he is being asked, which together determine what concrete alternatives he is deciding between. He would be being irrational to some degree if he decided without knowing what an elected assembly was, or what sort of assembly was being proposed, and without trying to find out what the actual results of having such an assembly would be. But there is here, as in the previous case, no additional condition necessary for rationality over and above the ascertaining, with sufficient accuracy, of what he is deciding between. In particular, rationality does not consist in first finding out what the *right* way to vote would be and then voting accordingly. What the voter has to find out is what he is choosing between; there is no additional knowledge besides this which rationality demands.

I shall now ask to what extent the adoption of a moral principle or norm resembles the 'coffee' and 'referendum' cases. In those two cases there was, as we saw, a place for fact-finding in the ordinary sense, and also for logic, in the thought which led up to the choice. I said earlier that moral judgements share *some* of their features with factual statements. I shall, however, in what follows ignore this for the time being and ask what *would* be the position if moral judgements and principles (for example, the principle that one ought never to inflict pain on others for one's own enjoyment) were equivalent to universal prescriptions or prohibitions and had no factual content. Later I shall briefly ask what difference their factual content, if any, makes.

What we need to do, if we are to establish the rationality of moral decisions, is to give an account of morality and of the moral words which is purely formal and normatively neutral and can therefore be accepted by anybody whatever his normative opinions, or even if he has none as yet, and then to show why people who have accepted this account, and are using the words in that way (who are, for example, using the word 'ought' or 'morally ought' in such a way that when they ask, 'What morally ought I to do?' they are asking a *certain* question and not some different question)—to show why people who are asking this question will, the world being as it is, rationally give certain answers to it and reject others. It is not a question of the facts or logic determining what we are to choose; we have to do the choosing. Rather, the facts and logic determine between what we are choosing, and, if we understand this, we shall rationally choose one alternative rather than another.

Why this is will be clear to anybody with a like understanding. Let us ask, then, what it is about the moral concepts which makes it inevitable that when we understand the moral questions we shall adopt certain moral principles and not others. I have tried to explain this at length on pp. 212–30 and elsewhere; here I must be brief. The explanation lies in two logical, formal features of the moral concepts recognized by Kant: their prescriptivity and their universalizability. I say that moral judgements are prescriptive because in their typical uses they are intended to guide our conduct; to accept one is to be committed to a certain line of action or to prescribing it to somebody else. I say that they are universalizable because a moral judgement made about one situation commits us, on pain of logical inconsistency, to making the same judgement about any precisely similar situation. There is a third feature which, unlike the first two, distinguishes moral from other normative judgements, namely their overridingness; but to discuss this feature of them would take up too much space, and it does not affect the present argument (see *MT* 53 ff.).

Because moral judgements and moral principles have the features of prescriptivity and universalizability, the person who adopts one is in effect prescribing universally for all situations of a certain (perhaps minutely specified) kind. These situations will include not only actual ones, but hypothetical qualitatively identical situations in which the roles of the agents are interchanged. When, therefore, I ask what I ought to do in such and such a situation, I am in effect asking for a prescription for a situation of a certain kind, on the understanding that it is to apply to *all* situations of that kind, no matter what role I myself am to play in them (for example, that of murderer or of victim).

This does not mean that any of the roles carries a veto (see

p. 248). That is to say, although, considering some one distribution of the roles in isolation from the others, I may be disposed to reject the prescription because in that role I would be the victim, this does not commit me to rejecting it *simpliciter*. For it may be that the disadvantages to the person in that role are outweighed in sum by the advantages to the others. If this is the case, I may be willing to accept the disadvantages, were I in that role, as the price of the greater total advantages to the occupants of the other roles, any of which I might occupy. There are various ways of dramatizing this choice, the most illuminating of which, perhaps, is that suggested by C. I. Lewis (1946: 547), who bids us suppose that we know that we are, in a series of worlds, to occupy in succession, and in random order, all the possible roles of those affected by such a choice, and then choose (see also Haslett 1974: 87 ff).

This way of putting the matter, as has been generally acknowledged, leads to a form of utilitarianism; the person who chooses under these conditions will give equal weight to the equal interests of all the affected parties and will therefore seek to maximize the satisfaction of those interests in total. Thus, if moral principles were chosen in the awareness that they are universal prescriptions or prohibitions, everyone would choose these same utilitarian moral principles (or maxims realizing, in the actual world, the single utilitarian principle), provided that they were fully apprised of the consequences of accepting or rejecting them. We have to ask, in the light of this thesis, and of what I have said above, whether the adoption of such principles is a rational process.

I wish to maintain, as before, that if there is this understanding and this awareness of the consequences (provided as before by logic and by factual information as full as we can make it), there is no other element required for rationality. The three situations I have described are of course vastly different; but I wish to maintain that the two requirements I have mentioned apply to all three cases, and are the only requirements that apply. The differences between the cases spring simply from the fact that the questions asked are different. The first question, 'Shall I pour you a cup of coffee?', is one which expects as answer a simple imperative, for example 'Yes, pour me a cup of coffee (please)'. The second is more complex: for example, the answer 'Let there be a separate elected assembly for Scotland' is not a simple instruction to one person, compliance with which will have consequences, apart from trivial ones, for just one person; it is a very complex instruction which, if and only if the required majority votes in the same way, will have vast and far-reaching consequences for the citizens of Scotland, the rest of Britain, and perhaps other countries. The third case, in which a moral judgement or norm is being adopted (for example, when a person asks '*Ought* I to tell her the truth?') is distinguished further by the fact that the word 'ought' has stronger logical properties than the simple imperative: the person who answers 'Yes, I ought to tell her the truth', is not just issuing a simple instruction or prescription to himself alone; he is saying something which commits him, in consistency, to issuing similar prescriptions to *anyone* in an identical situation.

It is this last feature which makes the adoption of moral judgements, norms, or principles such a very different matter from the choice to drink or not to drink coffee. It is because, in adopting a moral prescription, we are implicitly prescribing that *anyone* in an identical situation should do the same, that there is a discipline imposed on moral decisions which is not imposed on our choice of what to drink.

The person who adopts a moral principle knowing what the principle is, and what its acceptance concretely involves, is being as rational as he could be. The universality of moral principles secures in addition (unlike what may happen in the two previous cases) that there will be, in practice, agreement between all those who rationally adopt moral principles, at any rate in cases (that is, the vast majority of cases) where the implementation of a principle affects the interests of many people, or even of more than one (*FR* chs. 8, 9).

As before, no part in rationality is played by a requirement that one should first ascertain what the right principle is, and only then adopt it. If one accepts a principle, one will be thereby signifying that one thinks it right (to adopt a principle, and to come to think it right, are the same thing, since a principle implies that it itself is right). I do not mean that any principle that I adopt must, in virtue of my adopting it, *be* right. My adopting it does not make it right, even for me. Whether it is right or not does not *depend* on whether I adopt it (see pp. 14–17). That is a form of subjectivism which I do not hold, though I am often accused of it by those who do not understand either the issue or what I have said about it— and these are in the majority. I am saying that, while the adopting of a principle is one and the same thing as coming to think it right, there is no place, antecedent to coming to think it right (i.e. adopting it), for a separate earlier task of ascertaining that it is right, which could be the province of some further cognitive activity beyond that of understanding what the principle is, and what its implementation would concretely involve.

When a principle has been adopted (especially if it is generally adopted by members of a certain society) the statements of the principle or of applications of it acquire what has been called a descriptive meaning. For example, if it is generally agreed that it is wrong to cause pain to others for one's own enjoyment, the word 'wrong' will come, in the language spoken by members of that society, to have such a descriptive meaning as makes it incorrect to call an act of this kind anything but wrong. Descriptivist philosophers brought up in this society (unlike, perhaps, those brought up in less humane societies) will then be likely to say, either that we are constrained to adopt this principle and no other that is inconsistent with it, because if we adopted some other we should be breaking the rules of our language, or that we are constrained to adopt it, because otherwise we are showing ourselves ignorant of the moral facts, which our moral cognition, if we exercised it, could assure us of (see pp. 100–7).

Both these kinds of philosopher have got things the wrong way round. If we had not adopted this principle but some other, then the so-called 'rules of our language' would have been different. And likewise, if we had not adopted this principle but some other, what are misleadingly called 'the moral facts' would have been different; for these are nothing but our strong dispositions to *call* certain acts wrong. It is of course a fact that we have these dispositions; but we would not have them but for a further fact, namely the fact that we have adopted the principle; and this would not have been a fact, if we had adopted a different one. To base 'moral cognition' on *this* fact (as, in effect, both these kinds of descriptivist do) really is to be a subjectivist. The fundamental decision, that which requires rational moral thought, is the adoption of the principle in the first place.

4
Principles

I AM not going to say much in this paper that is new. I am going to draw attention to some distinctions which are so obvious that no competent philosopher will have failed to make them. My only reason for mentioning them is that while reading moral philosophy (especially recent moral philosophy) I constantly come across arguments which seem to depend on a neglect of these distinctions; they therefore do seem to need emphasizing. I shall also have some positive things to say (though these will not be new either) which have a bearing on the controversies which have been taking place about what is called 'rule-utilitarianism'. The main thing I am going to say about principles is that they can be more or less *general*. The only person who does not find this an all too familiar truth is one who has failed to make the distinctions that I have in mind.

I must begin by explaining how I am going to use the word 'principle'. I intend, first of all, to confine myself to such uses as might be found in the writings of moral philosophers, and closely related uses. There are many other uses of the word, but it would be pedantic to list them. I think that, as used in moral philosophy—in Mr Warnock's recent book for example (1971), or Professor Rawls's (1971: ch. 2)—the word 'principle' signifies, first, something that we can act on, or in conformity with, or, on the other hand, in breach of. I propose, with apologies to those (no doubt including these writers) who do not like the term, to call this characteristic of the kind of principles that I shall be discussing their *prescriptivity*.

There are various ways of expressing these prescriptive principles, some of which by their grammatical forms make the prescriptivity extremely obvious. To take a non-moral example, we can speak of the principle 'Never plant fruit trees

From *Proceedings of Aristotelian Society* 73 (1972/3).

when the ground is wet'; the use of the imperative here shows the prescriptivity. Or one may speak of the principle, never to plant fruit trees when the ground is wet; here the 'never to plant' is similar to that in 'The lecturer at Wye College told us never to plant'; this also shows the prescriptivity of the principle. We also speak of the principle that one should never plant . . ., or that one ought never to plant . . .; if there is a difference in meaning between these expressions and the others (as no doubt there is) it will not, I think, affect what I have to say.

Another feature which the kinds of principles that I shall be talking about have, is their *universality*. I deliberately choose this word, and not 'generality'. Many writers who do not see the importance of the distinction I am about to make (and I think these include Professors Rawls (1971: 131 f.) and Marcus Singer (1961)) have used the word 'general' for something like (though not exactly like) the concept I am after; but it can lead to confusion with the quite different concept for which I shall myself be using that word (in accordance with its etymology). To make matters more difficult, Rawls uses 'universal' for yet another concept, the precise nature of which I fortunately do not need, for our present purpose, to try to clarify.

I shall use the word 'general' in the same sense as in H 1955a and *FR* 38 ff. The principle 'Never plant apple trees when the ground is wet' is less general than the principle 'Never plant fruit trees when the ground is wet', because apple trees are only one kind of fruit trees, and there are, or logically could be, other kinds. Thus the second principle tells us to avoid a certain procedure generally, in planting all kinds of fruit trees, whereas the first tells us only to avoid it in the specific case of apple trees. 'General', as I shall use it, contrasts with 'specific'. But both of these principles are, in the sense in which I shall be using the term, universal. I will explain shortly what this sense is. It will be obvious from this example that principles can be more or can be less general, as I said; generality in principles is a matter of degree. The principle never to plant apple trees in heavy soil when the ground is wet would be even less general, because heavy soil is only one kind of soil; it would, that is to say, be more specific than any

of those mentioned before. And the principle never to plant
trees of any kind in any kind of soil when the ground is wet
would be more general than any of them.

I am not sure how best to explain formally the meaning of
'general' as illustrated by these examples. We might try the
following: a principle p_1 is more general than another principle
p_2 if and only if it is analytically true that to break p_2 is, in
virtue of that fact, to break p_1, but the converse is not
analytically true. Obviously this definition will not enable us
to rank all principles in a single scale of generality, for some
will be impossible to relate to each other in this way (consider,
for example, the two principles 'Never plant apple trees when
the ground is wet' and 'Never plant trees in heavy soil when
the ground is wet'). For this reason it would be better to say,
instead of 'more general than', 'general relative to'; but I shall
stick to the less cumbrous expression, and shall in any case
ignore this complication, as irrelevant to my argument. I have
no doubt that my definition is not nearly elaborate enough
to form the basis of a complete account of the matter for all
kinds of principles; such an account would have to begin with
an explanation of 'general' as applied to *terms*, and would
have to consider all the possible *forms* of general proposition.
In what follows, I shall assume that the definition applies at
least to universal prohibitions, with which I shall be mainly
concerned.

Simplicity in principles often goes with generality; it is
usually possible to express more general principles in fewer
words than less general ones; but this is not always the case
(we have had examples already where it is not), and the
concept of generality is a more useful, because a more precise,
one than that of simplicity. However, it is probably the
simplicity of some very general principles that has endeared
them to moralists, as we shall see.

'Universal', as I shall use the term, has not much to do
with generality; the two concepts are certainly different ones.
But the term 'universal' itself has been used in a number of
different ways, of which I wish to distinguish two. I think
that many people who have done elementary formal logic
would call the following proposition universal: 'All John's sons
went to Harrow School between 1932 and 1942'. They would

call it universal because, if formalized, it would start with a universal quantifier. But this, though necessary, is not sufficient to define the stricter sense of 'universal' which is needed in moral philosophy. The proposition contains the expressions 'John', 'Harrow', '1932' and '1942' which either are, or require for their definition, references to individuals otherwise than by description. In the stricter sense of 'universal' a universal proposition is not allowed to contain such terms.

Rawls is right to say that 'deep philosophical difficulties seem to bar the way to a satisfactory account of these matters'. But all the same he owes us an explanation of what he means when he says that, besides proper names, 'rigged definite descriptions' are to be excluded from 'general' (in his terminology) principles. I have not seen anywhere a satisfactory account of what 'rigged' could mean here; and it looks to me as if Rawls, like many others, has taken a short cut. Definite descriptions of any sort do not prevent a proposition being universal in my sense; a reason why, in spite of this, 'rigging' is of no avail is suggested in *FR* 107—a reason which does not depend on an assimilation of some definite descriptions, but not others, to proper names, and therefore does not require a solution of the problem of *which* are to be so assimilated (see further H 1962: 353).

In a famous passage in her article 'Modern Moral Philosophy', Professor Anscombe says:

> If someone really thinks, *in advance*, that it is open to question whether such an action as procuring the judicial execution of the innocent should be quite excluded from consideration—I do not want to argue with him; he shows a corrupt mind. (1958: 17)

Since a number of writers (e.g. Bennett 1965) have discussed very fully and adequately Professor Anscombe's attack on what she calls 'consequentialism' (see also p. 181), I am going to discuss, not that issue, but some others raised by this passage which I think equally important. I shall be considering especially the words 'should be quite excluded from consideration', and 'he shows a corrupt mind'. In what sense, I want to ask, is such a mind 'corrupt' (for I shall argue that there is indeed a sense in which it is)? And what can be meant here by 'excluded from consideration'? In discussing these questions we shall find helpful the distinctions I have been making.

We may start by asking what it was that made Professor Anscombe choose this sort of example. I find a clue to the answer in something I once heard her say (I hope I am remembering her rightly). She was complaining of a tendency of modern moral philosophers not to admit that there could be any 'absolutely general' principles which were beyond question. The principle appealed to in the passage I have just quoted (that one should not procure the judicial execution of the innocent) is obviously an example of such an 'absolutely general' principle which most of us would consider it in some sense corrupt to question; and that, I think, is why she chose it. But what could 'absolutely general' mean?

It is clear, at any rate, that it cannot, as here used, mean 'universal' in the sense adopted above. A corrupt consequentialist who wanted to maintain a less general principle than hers might justly claim that his principle was every bit as universal as hers, in that it required that in *all* cases of a certain *kind*, not needing individual references for its determination, an action of a certain *kind* (viz., judicially executing the innocent) should be avoided. He might (following a suggestion in a footnote to this passage of Professor Anscombe's) specify the kind of cases as follows: they are cases in which the judicial execution of the innocent is *not* required in order to prevent a nuclear war. Let us call them 'non-nuclear-war cases'. The consequentialist's principle then is that in *all* non-nuclear-war cases one should avoid judicially executing the innocent. The difference between this principle and Professor Anscombe's is not that one is more universal than the other; in the strict sense of 'universal' the expression 'more universal' has no sense.

On the other hand, her principle is certainly more *general* than his, in the same sense as that in which the principle never to plant fruit trees when the ground is wet is more general than the principle never to plant apple trees when the ground is wet. But in that case, what could be meant by 'absolutely general'? Generality in this sense admits of degrees; and so it is natural to take 'absolutely general' to mean 'so general that nothing could be more general'—or, in my other terminology, 'general relative to all other principles'. But in this sense Professor Anscombe's own principle is not absolutely general either. Here are some principles that are more general, in order of increasing generality: One should not kill the innocent by any means; One should not kill anybody; One should not kill anything; One should not do anything. Only the last, perhaps, could qualify as absolutely general.

Any attempt to give content to a principle involves specifying the cases that are to fall under it; only a contentless principle, therefore, can be 'absolutely general', in the sense of 'entirely unspecific'. In order to avoid this difficulty, somebody might try the following move: 'absolutely general' means not 'having no specific content', but 'having no exceptions'. But this will not do either. In one sense of 'have exceptions', neither the consequentialist's principle nor Professor Anscombe's has exceptions; he says that, without exception, in *all* non-nuclear-war cases, one should avoid judicially executing the innocent. It is true that, *relatively* to Professor Anscombe's principle, the consequentialist's principle introduces an exception; it says that an exception is to be made to Professor Anscombe's principle in cases where nuclear war is threatened. But equally, Professor Anscombe's principle makes exceptions relatively to some more general principles; for example, her principle might be arrived at by taking the more general principle that one should not kill anything, and making exceptions to it in the cases of (1) plants; (2) brutes; and (3) the guilty. I do not think that it is worth going at length into this question of exceptions (though it would have been interesting to sort out the different senses in which we can make an exception to a principle—a task which I began in *LM* 50 ff.); I propose to take it, somewhat dogmatically, that this move merely restates the issue without contributing to its resolution.

Any principle, then, which has content goes some way down the path of specificity; the question is, Do we display virtue, and avoid corruptness of mind, by trying to go as small a way as possible? I shall argue (perhaps to some people's surprise) that there is much good sense in what Professor Anscombe says on this subject, if we can once get clear about the necessary distinctions.

Besides the distinction I have already drawn between universality and generality, there is another, closely related to it,
which we shall have to notice: that between two different *uses*
that we make of principles in our moral thinking. I wish to
consider briefly an argument, often brought against ethical
universalists like myself, which, as it seems to me, is founded
on a neglect of this distinction. It is often said that the
requirement that moral judgements be universalized (i.e.
applied to all cases like that originally judged) is powerless as
a weapon in moral argument, because no two cases are ever
exactly alike. This objection to universalism fails completely,
because the type of moral argument which the universalist
employs can rely just as well on hypothetical cases in which
the person we are arguing with would find himself the victim
of the action he is advocating, as on actual cases; and
hypothetical cases can be as like actual cases as we please in
all their universal properties. But there is another use of
principles in moral thought, quite distinct from this type of
argument, confusion with which has perhaps misled the critics
of universalism. This use of principles is that which occurs
especially in moral education, including what I will for brevity
call self-education.

We learn from experience, in morality as in other matters;
and we also learn by precept. The two kinds of learning are
not so different in practice as might be supposed; for the
precepts very often relate to experiences, and the point of the
experiences is that they lead to the adoption of certain precepts.
Learning from experience is not just empirical observation; it
is the adoption of precepts or principles as a result of our
reflection on what has happened to us. The making of moral
judgements (for example, deciding what we ought to do) is,
if the universalist is right, always a decision about cases of a
certain *kind*; the content of the judgement is one which could
be expressed without using individual references except, if
necessary, ones preceded by the word 'like', which has the
effect of turning the whole phrase containing it into a
description of a universal property, even though individual
references occur in it (H 1955*a*: 307; *FR* 11). So, if we, as a
result of reflection on something that has happened, have
made a certain moral judgement, we have acquired a precept

or principle which has application to all similar cases. We
have, in some sense of that word, learnt something. I shall
not now discuss the difficult question of how the principle
would be justified (into that, no doubt, we should have to
bring the other type of argument I mentioned just now, resting
perhaps on the consideration of exactly similar hypothetical
cases). The point is, rather, that if we are going to learn
something from our reflection on a particular case (at least,
if we are going to learn something *useful*) the principle that
we carry away with us cannot be one of unlimited specificity;
it must be to some extent general, as I have been using that
term. Granted that a principle can satisfy the requirement of
universality without being general in this sense, nevertheless
it will have to be to some degree general in this sense if we
are going to take it away with us and apply it to other cases.
For here it does make a difference that no two actual cases
are ever exactly alike; this means that if the results of our
thinking are going to be of use to us in the future, we must
have isolated certain broad features of the case we were
thinking about—features which may recur in other cases.

It is important not to exaggerate here. I do not mean that
in order to play a part in learning, principles have to be *very*
general. The degree of generality required will vary with the
sort of learning and the sort of learner. To take two extreme
examples: first of all imagine a person who is devoted to golf
and has played it from his youth, and will go on until he can
hardly shuffle round the course, getting all the time more and
more canny; he, we might say, is learning all the time how
to play better, and is in some sense acquiring ever more
sophisticated principles. No doubt, well before he reached
middle age, his principles got sufficiently complex for it to be
no longer possible for him to express them in words; but
principles they still are, in the sense in which I am using the
term. On the other hand, consider the situation in which a
man has very stupid staff in his office, and has despaired of
teaching them anything at all complicated; he may enunciate
and, so far as he can, enforce very simple principles (perhaps
even as simple as those of which, I think, Professor Anscombe
is enamoured), and be content if he has taught them, for
example, never to post letters unstamped.

In a situation in which there is an authoritarian Church or other *custos morum* seeking to pass on to new generations the principles (whether God-given or not) which it thinks valid, fairly simple and general principles will be favoured. The same is true of armies and of militarist societies generally (H 1972*c*: 175). But in both these cases there will be difficulties; the world is complex, and a rigid adherence to very general principles is likely to produce hard cases in which even those whose education in the principles has been thorough are likely to dissent from their particular application. This will be even more likely if they allow themselves to consider fictional cases—a practice which, as I have learnt from Professor Anscombe, was condemned by St Ignatius. Indeed, it would not be too much of an exaggeration to find, in the current prevalence of fiction as an art-form, the principal cause, or at least symptom, of the decline of moral standards which occasions so much concern.

But even if we leave fiction out of it and stick to what actually happens, it is evident that there will be such hard cases. All moral systems whose preference is for simple general principles have to deal with this problem. I do not want anybody to think that I am against simple principles; I think that they are necessary for the moral life and that to question them is often, though not perhaps, as Professor Anscombe seems to think, always, a sign of moral corruption. But it may be, all the same, that those who think like her make a serious mistake about their status, through failing to notice the difference between two *kinds* of questioning.

It must be readily agreed, even by a utilitarian, consequentialist opponent of hers, that the man who can say to himself without questioning or hesitation, 'Thou shalt not commit adultery', or 'Never, never tell a lie' is more likely, in the course of his life, to do what is optimific than one who is prepared to question these principles, in the sense of 'contemplate breaking them', on any but rather extraordinary occasions—and this, though it is easy to think up cases, and some indeed actually occur, in which such acts would be optimific. It is the case that, as the world is, occasions on which adultery and lying are for the best are extremely few; and it is also the case that human beings who are prepared to contemplate breaking these principles are likely to persuade themselves quite often that the situations that face them are included in these few, when they are not. Therefore even a convinced and consistent utilitarian, saddled with the problem of bringing up his children or of taking his own moral character in hand, can reasonably say that the course of instruction likely to have the best consequences will include the inculcation of simple principles like these (though perhaps the one about lying is a bit too simple and could with advantage be modified without sacrificing its teachability). And the man who has been so brought up will be a better man than a man who has been brought up by an existentialist or an adherent of situation ethics, at least in that he will more often do what is right. It might therefore be plausibly argued that to induce such a man to question the principles in which he has been brought up would be to corrupt him.

Butler and Moore (of both of whom Professor Anscombe disapproves) stressed this side of the matter, the first from a theist and the second from the opposite point of view. Butler wrote:

As we are not competent judges, what is upon the whole for the good of the world; there may be other immediate ends appointed for us to pursue, besides that one of doing good, or producing happiness. Though the good of the creation be the only end of the Author of it, yet he may have laid us under particular obligations, which we may discern and feel ourselves under, quite distinct from a perception, that the observance or violation of them is for the happiness or misery of our fellow-creatures. (1726: Sermon 13 n.)

A reason for Butler's view (though I do not recollect that he ever puts it this way) would be that we shall be *most likely* to do the best thing—i.e. co-operate with the will of a beneficent Creator—if we follow the maxims (the simple traditional ones) that our conscience reveals to us. Conscience thus has a utility; for although it can, as Professor Anscombe says, tell men to do the vilest things (as indeed can the simple principles which are its, and her, mainstay), it, and they, are much more likely, the world being as it is, to lead men to do what is right than minute reasoning about the individual case, provided that the schooling which leads to the adoption of the principles and the formation of conscience has been well thought out.

Moore makes this utilitarian justification of general principles explicit:

> It seems, then, that with regard to any rule which is *generally* useful, we may assert that it ought *always* to be observed, not on the ground that in *every* particular case it will be useful, but on the ground that in *any* particular case the probability of its being so is greater than that of our being likely to decide rightly that we have an instance of its disutility. In short, though we may be sure that there are cases where the rule should be broken, we can never know which these cases are, and ought, therefore, never to break it. (1903: 162)

The 'never' is too extreme; for there will be cases in which we know, or can at least be reasonably certain, that to depart from the rule would be for the best. And there will also be cases which are so much outside the ordinary run of cases that we may feel impelled to ask whether the general principles, sound though they may be for general use, ought not to be scrutinized before they are applied to these unusual circumstances. Into this category come a great many political situations (such as some of those on which Professor Anscombe has commented, as for example Truman's dilemma about dropping the bomb). It is not to be supposed that the simple general principles which are the soundest guide in private life can always be safely employed in political situations; and this is so, not because political decisions lie outside morality and are to be made only for 'reasons of State', but because political situations differ in morally relevant respects from private situations, especially in their complexity and in the size of the calamities that it is possible to cause. But even in politics it is less often right to depart from the simple principles of good faith, restraint in the use of force, and the like, than many politicians deceive themselves into thinking. And in ordinary private life it is very seldom so (see H 1972*b*: 178).

Are moral philosophers up to no good, then, when they persuade us to question these principles? I have already implicitly provided their defence against this attack when I said that the schooling which results in the adoption of the principles has to be well thought out. If the workmen and the auxiliaries in the Republic are to lead sound and optimific lives, the guardians at least will have to do some thinking;

and in this democratic time we most of us like to consider ourselves guardians. And to think is to question. This means that sometimes, when we are not ourselves faced with temptations to special pleading, and can get a little nearer to the point of view of the ideal observer or prescriber or, as Butler would no doubt say, of God, we ought to examine the principles themselves and ask whether they are such that their general inculcation would be for the best. And in doing this we have to employ a kind of reasoning utterly different from that which takes the principles as given and reasons *from* them (with however careful casuistry). It is the former kind of reasoning that I was trying to elucidate in my book *Freedom and Reason*; it has, if I am right, to consist in asking what we can prescribe for all cases *exactly* like a given one. Only when we have done enough of such thinking shall we be able with any confidence to generalize, and propound a body of fairly simple teachable principles which can be used in our actual lives when we are surrounded by temptations, and when it is therefore dangerous to question the principles too readily.

Those who have not had the time, or lack the ability, to do this kind of thinking will be well advised to abide by the principles of those who have done it. It is not a question for philosophers, what proportion of the population falls into these two classes; it depends on sociological and psychological facts about people's powers—which may alter in the course of their development, and vary from one sphere of morality to another, according to the extent of their experience.

There is thus a tension between, on the one hand, simple general principles, and, on the other, the necessity of dealing adequately with particular cases. The controversies which led to the emergence of rule-utilitarianism in its various forms were the latest manifestation of this tension. The act-utilitarian view, if suitably expressed (and I am not going to try to do this now), might possibly give a satisfactory account of the reasoning of God or the philosopher-king; but when act-utilitarian reasoning is employed by ordinary humans it may be expected to lead to trouble. They would do better to be guided by simple general principles or by their consciences for most of the time. So the reaction of the ordinary well-brought-up man to act-utilitarianism was to say that it would require him in certain cases (nearly all, significantly, fictional cases) to do things which plainly appeared to him, because he was well brought up, to be wrong.

Rule-utilitarianism was invented as an answer to this objection. But in stating it we shall get into a tangle, unless we observe the distinction between 'universal' and 'general' which I have been labouring. It has been pointed out by Professor Lyons (1965: ch. 3), and earlier in a less fully reasoned way by me (*FR* ch. 7 *s.f.*), that if the rules or principles of the rule-utilitarian are allowed to be as specific and ungeneral as we please, provided that they remain universal, then rule-utilitarianism has the same practical consequences as act-utilitarianism, and vice versa. For if what I have to do is to ask what rule, adopted for and observed in situations *exactly* like this one in all its specific detail, would be optimific, then the answer cannot be different from the answer to the question of what would be optimific in *this* situation.

I now think that this criticism misses one of the main points of rule-utilitarianism, which was to do justice to the *general* rules or principles beloved of the ordinary *bien-pensant* citizen. A difference between act-utilitarianism and rule-utilitarianism can be introduced by limiting the specificity of the rules, i.e. by increasing their generality. And this point is closely linked with the necessity of teaching the principles; for, as I said, principles of more than a certain degree of specificity cannot be taught. The principles, like the ones about lying and promise-breaking, which the ordinary man is trying to defend against the act-utilitarian, are simple general ones, such as he was brought up in, and is trying to inculcate in his children. The generality of these principles is, from his point of view, one of their merits. So, quite apart from the fact that a rule-utilitarianism which allowed unlimited specificity in its principles could be used to justify the very acts whose acceptability to act-utilitarianism caused the ordinary man to object to it—quite apart from all this, the ordinary man will be likely to have a further objection to this kind of rule-utilitarianism, namely, that it does not give him the simple general principles which he thinks to be essential to moral education and character-formation.

It seems to me that *some* form of utilitarianism is probably the right basis for moral reasoning; and we shall eventually get clear what form this is. But I am not going to try here either to propound an acceptable form of utilitarianism, or to answer all the objections that could be made to it. I am not selling a cure-all for the ills of utilitarians. I just want to suggest that this whole area would become much clearer if we used the distinction that I have been making in order to separate two different kinds of rule-utilitarianism. I shall call these two kinds 'specific rule-utilitarianism' and 'general rule-utilitarianism'. I apologize for introducing yet another division into the classification of kinds of utilitarianism; there are a lot of kinds already, and each new distinction causes them to double in number, so that the total increases exponentially. The two kinds I shall distinguish are (to make it more confusing) perfectly compatible with each other, provided that the roles which they play in our thought are carefully demarcated.

Specific rule-utilitarianism is distinguished by the feature that its rules are allowed to be of any degree of specificity (though, because they still have to be universal in the strict sense, they are not allowed to mention individuals otherwise than by description). General rule-utilitarianism, on the other hand, requires its rules to have a certain degree of generality. There will obviously be different grades of general rule-utilitarianism distinguished by the amount of generality that is required in the rules or principles. But I shall avoid this complication by taking just one of these grades—that which requires the principles to be at least general enough to be teachable and usable for the other related purposes that I have mentioned.

I believe it to be the case that a type of specific rule-utilitarianism can be found which is consistent with my own universal-prescriptivist theory of moral argument—indeed, I am optimistic enough to hope that it might be securely founded on such a theory, and thus on considerations of philosophical logic unsupported by any intuitions other than linguistic ones. But I shall not try to substantiate this ambitious claim now. Nor shall I try to answer all of the many objections to utilitarianism that are current, though I have hopes that they could be answered (see *MT* 130 ff.). Here I wish merely to try to mitigate the ordinary man's objection I spoke of earlier, which is to specificity in itself. My answer to this objection is not at all new, but it does have to be rather carefully explained and distinguished from other moves, because it involves a kind of rule-utilitarianism (namely *general* rule-utilitarianism) which is not only a totally different kind from that just considered, but, to make it worse, is quite compatible with it, and therefore can be combined with it in the total regimen which I am recommending, if only the roles of the two are carefully distinguished.

This form is the form hinted at in the quotations from Butler and Moore which I gave earlier. The rules or principles of this kind of rule-utilitarianism are of limited specificity. It is hard to say *how* limited; but, roughly, they have to be sufficiently general for the ordinary man to build them into his character and into those of his children in such a way that they will not be in doubt as to what they should do in the moral situations that they are likely to meet with, unless they are rather unfortunate. A great deal of morality is concerned with such principles. A man of good moral character is a man who has such principles (not, of course, *any* such principles, but the right ones) firmly implanted in him, so that he does not, for example, hesitate about whether he should seduce his neighbour's wife or not. It is quite consistent even with act-utilitarianism (and *a fortiori* with the kind of specific rule-utilitarianism that we have been considering) to admit the utility of inculcating such principles, so that people do, without thinking, what is *likely* to be optimific. To do what they do may turn out, in extraordinary cases, not to be *right* by the act-utilitarian criterion; but even by the criterion what they do is *morally rational*, because the criterion, regarded as a guide to actual choices at the time that they are made, can only require people to do what maximizes *expectable* utility; and this, in nearly all cases, given the weakness of our human nature and the limitations of our knowledge, is likely to be what the sound general principles prescribe (see p. 224).

The kind of utility which these sound general principles

have is what has been called an 'acceptance-utility', whereas the utility of the principles of specific rule-utilitarianism is an 'observance-utility'. And acceptance amounts to more than mere verbal subscription; we have to be so imbued with these principles that we cannot break them without a sense of guilt. This explains the attractions of intuitionism (intuitionists are people who have seen the importance of such principles but not the necessity of having a rational way of selecting them); and it explains the difference between them and rules of thumb. Nobody feels guilty when he breaks a rule of thumb; and indeed the notion of 'rules of thumb' has confused people, if it has made them think that unless moral principles are epistemologically sacrosanct and applicable in absolutely all cases, however fantastic, they are 'mere rules of thumb'. There are in fact a great number of different statuses they might have besides these two; we do not need to be restricted to these two extreme positions.

An opponent of utilitarianism may describe a case (say, from some novel) in which adultery would be optimific, and claim that, according at any rate to act-utilitarianism and specific rule-utilitarianism, this would make it right in such a case to commit adultery. But the utilitarian (e.g. Moore) can now *join* St Ignatius, Professor Anscombe, Butler, and the ordinary man, and say that to consider doing such a thing *in practice* would show a corrupt mind; the good man would simply not think of it. One ought to abide by the general principles whose general inculcation is for the best; harm is more likely to come, in actual moral situations, from questioning these rules than from sticking to them, unless the situations are very extraordinary; the results of sophisticated felicific calculations are not likely, human nature and human ignorance being what they are, to lead to the greatest utility.

More might be said here about the utility of preserving such *institutions* as marital fidelity and the promise-keeping of which it is a special case, and of the *logical* inconsistency involved in accepting these institutions (as utility demands that we do) and yet not subscribing to their rules. And it may be pointed out that the two-level utilitarianism that I have been sketching has nothing to fear from Dr Hodgson's arguments (1967); for the general acceptance of sound general principles, though, as I have said, consistent even with act-utilitarianism, creates a strong initial presumption that people will keep their promises, tell the truth, etc., and thus makes it even easier for Mr Peter Singer to get started the virtuous spiral which he has so elegantly constructed (1972).

All that needs to be done, in fact, to show how the ordinary man's objection can be met, is to point out that the two kinds of utilitarianism that I have been speaking of can quite happily cohabit. We have simply to realize that they have epistemological statuses which are entirely different, and are designed to fulfil entirely different roles in our moral thinking. When we are playing God or the ideal observer, we can legitimately employ the specific kind of rule-utilitarianism. The highly specific principles which we shall then adopt will be the utmost that we can achieve by all the detailed and careful thought that we can command, within the limitations of our knowledge and the time available. And we shall have to do this sometimes, to the best of our ability, if we are going to try to make up our minds what are the best *general* principles to adopt and inculcate. For it is only by *testing* the general principles in specific situations (actual or hypothetical, but never fantastic) that we can satisfy ourselves that they *are* the best.

But when we are inculcating or, in difficult and tempting situations, trying to cleave to these general principles, we shall be wise to employ the other kind of rule-utilitarianism—that which limits the specificity of its principles for fear of indulging in special pleading. The first kind of rule-utilitarianism is for when we are doing philosophy, the second for when we are in moral trouble. The mistake of Professor Anscombe is, I think, to confuse these two roles; she tries to attach to the moral philosopher, who is only doing his job, an opprobrium which would indeed rightly attach to a moral agent in a situation of stress and difficulty who asked the same questions, or to anyone, even a philosopher, who suggested that he should.

5

Supervenience

I do not know who first turned the old word 'supervenient' to its new use which has become current in philosophy. I am certain only that I did not, but that it was already familiar when I was writing *The Language of Morals*. It has been suggested (among others by Professor Geach) that medieval translations of '*epiginomenon*' in Aristotle 1174^b might be the source. Cognate forms appear in Ross's English and Grosseteste's Latin translations. But I have been convinced by Mr Urmson that Aristotle's word does not mean 'supervenient' in the modern philosophical sense, being nearer in meaning to some of the traditional senses given in the *OED*. This would not, of course, rule out Geach's suggestion, for some modern might have misinterpreted Aristotle.

My own first use of the word, so far as I can determine, was in a paper, never published, which I read to the Oxford Philosophical Society in 1950. This was in the course of an attempt to find clear logical criteria for distinguishing between evaluative and purely descriptive words. I thought at that time that this characteristic of value-words could be used for that purpose. I even tried in the same paper to use it in order to refute ethical descriptivism, in much the same spirit as that in which Dr Blackburn has more recently had recourse to it in his campaign (which of course I support) against ethical realism (1971, 1981, 1984, 1985). But I came to think that both moves were mistaken. For supervenience is a feature, not just of evaluative words, properties, or judgements, but of the wider class of judgements which have to have, at least in some minimal sense, reasons or grounds or explanations. And, as we shall see later, it is possible, at a certain cost in queerness, to remain a descriptivist or a realist, even of a non-naturalist stamp, and still believe in supervenience.

From *Proceedings of Aristotelian Society* suppl. 58 (1984).

However, it is worth citing that early paper of mine, if only for the sake of the example I used. I asked my hearers to imagine two college rooms in the same block, identically shaped and furnished and with indistinguishable outlooks. Then I contrasted the three statements:

(1) XIII 3 is a nice room, but XII 3, though similar in all other respects, is not a nice room;

(2) XIII 3 is a duck-egg blue room, but XII 3, though similar in all other respects, is not a duck-egg blue room;

(3) XIII 3 is a hexahedral room, but XII3, though similar in all other respects, is not a hexahedral room.

I then, after some careful restrictions on what could count as 'other' respects, maintained that (1) was self-contradictory, but not (2). (3), I said, was also self-contradictory, if 'other respects' were taken to include the fact that it was bounded by six plane surfaces. My argument was directed to bringing out the differences between the reasons for which (1) is self-contradictory and those for which (3) is self-contradictory. In the course of it I pointed out a second feature, that someone could say 'XIII 3 has the following characteristics (giving a complete description of the room, except as regards its niceness) and it is nice'; and then he could change his mind, and say 'XIII 3 has the following characteristics (giving the same description as before) only it is not nice.' He would then, I said, be contradicting what he said before; but neither of his remarks taken by itself would have been internally self-contradictory. In this, 'nice' behaves like 'duck-egg blue'. On the other hand, if 'hexahedral' were substituted in these two remarks for 'nice', one or the other of them *would* be internally self-contradictory, provided that the 'complete description' determined whether or not the room was bounded by six plane surfaces. Thus these two tests suffice to distinguish 'nice' from both 'duck-egg blue' (which it resembles on the second test but not on the first) and 'hexahedral' (which it resembles on the first but not on the second).

The tests between them, I still think, provide all the data that an explanation of the phenomenon of supervenience has to account for. And it is significant that these essential features

appear even with a word like 'nice'. Though things have to
be nice *because* of their other properties, one might think that
in using it to talk *de gustibus* one was not bound by such logical
restrictions as when making moral judgements for which
weightier reasons of principle have to be given; but one is.
This should be enough to discourage those who want to
draw too ambitious conclusions from the phenomenon of
supervenience in other fields.

Recently it has been suggested by Professor Davidson (1980:
214, 253) that the notion of supervenience might have an
application in the philosophy of mind; and he and others have
drawn parallels with other fields too, among them the relation
between primary and secondary qualities, and between being
H_2O and having the properties which water has. It is easy to
see the attraction of such an idea. When one has on one's
hands a somewhat mysterious relation between two things, it
is very natural to cast around and look for analogous mysterious
relations between other things which might have the same
explanation. However, I shall be arguing that Davidson, at
least, ought to resist this temptation—or anyway that, even if
he does not tell Satan to get behind him, he ought to use a
long spoon in supping with him. One reason is that in fact
the relation in moral philosophy is not mysterious. It is simply,
under another name, one of the main constituents of our old
friend universalizability. I shall be saying shortly what the
others are. Anybody who understands the situation in ethics
can explain very easily why, and in what sense, evaluative
properties supervene on descriptive properties.

The second reason is that, when this has been done, it
becomes unclear how the supervenience phenomenon, even if
it occurs in the case of mental events, will serve the purposes
of 'anomalous monists'. As the link with universalizability
shows, supervenience brings with it the claim *that there is* some
'law' which binds what supervenes to what it supervenes upon.
It does not tie us down to any particular 'law'; that may be,
as we shall see, optional. But, essentially, what supervenience
requires is that what supervenes is seen as an instance of some
universal proposition linking it with what it supervenes upon.

Let us then clarify this by asking what the supervenience
relation amounts to in morals. I must first stress a distinction

which is not new (it is already implicit in the 1950 paper which I have cited and in *LM*), but failure to make which can confuse. I think it is the same distinction as has been made formally and very clearly in other terms by Dr Blackburn; and I also think that it corresponds at least roughly with a distinction that Professor Kim (1982, 1983) now wishes to draw between 'strong' and 'weak' supervenience. I should perhaps mention here that, as Professor Haugeland (1982 *s.f.*) has kindly pointed out, what I have always had in mind is not what Kim now calls 'strong' supervenience. It is nearer to his 'weak' supervenience; his 'strong' supervenience has much more in common with the relation in the example just used between 'hexahedral' and the spatial properties (a relation which, in the 1950 paper and in *LM*, I carefully *distinguished* from that of supervenience which characterizes 'nice' and 'good').

The distinction is best approached via an understanding of a certain form of reasoning, of which practical syllogisms are one example. A typical practical syllogism has one universal premiss, one singular premiss subsuming a particular case under the universal premiss (one might call this the sub-sumptive premiss), and a singular conclusion. There are also inferences of the same form with descriptive premisses and conclusion, like the well-known one with the conclusion that Socrates is mortal. Let us call the two premisses and the conclusion of one of these inferences 'p', 'q', and 'r'. In full the inference will be of the form

p: For all x, if Gx then Fx
q: Ga
So r: Fa

We have to distinguish between two theses, the first much easier to state than the second. It is the second, not the first, that supervenience requires. The first is:

(1) Necessarily if q then r.

Note that, if we took as the universal premiss not 'p' but 'necessarily p', then (1) would follow directly. But I shall be arguing that the universal premiss, whose existence is neces-sarily posited when we ascribe a supervenient property, does not itself have to be a necessary truth—at least not in the sense that we are constrained logically or in any other way to subscribe to it. I did not have to like that kind of room or call it nice. If I call one room of that kind nice, there must be some universal, though perhaps highly specific and by me unspecifiable, aesthetic attitude that I have; in other words I have to be subscribing to some universal premiss from which, in conjunction with facts about the room, it follows that the room is nice (*FR* 139 ff.). But my tastes might have been different.

The second thesis (the supervenience claim, which has to be distinguished from (1)), is much harder to formulate satisfactorily. It, like (1), claims to state a necessary truth (another reason for the confusion). I suggest the following:

(2) Necessarily, if *r*, then there is a valid inference of the '*p*, *q*, so *r*' form, the two premisses of which hold.

This is what is involved in the claim that '*r*' ascribes a supervenient property; it is not, of course, universally true whatever '*r*' is, but is what distinguishes '*r*'s which ascribe supervenient properties from those which do not. Note also that in order to separate off cases of 'substantial supervenience' from cases which are supervenient in only a trivial sense we have to insist that the universal premiss should not be analytically true, or true in virtue of the meanings of words. In this trivial way a great many descriptive properties are supervenient (indeed all, if we admit even unformulated meaning-rules as universal premisses) for the same reason as all descriptive statements are trivially universalizable (*FR* 23). The statement that this tomato is coloured is (in virtue of the meaning of 'coloured' and 'red') derivable by an inference having as premisses 'All red things are coloured' and 'This tomato is red'; and a similar game could be played with 'hexahedral' in the example used earlier. In what follows I shall, except where indicated, use 'supervenient' in such a way as to exclude these trivial cases.

I say that the premisses 'hold', and not that they 'are true', because the doctrine I shall be maintaining is meant to apply to all inferences to this general sort, whether their premisses and conclusions are descriptive or prescriptive. I shall not argue whether some prescriptive propositions can be called true or false, though in fact some can (see p. 26). Also, I do not intend that 'hold' should necessarily be taken in a realistic sense. For the purpose of my present exposition, all I am doing in saying that a premiss holds is to subscribe to it (see *LM* 191).

But we are not at an end of the problems presented by the word 'necessarily' at the beginning of both (1) and (2), and also of the revised premiss 'Necessarily p'. On my own view of supervenience, the 'necessarily' at the beginning of (2) means conceptual or logical necessity, simply because supervenience is, on my view, a logical property. But I concede that other views might be held (for example that it is a case of 'presupposition', or else that some more substantial form of necessity than logical is involved). The necessity of the 'p, q, so r' inference itself (what makes it valid) is also logical necessity. My view is, however, neutral so far on what type of necessity is implied by the 'necessarily' at the beginning of (1) and of 'Necessarily p'. The school of moral philosophers known as 'naturalists' accepts (1) for moral cases, and construes 'necessarily' there as implying logical or conceptual necessity. (1) is supposed by them to be true in virtue of the meaning of some moral word, and correspondingly for them the necessity implied by 'Necessarily p' in the revised premiss is of the same sort. They thereby make the supervenience of moral properties merely trivial; moral judgements are then universalizable only in the trivial sense in which purely descriptive statements are.

Ethical realists of a non-naturalistic sort like Moore will construe the 'necessarily' in (1) and in the revised premiss as implying synthetic a-priori necessity. Others may opt for metaphysical necessity, if they know what that is. In certain contexts the necessity of (1) and the revised premiss may be construed as physical or causal necessity, as we shall see. Our account is general enough to cover all these interpretations. By contrast, for the necessity in (2) I shall, for simplicity's sake, stick to conceptual or analytic necessity until someone shows that we need other kinds.

Those who reject naturalism are thus left with a number of possibilities. Moore opted for the one just mentioned, that of claiming necessity for 'p', and thus accepting (1), but at the same time rejecting the view that the necessity involved is merely conceptual. Dr Blackburn, and I myself at one time, have thought that the supervenience of moral properties could be appealed to in order to refute such a view, and thus, having knocked out both the naturalistic and the non-naturalistic varieties of realism, to establish anti-realism (or in my terms non-descriptivism) on a secure basis. I had given up this hope by the time I wrote *The Language of Morals*, and sought other means of impugning descriptivism. My reason was that it does not seem to me impossible that someone should maintain, as Moore did, that 'Necessarily *p*' states some kind of synthetic a-priori truth. This leaves the relation between descriptive and moral properties looking queer. It is, as Blackburn says, 'an opaque, isolated, logical fact, for which no explanation can be proffered' (1971: 111). This is a sitting target for Mackie's 'argument from queerness' (1977: 38). But that argument does not rely on supervenience—only on that robust sense of reality which the realist lacks. He can, if we are prepared to swallow it, go on saying, without offence to supervenience, that there just is this *sui generis* non-natural property which all things of a certain kind necessarily (but not analytically) have. He will say this if he accepts (1). If, on the other hand, he rejects (1) but accepts (2), he can say something even queerer, that there just is this *sui generis* property which all things of a certain kind have, though not necessarily, and which is such that, if anything does have it, then anything else which is just like that thing in other respects must have it too. Like Blackburn, I find this hard to swallow, but others may have stronger stomachs (stomachs these days are getting stronger).

Let us, before we proceed, briefly notice how the inference-schema that I have been using accounts for the supervenience-phenomenon, and in particular for the manifestation of it to which Davidson appeals, namely that we are not logically permitted to make divergent moral judgements about cases which we admit to be similar in all their descriptive properties. The explanation is that, once it is claimed that there is *some* universal premiss (even if we cannot say what it is) which holds, and which, in conjunction with a subsumptive premiss which also holds (even if we cannot say what this is either), entails that the case has the moral property, it will follow that any other case just like this one in other respects will have the same moral property; for it too must be subsumable under the same universal premiss.

The 'just like' is important. If the second case diverged in some feature which made a difference, then it would not be subsumable. But if it is just like the first case, then if the universal premiss holds for all cases specified in it, and the subsumptive premiss says that the first case is as specified in it, then any case just like the first must be equally so specifiable and subsumable, and therefore, by an identical inference, have the same moral property as the first case. It must be added that we must not, at this level of thinking, set limits on the specificity of the specifications in the universal premiss. It has to be universal but need not be general (see p. 50). Even small differences in the descriptive properties of the case may make a difference to its moral properties.

I have now said all I have time to say about moral judgements in particular. Let us now turn to some other possible parallels, and first to the most obvious, the case of causal explanation. The well canvassed 'covering law' theory of causal explanation could be put in terms of supervenience, and of the schema we have been using. To say that an event *A* caused an event *B* (*A* and *B* being particular events, not kinds of events) would then be to say that *there is* some logically valid inference with a universal premiss and a particular subsumptive premiss, such that both premisses hold, and together they entail that, if *A* happened, *B* would happen. I am not going to argue either for or against this theory of causal explanation; I think that it, or something like it, is almost certainly true of some kinds of causation (which is to say that the words 'cause' and 'explain' are sometimes used in such a way that they imply supervenience), but I shall not discuss whether there may not be other kinds or uses which do not have this implication. At any rate in the cases which do have it, the supervenience phenomenon is identical with that in morals, except that the individual in question is an ordered pair of events instead of a single action, person, or other subject of a moral judgement, and that the universal premiss, instead of being a moral principle of some sort, is

some kind of descriptive universal proposition which is claimed
to be true (e.g. a 'law of nature').

I wish to draw attention to some other similarities between
the moral and the causal cases (both of which I have sketched
very crudely, leaving out many needed qualifications). The
first similarity is that there is in both cases a restriction on
the form of the universal premiss which I have so far not
mentioned. This is that it is not in either case allowed
to contain references to individuals. The doctrine of the
universalizability of moral judgements standardly imposes this
requirement, which is the second main element, besides
supervenience, in the doctrine. Supervenience by itself does
not impose the requirement; it only says that there has to be
some universal premiss (which might be universal in some
weaker sense not requiring the elimination of individual
references, but only universal quantification). However, it is
generally held that moral principles have to be universal in a
strong sense which excludes such individual references, and
that the same is true of causal 'laws'.

A second similarity is that neither in the moral nor in the
causal case does the universal premiss have to be a necessary
truth, at any rate in an important sense of 'necessary'. To
illustrate this, imagine an ethical non-descriptivist of a more
extreme sort than myself, who thought that moral principles
could be just universal pronouncements made *ad libitum* by
any speaker, without any requirement to advert to the facts
of the case (contrast *MT* 88). He could, even so, believe in
supervenience in the sense in which I have just been ex-
pounding it. He would have to agree that a speaker who
made a moral judgement, but denied that he subscribed to
any principle from which, in conjunction with the facts of the
case, the moral judgement followed, would be abusing the
moral words he uttered. But such an extreme non-descriptivist
would leave it open to anyone to derive his moral judgements
from any moral principles he cared to frame and embrace,
provided that he applied them consistently. So the principles
could hardly be called necessarily true. This is even clearer in
the 'nice room' case described above. Niceness is supervenient
on the descriptive properties of the room; but we are not

constrained as to the kinds of room, liking for which we express by calling them nice.

Essentially the same point can be put by observing that expressions like 'because of' and 'in virtue of', both in moral and in causal contexts, though they imply supervenience, by no means imply necessity in the universal premiss. There is, indeed, a sense of 'necessity' in which they do imply it, as we shall see. But at any rate there is a sense in which things can be nice because they are as they are, without it being compulsory on us to like, and call nice, that kind of thing. There is, all the same, a necessity *that there be* a universal premiss (itself perhaps optional) from which, in conjunction with the subsumptive premiss, the conclusion necessarily follows. To use an example I have used before (H 1963*b s.f.*): the food was poisonous because it contained cyanide; and to say this is to say *that there is* some universal premiss which holds (which might be, in this case, 'Everything containing cyanide is poisonous') and some subsumptive premiss which also holds (e.g. 'This food contains cyanide') and that the two premisses together logically entail the conclusion 'This food is poisonous'. It is not to claim that the universal premiss holds necessarily (except in the sense to be mentioned shortly). There could be a world in which cyanide was not a poison.[1]

However, it does seem that, at least in the moral and causal cases, the universal premiss, though it does not need to hold necessarily, has to be nomological in character (as the premiss about cyanide was: it implies that if any food had contained it, it would have been poisonous). I have argued that the universality of moral principles requires them to apply to hypothetical cases as well as actual (*MT* 113), and the same seems to be true in the causal case. It is easy to confuse nomologicality with holding necessarily, but they must be distinguished.

That the universal premiss does not, for supervenience, have to hold necessarily means that someone who had embraced an extreme descriptive theory of science of a Machian sort

---

[1] I have avoided in this paper any use of the fashionable 'possible worlds' terminology, although, used carefully, it can be helpful. I have done so because when not used carefully, especially when coupled with realist prejudices, it can lead to confusions. That would have to be the subject of another paper.

could still believe in the supervenience of causal properties.
His 'scientific laws' would be just descriptions, universal in
form and nomological in character, of what goes on in the
world, and not in at any rate one sense necessary truths (God
could have made the world otherwise); but the person who
attributed causal properties to events would still, on such a
view, be committed to the existence of *some* true universal but
contingent nomological propositions. The same would be true
of a Humian who believed in constant conjunction but no *in
rebus* necessity.

It must be granted that if we *meant* by 'physical necessity'
simply that such universal nomological propositions hold (and
perhaps we sometimes do), then in a sense the propositions
themselves might be said to hold necessarily; but this could
be misleading. A less question-begging way of putting the
matter would be to say, what is undoubtedly true, that if the
universal premiss holds, then we only need the subsumptive
premiss in addition in order to infer the conclusion by a
logically necessary inference. It is easy to see how this could
lead to the thought that in some sense the universal premiss
itself is necessary, since it justifies this necessary inference. It
might be held, alternatively, that the universal premiss holds
necessarily in some other sense of '(physically) necessary'. Into
these questions in the philosophy of science I shall not go
further, beyond saying that we have not yet found, so far as
I can see, any need to talk in this area about *metaphysical*
necessity. In morals, likewise, some might say that universal
moral principles hold necessarily; and others might prefer to
say that they do not hold necessarily, but justify a necessary
inference from themselves, plus a subsumptive premiss, to a
moral judgement as conclusion. For myself, I prefer the second
way of putting the matter. The important point is that
supervenience by itself does not settle it one way or the other,
either in the moral or in the causal case.

Now I come to a much more precarious case, that of the
relation between statements about 'natural kinds' like water
and statements about the physical properties or structures
which underlie them. I could, I think, say some of the
same things about the relation between these same physical
properties and 'secondary qualities' like redness; but I shall

not have room. It is commonly said that the property of being water supervenes on the chemical (or ultimately on the physical) property of being H_2O. What would this imply? According to the account I have given it would imply that anyone who said 'That stuff is water' would be committed to holding that there was *some* universal principle which held, according to which *there is some* physical or chemical structure such that anything which has it exhibits the observable properties which that stuff exhibits, viz. those of water. He would not be committed to any view about what the universal principle or what the physical or chemical structure specified in it was; that would be a matter for empirical investigation. But if he denied that there was any such principle or structure, then he would be doing something wrong (perhaps misusing the word 'water' or showing a misunderstanding of the concept).

As it stands this view seems to me to be obviously false (which is why I have not been so bold as to ascribe it to anyone). It is false because the word 'water' came into use long before anybody had heard of chemical properties or natural kinds, and still retains in most circles the sense which it then had. The dictionary can perhaps help us here. According to the *OED* there are two distinct relevant senses of 'water'. The first is 'The liquid of which seas, lakes, and rivers are composed, and which falls as rain and issues from springs; when pure, it is transparent, colourless (except as seen in large quantity, when it has a blue tint), tasteless, and inodorous. Popular language recognizes kinds of "water" that have not all these negative properties; but (even apart from any scientific knowledge) it has usually been more or less clearly understood that these are really mixtures of water with other substances.' It is to be noted that there are really two definitions here, one by extension and one by description. They pick out the same stuff only contingently (the rivers might all run red, or run blood). But in the world as it is the extension nearly always tallies with the description, and that is enough for the dictionary.

By contrast the definition which the *OED* gives of the second sense of 'water' does not even in the world as it is pick out the same stuff as the two definitions of the first sense: 'The substance of which the liquid "water" is one form among several, now known to be a chemical compound of two volumes of hydrogen and one of oxygen (formula H_2O); in ancient speculation regarded as one of the four, and in prescientific chemistry as one of the five elements of which all bodies are composed.' The 'H_2O' definition lets in ice as water, for example, which the extensional definition of the first sense does not (the sea is not composed of ice, though if the climate got a lot colder it might be). And the descriptive definition of the first sense does not either, because ice is not a liquid. So the dictionary is obviously right to say that there are two senses. But there is more to it than that. That the senses are different is clear for another reason too, similar to that already given for rejecting the supervenience thesis for water as crudely stated: the word 'water' was in use long before they had heard of H_2O. The first citation in the *OED* is dated 1050; and if in 1066 Harald referred to the stuff over which the Normans were invading England as 'water', he did not mean 'H_2O'.

What has happened is that, when it was discovered that water was composed of H_2O, a new use of the word came in alongside the old, as the *OED* correctly records. But the old has survived as an alternative. If a chemist says 'water' he may well mean 'H_2O'; when an ordinary man says 'water', he may well not. But chemists are ordinary men too for most of the time; if they were parched with thirst and begged for water and you directed a jet of steam at them they would not thank you. And most ordinary people in advanced countries have by now heard of the chemistry. So things have got mixed up enough to confuse philosophers. However, there is no ground in these linguistic phenomena for saying that there is anything mysterious (anything requiring reference to essences in any but a nominal or physical sense) about the relation between H_2O and water. We do not need to invoke any metaphysical necessities to account for it.

Let us ask what we would best say, in the light of this history, about the supervenience, or otherwise, of the property of being water upon the property of being H_2O. I have derided the idea that, as 'water' is currently used, there is this supervenience. In the primitive sense, when we say that something is water, we do not imply that there is *any* (let alone any particular) chemical or physical structure such that stuff which has it is always water and that stuff has it. That is what we should have to be implying if it were a classic case of supervenience. But in the dictionary's second sense, the scientific sense, we have a choice. If the dictionary had just said 'H_2O', the choice would be easy. Being water in this second sense would then be entailed logically by being H_2O (and vice versa). So the property of being water would be supervenient on that of being H_2O only in the trivial sense that I said I would not use. Certainly seekers after natural kinds have been interested in supervenience in a more substantial sense; they are not saying merely that 'water' *means* 'H_2O'.

However, that is not all that the dictionary says. From what it says about 'ancient speculation' and 'prescientific chemistry' it looks as if there is justification for saying that there was a time when 'water' had a sense that was neither 'H_2O' nor 'The liquid of which seas etc.'. Perhaps, in that sense, it *was* the name of a natural kind and *did* imply supervenience, and the existence of an only vaguely specified underlying structure. Our account of supervenience is able to accommodate such a sense if it once existed; but it would be absurd to claim that it is the only, or even a common, current sense. If anybody *does* use 'water' in that sense, being water, as he uses the word, is a supervenient property.

Is there need here to speak of any other kind of necessity than physical on the one hand and logical or conceptual on the other? I do not think so. The 'law' that is in the offing when we say that what is H_2O must be water is either a conceptual truth, in that the two expressions mean the same; or it is a physical law, part of physical and chemical theory, according to which stuff which has a certain chemical structure always has the observable properties of water in the *OED*'s first sense (or, we have to add, of ice or steam). Even those who maintain the popular and plausible view that there is no hard and fast division between what is true by definition (or in virtue of meaning) and what is true as a matter of fact do not need to invoke any kind of non-conceptual or metaphysical necessity here. Indeed, their doctrine, above all, removes the need for anything in between physical and conceptual necessity, because it has not only precluded there being any space in between them for it to occupy, but denied that there is any boundary.

In short, the following statement is true by logical necessity: If anything has a property which is supervenient causally on another, then there is a principle which holds, such that from it, in conjunction with a subsumptive premiss which also holds, the conclusion that the thing has the supervenient property can be inferred by logical necessity; and it is possible, but not absolutely compulsory, to say that the principle itself holds of physical necessity. With all these necessities around, it is not surprising that some have found a place for metaphysical necessity; but I do not see any necessity for this—at least none which arises from the phenomenon of supervenience.

I have not left myself room to say as much as should be said about my last topic, the use of the concept of supervenience in the philosophy of mind. But on the face of it it looks as if the concept, as I have been exploring it, is not going to be of much help to the anomalous monist. For at the very least, if mental events are supervenient in this sense on physical events, there are going to be some true universal propositions, although we may not be able to say what they are, which link the two. It is not enough that there should be merely physical laws that enable us to predict the mental events which, on this view, are token-identical with physical events. The laws will have actually to mention mental events, and indeed, since they are universal propositions, not individual mental events but kinds of mental event. Otherwise the inference which supervenience says is possible will not go through. For the inference is, as we saw, of the form 'For all x, if Gx then Fx, but Ga, therefore Fa'. Here 'Fa' has to be a description of a mental event: it is described as an instance of a kind, 'F'.

The question of whether the 'laws' whose existence the anomalist denies are biconditionals or merely one-way conditionals does not seem to me crucial. Nobody gets called an anomalist about cars because their deceleration can be caused by braking, release of the accelerator pedal, or any number of alternative defects in the transmission, petrol supply, electrical system, etc. So why should one be called this if one thinks that pains can have alternative neurological causes? The really crucial question is whether there are even one-way laws, going some of them in the physical–mental direction and some in the mental–physical; and to at least the former sort the believer in supervenience seems, on the face of it, to be committed.

As we also saw, supervenience does not require the universal premiss to be universal in quite the strong sense in which it has to be in morals; the law might mention an individual person. But Davidson does not, I am sure, want to say that, when we say 'He is in pain', the true universal proposition we are positing could be a proposition true only of that individual, so that your pain could have a physical correlate in your nervous system whose precise reproduction in my nervous system was unaccompanied by pain; for he explicitly says 'there cannot be two events alike in all physical respects but differing in some mental respects' (1980: 214). He could, alternatively, say that the universal premiss in question does not hold necessarily; but, as we have seen, a similar view could be put forward about physical events, and there seems to be no basis, so far, for differentiating the two kinds of events in this respect. He could try saying that the laws in question, though universal, are not nomological. But in that case we should be faced with the possibility that our mental states have been uniformly correlated with our own and other people's physical states up to now, but that one day soon the correlation might simply collapse. This would please the indeterminists, but I can see no more reason for fearing a 'breakdown of induction' in the mental case than in the physical, especially if one is a monist. Or else he might say that the analogy with the supervenience of moral and causal (including natural-kind) properties breaks down, and that he was speaking of supervenience in some different sense. But in that case it might have been clearer if he had used another word, and, in telling us what he meant by it, had not appealed to the analogy.

6

Ontology in Ethics

THERE is a long-standing dispute between two main types of ethical theory, which, nevertheless, is not always stated in the same terms. It is the purpose of this paper to ask whether it matters in what terms we formulate it. I shall argue that one way of posing the issue has advantages over the others, if we want to get to the root of the matter. This is because all the others pose it in terms which, for want of clarity and other reasons, leave it undecidable unless in the end we have recourse to the preferred way.

Here is a list of the formulations that I shall be considering, with, in brackets, indications of the type of distinction that each purports to be.

(1) Realism vs. anti-realism (ontological)
(2) Moral judgements as expressing beliefs vs. moral judgements as expressing attitudes (psychological)
(3) Cognitivism vs. non-cognitivism (epistemological)
(4) Descriptivism vs. non-descriptivism (logical or conceptual)

In his splendidly invigorating book *Ethics: Inventing Right and Wrong*, John Mackie opted on the whole for the first way of stating the issue, though he did not favour the *words* 'realism' and 'anti-realism', preferring such names for his own theory as 'subjectivism' and 'scepticism'. This choice of words is perhaps to be regretted; for 'subjectivism' has many different meanings between which people will go on being confused in spite of Mackie's ample explanation; and a 'sceptic' is hardly what he was, since, like Hume, he allowed plenty of room in his theory for the holding of moral opinions, and certainly had strong ones himself, which guided his conduct more firmly than those of many of us. He explains his use of 'scepticism'

From *Morality and Objectivity: Essays in Memory of John Mackie*, ed. T. Honderich (Routledge, 1985).

too; but it is hardly the usual one. However that may be, he undoubtedly thought of the main issue as ontological. He says, 'What I have called scepticism is an ontological thesis, not a linguistic or conceptual one' (1977: 18); and he would surely have insisted that it was not an epistemological nor a psychological nor a logical one either, though it might have close relations with such theses.

It is to be noted that it is not necessary to take the same side in all formulations of the dispute, as might be thought by one who was confused by the use of the muddling words 'objectivist' and 'subjectivist' to label the two sides regardless of the different formulations. To take different sides can, however, in view of the close relation between the formulations, lead to difficulties. Mackie himself illustrates this. He adheres to the left-hand side of the fourth formulation, although he has adhered to the right-hand side of the first; he is, that is to say, a descriptivist but an anti-realist:

If second order ethics were confined, then, to linguistic and conceptual analysis, it ought to conclude that moral values at least are objective; that they are so is part of what our ordinary moral statements mean; the traditional moral concepts of the ordinary man as well as of the main line of western philosophers are concepts of objective value. (1977: 35)

The fact that Mackie takes different sides on these two formulations is indeed the root of his 'error theory'; for he has attempted to saddle the ordinary man with moral concepts such that nothing said in terms of them could possibly be true if anti-realism were correct.

The ontological way of posing the issue is now the most popular, and is also the most primitive. It goes back to Plato at least, and has recently come back strongly into fashion after a period of neglect, so that many people now use the expressions 'realist' and 'anti-realist' as if it were perfectly plain what they mean (which is far from being the case). This is in conformity with a similar recent trend in philosophical logic generally, where the words are now much used. I shall not be so bold as to express any opinions about their use in other fields such as the philosophy of mathematics, although I suspect that it has caused trouble there too. The trouble it has caused in ethics is enough for one paper.

What then does 'ethical realism' mean? On the face of it, it means the view that moral qualities such as wrongness, and likewise moral facts such as the fact that an act was wrong, exist *in rerum natura*, so that, if one says that a certain act was wrong, one is saying that there existed, somehow, somewhere, this quality of wrongness, and that it had to exist *there* if *that* act were to be wrong. And one is saying that there also existed, somewhere, somehow, the fact that the act was wrong, which was brought into being by the person who did the wrong act (or should we say that the fact that the act *would* be wrong *if* he did it existed even before he did it?).

It is easy and perhaps even legitimate to caricature ethical realism in this way; for it is not clear what else the term could mean. But we are not much the wiser. First of all, there is a quite general problem about the existence of qualities and facts of all kinds. The word 'exist' is, admittedly, notoriously treacherous. There are said to be both different senses of the word, and different kinds or levels or even orders of existence or being. We have to distinguish at least two ways in which we can speak of senses of 'exist' or kinds of existence. One of them need not detain us for long. For a cow to exist is obviously not the same as for a horse to exist; but this is merely because a cow is a different sort of thing from a horse. We do not need, in order to account for this difference, to distinguish between senses of 'exist' or kinds of existence (see Quine 1953: 2 ff.). It is possible to extend this move in order to deal with kinds of things that differ from one another much more than cows and horses do. So, if one philosopher claims that numbers exist in a different sense from cows, or that the existence of numbers is a different kind or order of existence from that of cows, another philosopher may well reply that no distinct senses or orders are required; it is simply that numbers are different from cows.

However, even if we agree with this second philosopher, there remains a way in which we can usefully distinguish between senses of 'exist'. (1) In one of these senses it is all right (e.g.) to say 'The quality of redness exists', if we can *meaningfully* say of something that it is red. (2) In another, somewhat stronger, sense, it is all right to say that it exists, if we can *truly* say of something that it is red. (3) There is also a sense of 'exists', not the same as either of these, in which it is all right to speak of something existing, if it can be *referred to*. This is so (to speak roughly) if an expression referring to it can occur in the subject-place in a true, or even a false, statement. This sense does not for our purposes need to be distinguished from a closely related sense in which it is all right to speak of things of some kind existing if variables which range over things of that kind can be quantified over in true affirmative existential statements, or even in false ones. Thus the Queen of England exists if we can say something true or even false about her, and the King of France does not exist because we cannot; and cows exist because we can begin true statements or false ones with the words 'Some cows'. In this sense, the property redness exists because we can say 'Redness is a colour-property', and properties exist because we can say 'Some properties are not instantiated.' This is obviously a very weak sense. It would take a hardened anti-realist to say that wrongness does not exist in this sense; for we can certainly refer to wrongness, as when we say 'The wrongness of Smith's act is such that he ought not to be allowed to profit from it.'

It is to be noticed that all these three senses of 'exist' (which we might call formal senses) have been defined in terms of what we can or cannot rightly say—which means, here, what the logical rules governing the words or concepts allow us to say. This in itself ought to give the ontologist pause. For it may turn out that the problem of whether wrongness exists is after all a conceptual one—a problem in philosophical logic not metaphysics. Or it may turn out that *all* ontological problems are really conceptual ones, and that metaphysics is not to be distinguished from philosophical logic. Without entering into this old general question, I will merely express the hope that in ethics it might turn out that this is so—that is, that when we are discussing so-called ontological questions in ethics, we are really discussing the same questions as can also be put in conceptual or logical terms; and then it would have to be asked which were the most perspicuous terms to put them in. That indeed is the question I wish to pose in this paper.

But it is not clear that any of these formal senses of 'exist' is being used when the ethical realist claims that wrongness exists *in rerum natura*, or the anti-realist denies this. At the beginning of his book Mackie uses, not this expression, but the phrase 'part of the fabric of the world' (1977: 15, 21). I am sorry to say that he gets this expression from me, but from a passage in which I explicitly say that I cannot attach a sense to it in this context (H 1972c: 47). It raises all the same questions. It is probable that most anti-realists, perhaps including Mackie, would not mind saying that wrongness exists in one of these formal senses, and would wish to deny it existence only in some more 'material' sense. Reverting to the two philosophers mentioned above, it might be that the anti-realist is like the first of them: he thinks that, even if wrongness exists in *some* sense, it exists in a different sense from cows. A realist follower of the second philosopher might reply that it exists in the same sense, but is a different sort of thing from cows.

But if this is what they say, there is really no reason why they should quarrel. There would be a substantial dispute between them if the realist were claiming that wrongness was like cows, tangible and spatially located; or, to use the alternative formulation in terms of existence, that wrongness exists in the way that cows exist, by being encounterable. But he is not claiming either of these things. He may be claiming that we might somewhere encounter someone doing a wrong act; but the anti-realist, unless, unlike Mackie (1977: 16), he is also an amoralist who refuses to make the moral judgement that any act is wrong, will not deny that.

In other words, if expressions like '*in rerum natura*' and 'part of the fabric of the world' are taken in a strong sense which lets cows in but keeps numbers out, the realist can admit that wrongness is not *that* sort of thing, or does not exist in *that* sense. But if these expressions are being used in some weaker sense which lets numbers in as well as cows, then I can see no reason why the anti-realist should not admit that in *that* sense wrongness exists, at any rate provided that he admits that some acts are wrong (cf. sense (2) above), or that he at least admits that it makes sense to say that they are (cf. sense

(1) above), or that one can say something about wrongness, putting the word in the subject-place (cf. sense (3) above).

It might be objected that in defining senses (2) and (3) above, I made essential use of the notion of truth. For redness to exist (sense (2)) we had to be able to say *truly* of something that it was red; and for redness to exist (sense (3)) 'redness' had to admit of being a subject-term in a true or false statement. So, it might be claimed, wrongness will not exist on either of these definitions if statements containing the words 'wrong' and 'wrongness' cannot be true or false; and they cannot be true or false if the notion of truth does not apply to them. So an anti-realist could insist that wrongness did not exist in either of these two senses, because the statements in question cannot be either true or false. He might add, in view of the close connection between the notion of truth and that of meaning, that in that case it would not exist in sense (1) either.

This objection, however, is not to the point when we are discussing, as we now are, whether there is an *ontological* issue of substance between the realist and the anti-realist. For even if the question whether moral judgements can be called true or false is a fundamental question in ethics (as some think it is), it is not an ontological but a conceptual question. It is not a question about the existence or non-existence of anything. So, if the realists and the anti-realists were to claim that the issue between them is a serious one because it hangs on the answer to this serious conceptual question, they would be admitting that the issue is not really ontological but conceptual. They might as well give up calling themselves realists and anti-realists, and start calling themselves descriptivists and non-descriptivists instead. This is what I shall in fact be proposing, though I do not think that the most perspicuous way of stating the issue between the descriptivists and the non-descriptivists is by asking whether moral judgements can be true or false (on this see p. 26).

To sum up so far: it is unlikely that the formal senses of 'exist' are going to be of any use in setting up an ontological dispute between the realist and the anti-realist, because the latter can agree that in those senses moral qualities exist; but nor is the supposed stronger 'material' sense, because in that sense the realist would be unwise to claim that they exist, and does not need to.

It is now time to turn briefly to the other possible formulation of realism, that which insists on the existence of moral facts. The dispute is likely to collapse in the same way as before. Consider again the three formal senses of 'exist'. There seems to be no sense of 'exist' analogous to sense (1) above in which facts can be said to exist, because we do not establish the existence of facts, as we do of properties in this sense of 'exist', by making meaningful statements, but only by making true ones (or by its being the case that they could be made). In a sense analogous to sense (2), the fact that an act was wrong can be said to exist, if someone can truly say that that act was wrong. In a sense analogous to sense (3), the fact that an act was wrong exists, if the fact can be referred to by putting, e.g., 'the fact that it was wrong' into the subject-place in a true or false statement.

But the realists and the anti-realists have no reason to fall out over any of this, unless they are really disputing about the conceptual, not ontological, question of whether moral statements can properly be called true or false—in which case they should rename themselves descriptivists and non-descriptivists, as suggested already. By all means let them, if they wish, formulate their dispute as one about whether moral statements are factual or not; but let them recognize that this is not an ontological question but a conceptual one about the logical character, or role in our discourse, of these statements.

As to the question whether moral facts are part of the fabric of the world, or exist *in rerum natura*, that is a question that could be asked about *any* facts, and I shall not go into it. Actually, I agree with those who have argued *contra* the *Tractatus* that 'the world is the totality of things, not of facts' (cf. Strawson 1950: 133 ff.). I do not believe that we encounter facts in the world, spatially located. But since this is a general question in metaphysics, and what we say about it will apply to the fact that there is a cow in the field as well as to the fact that Smith's act was wrong, any dispute about it is not going to divide *ethical* realists and anti-realists in particular. If an ethical anti-realist is against admitting the existence of moral facts because he is against admitting the existence of any facts, his dispute with the realist is not a dispute in ethics. For there to be a dispute in ethics, one side must say that some facts exist, but not moral ones, and the other side must say that both sorts exist. In that case, the dispute is disposed of by what I have said already.

So far we have been talking about the property of wrongness, and the fact that an act was wrong, in just the same terms as the property of redness, and the fact that a thing is red. Everything that I have said about one of these pairs of expressions could be said about the other. Now it is time to ask whether there are things we should say about moral properties and facts which we should not say about 'ordinary' properties and facts. There is an old move, and an old answer to it, which used to be current in moral philosophy. The move has been revived; and perhaps the answer should be too. It is not my present business, however, to decide whether the answer is effective, but only to point out, what is fairly obvious, that neither the move nor the answer to it is ontological, both being epistemological or conceptual.

It is tempting, and initially useful, to compare moral qualities with what, following Locke, have been called 'secondary' qualities. Redness, which I have been using as an example, is one of these. The move is to claim that all the reasons given by anti-realists for singling out moral qualities as special in some way can equally be given for singling out secondary qualities as special in the same way. Thus, if the wrongness of an act is said to be the 'product' of an attitude on the part of the person who thinks it wrong, so also the redness of a thing can be said to be a 'product' of the visual reactions of a perceiver. In neither case, of course, is it the product solely of the attitude or reaction; in both, the primary or the non-moral qualities of the act or thing are partly involved. In both cases, on this view, the wrongness or the redness can be said to be the joint product of properties of the object or act (which are themselves not identical with the quality of wrongness or of redness) and of reactions in the perceiving or thinking subject.

The usefulness of this move to a realist is thought to be the following. If the anti-realist claims that so-called moral 'qualities' are nothing but reactions in an observer or thinker produced by the non-moral properties of an act, in conjunction with his prior dispositions or attitudes, the same can be said of all secondary qualities. So the distinction which the anti-realist is trying to make between moral properties and qualities like redness disappears.

The answer to this move has two parts. The first is to point out that, on this interpretation of what they are saying, both parties are misconceiving the issue between them in a common but by now inexcusable way. They are both speaking as if the anti-realist were advocating an 'old-fashioned' subjectivism of a kind which Mackie rightly disavows (1977: 17; see p. 19). This is the consequence of talk about moral qualities being the 'products' (in part) of attitudes, dispositions, or reactions of a thinking subject. Many people, because they have not even begun to understand the issue, seem unable to conceive that the anti-realist could mean anything else but this; but there is no reason why we should follow them. They only think this because they have not rid themselves of the prejudice that everything we say of anything has to be the ascription of some sort of descriptive property to it: if not an 'objective' property of the thing, then a 'subjective' property consisting in some relation the thing stands in to a subject (e.g. that of arousing an attitude in him). This is an old and tedious mistake, which it was the achievement of the early non-descriptivists to expose; when we say something moral, we do not have to be ascribing any kind of property, subjective or objective.

It is worth while pointing out, in this connection, that realists who make this move are in acute danger of falling into a most implausible type of relativism (see pp. 100, 113). For if they treat wrongness as fully analogous to redness, the statement that an act is wrong will be refutable by showing that it is not called wrong by people, conversant with the language, who view it under normal conditions. This is what we do with the statement that a thing is red. In the latter case, there is no room for anything as an explanation of deviance, except either a mistake about the meaning of a word or a fault in observation. If 'wrong' were treated in the same way, we should be able to squash a person who said it was wrong to eat meat by pointing out that everybody else, all those conversant with the use of the word, see nothing wrong in it even when fully informed about the character of the act. So the vegetarian will have to accept that he either is morally colour-blind or does not know English. The only way to get our moral judgements right is to say what others who speak our language say in the same circumstances (see p. 106).

This brings us to the second part of the answer to the realist's move. Even if there is an analogy between moral qualities and secondary qualities, those who press the analogy will fall into this kind of relativism unless they notice that there is also an important difference. The reactions which, according to this sort of phenomenalist view of morality, 'produce' the moral quality are attitudes such as approval and disapproval. But these, unlike the perception of something as red, are subject to our reasoned choices. We can ask, and rationally answer, the question 'What attitude shall I take up to meat-eating?' There is nothing corresponding to this in the case of redness. This fact is reflected in another, that to call an act wrong is to condemn it, and thus to engage our wills and those of any who agree with us in antagonism to the act.

The difference between moral and 'ordinary' properties lies not in any supposed difference in what 'produces' them, but in the different kinds of semantic or linguistic conventions which determine when we can ascribe them. The ascription of redness, for example, is governed by conventions which do not allow two people, faced with the same object in the same light in normal circumstances, to say, one of them that it is red and the other that it is not. One of them must be in breach of the conventions. He is in breach of them even if his mistake is due to colour-blindness. But the ascription of wrongness is governed by conventions which do allow you and me, confronted by the same act in normal and identical circumstances, to go on saying, one of us that it is wrong and the other that it is not wrong, if that is what we respectively think. We can reason about it in the hope that one will convince the other; but neither of us is constrained by our observation of the facts of the case and the correct use of words.

But we have now got right away from the supposedly

ontological question which allegedly divided the realist and the anti-realist, and on to questions about language and the conventions for the ascription of properties. It is not my purpose in this paper to settle these questions by coming down on one side or the other in any of the issues (realist/anti-realist, cognitivist/non-cognitivist, etc.) that I have listed, although it is well known what side I in fact support. I aim only to indicate which of these formulations best locates the main issue and gives us some hope of understanding it. I have said enough, perhaps, to show that the ontological way of putting the issue, which is associated with the names 'realist' and 'anti-realist', is *not* the best way of putting it. As soon as we start discussing the question in any penetrating way, it collapses into questions of a non-ontological sort. We cannot understand what on earth the parties to the ontological dispute are claiming until we restate the issue in terms which are not ontological.

In the light of what I have said, it appears that we do not need to worry about whether moral facts or moral qualities exist. Doubtless they exist in some of the senses I have listed, but not in others. At least, they are not part of the fabric of the world, and do not exist *in rerum natura*, if those terms are used in the strict sense that they certainly are by Mackie. I have heard realists agree that they do not: 'Of course', they say, 'moral properties are not physical properties and moral facts are not physical facts; but all the same they are real properties and facts.' An anti-realist, on his part, can easily agree that they exist in some of the other senses, or even exist *in rerum natura*, if that term is taken more liberally. That is not the way to get to the bottom of the problem.

What should concern us, rather, is how we should rationally determine, or satisfy ourselves, whether an act is wrong. People become realists, and insist that the quality of wrongness has to be part of the fabric of the world, because they think that, unless this is so, there will be no way of rationally deciding such questions. But are they right to think this? They think it, only because they are the victims of a prejudice which is almost universal among moral philosophers.

The prejudice is one about rationality. It is thought that only procedures leading to the making of statements can be rational (see p. 99). Hume summed up this prejudice in his famous remark that

Reason is the discovery of truth or falsehood. Truth or falsehood consists in an agreement or disagreement either to the *real* relations of ideas, or to *real* existence and matter of fact. Whatever, therefore, is not susceptible of this agreement or disagreement, is incapable of being true or false, and can never be an object of our reason. (1739: III. i. 1)

Mackie, in this as in so much else, seems to have been a follower of Hume. That this is a mere prejudice should be apparent to anybody who reflects that we can rationally decide what to do, or what to ask or advise others to do (see p. 35). In other words, thought-processes which have as their end-products prescriptions can be rational (or irrational). There will be factual elements in the reasoning (i.e. rationality demands congnizance of the facts—see *MT* 88); but even given this cognizance, whether the whole process is rational or irrational, or whether the conclusion is rationally or irrationally arrived at, does not depend solely on the rationality of the fact-finding part of the process. What Hume calls 'the relations of ideas' have to be rationally ordered too, and these ideas will include some prescriptive ones. Indeed, they must, if the conclusion is to be prescriptive. It is thus entirely possible to arrive rationally at a moral conclusion even though that conclusion is not a statement of fact about what is the case *in rerum natura*. Ethical rationalism does not, therefore, demand ethical realism.

If this is once understood, we are free from the need to engage in ontology of any sort in order to do ethics. The ontological issue has dissolved into an epistemological or logical one: how to give an account of moral thinking which allows it to arrive in a rational way at conclusions which are practical and prescriptive. We can admit that there exist moral qualities and facts in some of the senses listed above, but see that this is beside the main point. A philosopher who affirms that they exist has done absolutely nothing to solve the main problem, namely how we determine that they exist in a particular case—in plainer words, how to determine, for example, that an act *is* wrong.

I started by listing various ways in which the distinction between types of ethical theory could be put. Of these, we can perhaps now leave behind the terms 'realism' and 'anti-realism', as concealing the main issue. We are left with the distinctions in psychological terms (beliefs/attitudes), in epistemological terms (cognitivism/non-cognitivism) and in logical or conceptual terms (descriptivism/non-descriptivism).

The psychological way of putting the distinction can perhaps be set aside fairly rapidly. This is because the beliefs and attitudes in question will share the property of intentionality which all mental states have. It will be impossible to characterize them fully and perspicuously without introducing a proposition or 'that'-clause which gives the content of the mental state. For example, it is commonly and rightly held that to describe a desire we have to characterize it as the desire *that* such and such a thing should happen. This is obviously so with moral beliefs or attitudes. Whether we speak of the belief that an act would be wrong, or of an attitude of disapproval of the proposed act, we have, in order to characterize the mental state in question (to say what in particular the person who is in it is thinking, or what is going on in his mind) to say that he is thinking *that* the act would be wrong.

Thus the full explanation of these psychological states demands a logical or conceptual or linguistic explanation of the words in which what he is thinking would be expressed if it were expressed, or of what he would be saying if he said that the act would be wrong. This can be illustrated by the controversies between the early emotivists and their opponents. Suppose that an emotivist (Professor Ayer for example in *Language, Truth and Logic*) were to say that 'It would be wrong' is to be analysed as an expression of disapproval of the act. And suppose that an opponent protested that at least this sentence has the grammatical form of an indicative and therefore must express a belief. This will not serve to refute the emotivist or even put him off his stride. In order to determine the issue between those who say that this grammar is only superficial and those who maintain that it truly represents the logical character of the judgement, we shall have to engage in conceptual study, and only when that is complete shall we know whether, when the man said it, he was expressing a belief or an attitude. The psychological way of putting the distinction, therefore, will always for its full explanation require the logical or conceptual.

I wish to say in passing that in my own view the grammar is *not* superficial, but that those who rely on it for an argument are. There are descriptive elements deeply embedded in moral statements, along with the prescriptive, and they need a full account of what Stevenson called the descriptive meaning of the statements to explain them. An initial dogmatic insistence that the statements are descriptive in form gets in the way of this necessary explanation, whose upshot is that moral statements are a hybrid, sharing some of the characteristics both of pure descriptions and of pure prescriptions. All this I have treated of elsewhere; and it needs to be understood if we are justly to assess Mackie's view that people making moral judgements claim to be 'pointing to something objectively prescriptive' (1977: 35; see *MT* 78 ff.).

If, then, the psychological way of putting the distinction, like the ontological, collapses into the logical or conceptual, we are left with the epistemological and logical-conceptual ways as the only remaining possibilities. I shall now argue that the epistemological in turn collapses into the logical-conceptual, and that for clarity we should cease to speak of cognitivism and non-cognitivism and use instead the terms 'descriptivism' and 'non-descriptivism'. The reason for this is that a solution to the epistemological problem of how we can determine rationally whether an act would be wrong depends on a solution to the logical or conceptual problem of what we are saying when we say that it would be wrong. One does not have to be an old-fashioned verificationist, nor even (which is different) hold a purely truth-condition theory of meaning, to be sure that the logical character of an utterance, and the rules which govern our reasoning about it, are closely linked. If it is by reasoning that we determine whether we should accept what has been said, the epistemological question of how we determine this must be inseparable from the logical question of what we are saying and its implication-relations with other things we might say. This could be denied only by a very extreme intuitionist who thought that we needed no reasoning, no rational thinking, to determine the moral character of acts, but just saw intuitively that they were right or wrong. But even he would have taken a stand on the logical character of moral judgements, assimilating them to judgements of perception immune to thought. The issue between him and a rationalist would still be a logical one.

There is, however, a danger to be guarded against here, signalled by the reference in the last paragraph to the verification and truth-condition theories of meaning. It is right to say, as I have, that the logical character, even the meaning, of moral statements is closely tied to ways of reasoning about them. But it is wrong to say that their meaning, in conjunction with the non-moral facts, determines their truth or falsity. The ways of reasoning which their logical character imposes on us do not consist simply in comparing a moral statement with the non-moral facts and then pronouncing it true or false in accordance with truth-conditions or verification-rules. To think this is to be a descriptivist. A prescriptivist like myself will think that we have first to understand the statement (its logic and conceptual character as well as its content), and thus the forms of thought which are appropriate to determining whether to accept it, and then do some thinking in accordance with these forms of thought. They may require much more than a bare comparison with the non-moral facts. I have tried to explain elsewhere what they do require (*MT* chs. 5, 6).

My conclusion is that, for any penetrating thinker, both ontological and psychological questions about ethics are bound to give place to a combination of logical and epistemological questions intimately related to one another. The reason why I much prefer the term 'descriptivism' to the term 'cognitivism', and somewhat dislike being called a non-cognitivist, is that this term would seem to imply that I recognize no rational procedure for deciding moral questions. It depends on how much one reads into the word 'cognitive'. For many psychologists, belief as well as knowledge counts as a cognitive state. The psychological argument, just set aside, between those who call moral convictions beliefs and those who call them attitudes was superficial, not only for the reason given (intentionality), but because one could very well call them beliefs and yet maintain that they were radically different from ordinary factual beliefs. The same trouble will infect the word 'cognitive' if a belief is to count as a cognitive state. Even an emotivist might hold that in this wide sense of 'cognitive' moral attitudes were cognitive states. But in a narrower sense of 'cognitive', in which a mental state is not cognitive unless it consists in *knowing* something, an emotivist could not be a cognitivist, for he denies that there can be knowledge of moral truths.

My own position is that we can certainly speak of knowing that an act is wrong, just as we can speak of someone saying truly that someone did something wrong (see p. 26). But I would immediately add that this is because such utterances have in most societies a fairly firm descriptive meaning attached to them, so that we know at once what non-moral properties would be accepted as substantiating the claim that an act was wrong, and can therefore, when we know that an act would have these properties, readily say that we know that it would be wrong and that it is true that it would be wrong. But to recognize this should not lead us to ignore the much more important question of how we are to decide whether society is right to give the word this particular descriptive meaning, thereby selecting certain kinds of act and not others for condemnation.

It is this latter question (how to decide) which should engage us. It is an epistemological question—a question in the theory of knowledge in a wide sense of 'knowledge'; not a question of how to find out facts, but one of how to determine questions (in this case prescriptive questions) rationally. If to think that they can be determined rationally is to have an epistemology or theory of knowledge, then one who thinks this, as I do, should perhaps be labelled a cognitivist. But I do not recommend the label, because those who are unable to envisage any other kind of reasoning than factual will think that if I am a cognitivist I must be a descriptivist, which I am not.

In conclusion, I should like to defend briefly my use, here and above, of expressions such as 'logical and conceptual'. I belong to the school of thought which holds that to study the logical properties of words and to study concepts are the same study. Formal logic, on this view, is the formalization of the rules governing words (especially but not only the so-called 'logical' words) which partly determine the meanings of those words (determine it wholly if they are purely logical words like 'all'). I would wish to maintain that 'ought' and 'wrong' are in this way purely logical words, being natural-language versions of deontic-logical signs. But a lot of this could be given up, without abandoning the essential point, that to understand what someone who has made a moral statement was saying we have to understand what he was implying, what would be consistent or inconsistent with what he said, and the like. In this field at least, logical and conceptual analysis are inseparable, and that is why I have not tried to separate them.

7
How to Decide Moral Questions Rationally

I F we look back over the development of moral (and also of legal) philosophy over the past fifty years or so, we can see it as the unfolding of the consequences of a fundamental mistake. Almost the first thing that happened to me when I started doing moral philosophy was that I saw that it was a mistake. I have been trying ever since to make people see that it is a mistake. But I have not been very successful. Let me now try to explain again what the mistake is.

It is the mistake of thinking that the only possible exercise of reason is in determining facts or discovering truths. That there can be practical as well as theoretical reason was a cardinal thesis of Kant; and Aristotle, with his concept of *phronēsis*, or practical as opposed to theoretical wisdom, showed that he thought the same. But now nearly everybody, whether or not he calls himself a rationalist, seems to agree in thinking that *if* one wishes to be a rationalist (if, that is to say, one wishes to find a place for rationality in moral thinking), one has to be a descriptivist (that is to say, one has to believe that there are moral facts to be discovered). This almost universal mistake has had the most harmful consequences in recent moral philosophy, which it is my purpose in this paper to explore.

The effect of the mistake has been to preclude its victims from finding an account of moral thinking which has any hope of showing it to be a rational activity. The reasons for this are simple. If one thinks that the only function of reason is to discover facts, then obviously one will think that in order to make moral thinking a rational activity one has to show

From *Critica* 18 (1987). Original Italian version in *Etica e diritto: le vie della giustificazione razionale*, ed. E. Lecaldano (Rome, Laterza).

moral judgements to be some sort of factual or descriptive judgements. But both of the possible types of theory which claim to show this turn out to be dead ends, each of them leading in its own way into a kind of relativism that would be wholly unacceptable to most of the adherents of these 'objectivist' views. I shall explain in a moment how this comes about. On the other hand, if one makes the mistake, but at the same time realizes that moral judgements are *not* (or at least not purely or primarily) statements of fact, then one will be led into a completely irrationalist view about moral thinking: one will be led to think that since the only possible exercise of reason is in discovering facts, and since there are no moral facts to be discovered, reason cannot be used in establishing them; they must therefore be the province of the irrational emotions or, as Hume called them, passions.

Those who take the first horn of this dilemma, and say that moral judgements state facts and that therefore they can be rational, fall into two main schools. We have, first, various so-called 'naturalist' theories. The distinguishing feature of these is that they hold that moral judgements are equivalent in meaning to factual statements of some ordinary non-moral kind. They can therefore be established by whatever methods are appropriate to discovering facts of that ordinary non-moral kind. It is difficult to find convincing examples of such theories. A simple example—a theory which has probably never been held in this simple form, though James Mill and indeed Bentham made occasional remarks which might lead one to suppose that they held it—would be a theory which held that 'right action' *means the same as* 'action which maximizes pleasure', and that 'maximizing pleasure' is a description of an observable empirical property of actions. That it is impossible to find convincing statements of any naturalist theory has not prevented people to this day going on claiming that moral judgements do state facts which are open to discovery by the normal processes of observation not involving any special power of moral cognition.

Secondly, we have various kinds of 'intuitionist' theories, according to which moral judgements are statements of fact indeed, but statements of a special kind of fact which is not open to ordinary methods of discovery, but requires a special kind of moral thinking to ascertain it. Such a crude statement of the intuitionist view would not be acceptable to many modern moral philosophers; but if one looks carefully at their arguments one can see that at many crucial points they make appeal to intuitions (sometimes called 'moral convictions') which are unsupported by argument. This is true of John Rawls, Robert Nozick, Ronald Dworkin, Bernard Williams, and Stuart Hampshire, for example. To these I fear that we must add Hilary Putnam (1987). The arguments of such writers will not survive scrutiny, unless the scrutiny is conducted by sympathetic people—that is, by people who already share the writers' convictions. Against those who do not, no arguments are provided. So we are bound to conclude that they are placing reliance on their ability to discern the moral truth without argument, by exercising their power of moral cognition, and think that all who similarly exercise it will come to the same conclusions. This, though, is clearly false, because, to take an obvious example, Rawls and Nozick come to radically opposed conclusions by exercising their respective moral intuitions. However, to find writers who actually *avow* intuitionist views, one has, with a few exceptions, to go back to the previous generation, to people like Ross and Prichard. But in spite of this it is fair to say that the majority of moral philosophers today, at any rate in the English-speaking world, are some kind of crypto-intuitionists.

Those who take the second horn of the dilemma, and say that moral judgements are *not* statements of fact, and that therefore moral thinking *cannot* be a rational activity, include mainly the emotivists, such as Hägerström, Carnap, Ayer, and Stevenson. The view is not held by many people nowadays, largely because by now those who think that moral judgements are not (or not purely) statements of fact have disabused themselves of the mistake I am exposing, and come to see that the denial that there are moral facts does not entail that moral thinking has to be irrational. But the people who see this are still relatively few. It is much more common to find their *opponents* (who think that there are moral facts) accusing those who deny this of irrationalism, because they, the opponents, are the victims of the mistake and do not see the possibility of a rationalist, but non-factualist and non-descriptivist, theory.

Let me now explain, as I promised to do, how both sorts of factualism or descriptivism are bound to collapse in their different ways into relativism. I will start with a naturalist. Let us suppose that he maintains that, for example, the sentence '*X* (some act) is wrong' means the same as '*X* is *F*', where '*F*' stands for some factual or descriptive predicate, such that the statement that *X* is *F* is verifiable by some ordinary fact-finding procedure. Now consider the position of someone who disagrees with him about some fundamental moral question. Suppose, for example, that '*F*' stands for 'not pleasure-maximizing'. The two will then be thinking, one of them that all acts which do not maximize pleasure are wrong, and the other that some acts which do not maximize pleasure are not wrong. The first of these two people, the naturalist, will maintain that his own opinion is true by definition, because 'wrong' *means* 'not pleasure-maximizing'. The second, however, is not going to be defeated so easily. Since what he thinks is that there are some acts which are not pleasure-maximizing but yet are not wrong, he cannot be using the word 'wrong' in such a way that it is logically impossible for this to be the case. He can present himself as a standing counter-example to the naturalist's definition.

It then becomes a question of whether one, or whether the other, of them is correct in his use of the word 'wrong'. Let us suppose that they set out to decide this question in what seems the only possible way, by linguistic research—that is, by examining the way the word is used by speakers of their language. It will be the case that the people of their linguistic community are divided into two classes, one of which uses the word 'wrong' in the same way as the naturalist, to mean 'not pleasure-maximizing', while the other uses it in some different way, or in a variety of ways. The object of their investigation is to determine the relative sizes of these two classes. They know already that neither of them is empty; for one of the disputants is a member of the first class, and the other of the second.

People of the first class think that whatever acts are not pleasure-maximizing are always wrong, and people of the second class do not think this. But is this really no more than a disagreement about the use or meaning of the word 'wrong'? Obviously not. It is a *moral* disagreement of substance between the two classes of people. But it is worth exploring the consequences for the naturalist of his thinking, as he does, that it is just a verbal disagreement.

Why do I say that naturalism collapses into relativism? Let us suppose, for the sake of simplicity, though it makes no difference to the argument, that the two classes of people are both fairly numerous, and that they are divided geographically. Everybody living south of a certain latitude within the country in question says that whatever is not pleasure-maximizing is wrong, and everybody living north of the same latitude disagrees with this. According to the naturalist, the first lot *have* to think what they think, because they *mean* by 'wrong', 'not pleasure-maximizing'. If somebody living north of the critical latitude were to migrate to the southern part of the country and were determined, in order to be able to communicate with his new neighbours, to learn to speak the language precisely as they speak it, he would have to *change* his use of the word 'wrong', so that he too would become constrained to think that whatever did not maximize pleasure was wrong.

There are two possible interpretations of what has happened. One of them is not open to the naturalist: it is the one which I said just now is obviously the right interpretation. This is that the disagreement is not just a linguistic disagreement but a substantial moral disagreement. But this the naturalist cannot admit. He has to say that it *is* just a linguistic disagreement. He has to say that the people in the southern part of the country *mean* by 'wrong', 'not pleasure-maximizing'. What he will say about the people in the north I do not know. Possibly he will say that they use the word in a different sense. Possibly he will say that they are somehow mistaken to use it in this sense; but if that is the sense in which they do use it, it is hard to see how he can say this. It would be like the Americans saying that Englishmen are wrong to use 'solicitor' to mean what Americans mean by 'attorney'. The English would justly retort that that is how they do use the word in their country, and who are the Americans to tell them to use it in some other way?

However, whatever the naturalist says about the people in the north, he will have to say that, on his view, the person who goes to the south and learns to speak the southern language will have come to think that whatever is not pleasure-maximizing is wrong. This is the relativism into which, as I said, naturalism inevitably collapses. It ties moral opinions to the meanings of the moral words, the effect of which is that we have to adopt the moral views of those who use the words. Otherwise we are linguistically at fault. I have chosen too simple an example. But if one took some more sophisticated example of a naturalist position, exactly the same thing would happen. Naturalism reduces moral disagreements to linguistic disagreements, and the result is that we become constrained to adopt the moral opinions of those whose language we are speaking.

I come now to the intuitionists, whose doctrine collapses into a different sort of relativism. Here too we must start with the fact of moral disagreement. Let us suppose again that two people disagree about some important moral question. According to the intuitionist, each of them is using his moral intuition, and, since they disagree, one of them must be using it wrongly. One thing at any rate is clear, that both of them have moral convictions of the sort that intuitionists appeal to. The convictions may be strong ones, so that each will say, 'I know I am right'. The question is, whether the intuitionist has left himself any way of deciding *which* is right. Since he has no appeal except to convictions, it would seem that he has not.

To put the point another way: there is no dispute about the *phenomena* of the moral life between this intuitionist and someone who thinks that the moral convictions are just feelings or attitudes. What this second person will say is that the two disputants have different attitudes, or feel differently about the matter. Unless the intuitionist can produce some way of deciding which of the two convictions is the correct one, does his theory differ in any important respect from that of the person who speaks of attitudes and feelings? I cannot see that it does.

To this an intuitionist is likely to reply that the intuitions or convictions to which he appeals are not just *any* convictions that anybody happens to have, but the convictions of morally well-educated people. If this is so, then one of our two disputants must have been badly educated morally. But which? It is easy to think of cases where different cultures bring up their children differently. For example, in many circles in India, meat-eating is considered wrong, and children, when they get to the age at which they ask such questions, are led to think that it is sinful. By contrast, in most, but not all, circles in the West it is regarded as perfectly legitimate. What will the intuitionist say about two people, one from each of these cultures, who are in dispute on this question? There may be no doubt about the strength of their convictions, nor any doubt that these convictions are the result of their education. But which was the good education? The intuitionist has left himself no way of deciding this question.

The same trouble arises at a more theoretical level. An intuitionist who (as is usual) calls himself a cognitivist or a realist will often say that moral qualities are really no different in status from perceptible qualities like redness. Just as those who have learnt the use of the word 'red' and have normal eyesight can say which objects are red, so those who have learnt the use of the word 'wrong' and have normal moral reactions can say which actions are wrong. But if we try out this theory on the dispute about meat-eating we shall see into what trouble we get. It turns out that the two disputants have *different* reactions to meat-eating. Which of these reactions are the *normal* ones? If such a dispute arose about the redness of some object, then we should have to say that one of the disputants was either colour-blind, or mistaken in his use of the word 'red'. But in the case of wrongness the intuitionist will not say (because he is not a naturalist) that the dispute between the two people is a verbal one; he will say that it is a difference between the moral reactions that they respectively have. He is required by his theory, therefore, to say that one of them (though he has not told us how to say which) is 'morally colour-blind', that is, that he has the wrong moral reactions to the facts about meat-eating on which they are both agreed.

However, it is clear that the case of redness and the case of wrongness are quite different. This can be seen from the fact that in many cases we allow moral disagreements to continue without insisting that one of the parties must either be misusing the moral words or be morally colour-blind. They just disagree about a moral question. I shall ask later how we are to do the thinking which would resolve such disagreements. But for the moment let us be clear that this case is not like that of redness. The person who says that an object seen in a normal light is red, when everybody else agrees that it is not red, is constrained to admit that he either does not know the use of 'red' or has made a mistake. In the face of this general dissent from his statement, he has to withdraw it. But the man who says that eating meat is wrong can stick to his opinion, even if nobody agrees with him; he does not have to admit that he has misunderstood the word 'wrong' or has a faulty moral faculty. He is using the word 'wrong' in just the same way as everybody else (otherwise it could not be used to express their disagreement: when he said that meat-eating was wrong and they said that it was not wrong, they would be meaning different things by 'wrong' and so their statements would not really contradict one another). He just thinks wrong something that all the rest of them do not think wrong (in the *same* sense of 'wrong'). Do the vegetarians have to adopt the views of all the rest just because they are a minority?

Note that although vegetarians in the West started by being in a very small minority there are now many of them, and they are increasing. The same is true of pacifists. Can we say that at any stage in this process the vegetarians or the pacifists could be ruled out of court by pointing out that they are in a small minority? That really would be relativism.

It is no accident that both naturalism and intuitionism, when faced with moral disagreements, collapse into relativism. The basic reason is the same in both cases. It is that both, seeking some source of moral authority, find it in something that is relative to particular cultures. The naturalist finds it in linguistic usage. But this obviously varies from one culture to another, with the result that, by tying correct moral judgement to the correct use of the moral words, he binds our morality to the culture of the people whose language we happen to speak. The intuitionist, on the other hand, finds his moral authority in the moral convictions of people. But these vary according to the attitudes, engendered by the upbringings, that are favoured in particular places. Here too there is no firm ground on which to stand.

So far as I can see, naturalism and intuitionism are the only two possible kinds of descriptivism (though there are of course many thinkers who are so unclear that it is impossible to say to which school they belong). It is therefore time to ask whether we ought not, in our search for moral rationality, to abandon descriptivism altogether, and whether, if we do, we can find any form of non-descriptivism that will serve our rational purposes. I have maintained in many places that we can. Those who have not followed these disputes may find it surprising that a non-descriptivist could be a rationalist; but that is because they are the victims of the mistake I have been trying to expose. I think I have Kant on my side.

Suppose, therefore, that we abandon once for all the claim that moral judgements are mere statements of fact, and seek for a rational form of non-descriptivism. What then can we do to provide rational moral arguments? I have suggested in my writings that the first thing we have to do is seek an understanding of the moral words or concepts (see p. 175). This understanding will bring with it a grasp of the logical rules which govern our moral thinking; for to understand a word is to understand the implications of propositions containing it. However, the meaning and the logic of the moral words that we do discover is not primarily a descriptive meaning but a prescriptive. We do not discover that their meaning is tied to the truth-conditions of propositions containing them. Rather, we discover that to say of some act that it is wrong is to condemn it, or to prescribe the avoidance of it. At this point those who have made the descriptivist mistake will ask how, if that is what moral words mean, there can possibly be any moral reasoning. But I ask them to be patient.

When we are wondering whether to call some kind of act wrong, we are wondering whether to prescribe its avoidance. But there is more to it than that. We are wondering whether to prescribe its *universal* avoidance (in cases just like the one we are considering). In words which Kant might have used, we are wondering whether to prescribe its avoidance as a universal law. And analogously, when we are asking whether an act is obligatory, we are wondering whether to prescribe its performance, in just those circumstances, as a universal law. I have argued elsewhere, in highly Kantian style, that this requirement of universality in our moral judgements places severe constraints on the moral judgements or universal prescriptions that we shall be prepared to accept (*MT* chs. 5, 6). To take a simple case: if I had only to utter singular prescriptions, I might well be prepared to prescribe that I should snatch the food off other people's plates if I had a mind to it and was stronger than them. But if I ask whether I am prepared to prescribe that this should be done universally, including cases where I am the victim and am weaker, I unhesitatingly answer that I am not. So, reasoning in this way, we come to adopt a universal principle, acceptable to all of us, which condemns such behaviour. In my books I have elaborated this line of argument, using examples that are less simple and more serious. I have room now only to say very briefly how the argument goes. In doing so, I shall not be able to counter numerous objections which may occur to those who have not become acquainted with the places where I, and others also, have answered them.

The argument, although it has started from a Kantian view about the logic of the moral words, now takes a utilitarian turn. It is commonly thought that there are two schools of thought in moral philosophy called the Kantian and the utilitarian, and that these hold views diametrically opposed to each other. Those who say this show only how superficially they have studied Kant and the utilitarian writers. John Stuart Mill gives good reasons, in his essay *Utilitarianism*, for saying that the Kantian Categorical Imperative is satisfied by the utilitarian doctrine. After investigating the matter in more detail I have found this to be so, and indeed I am inclined to accept Mill's hint (1861: ch. 1) that it is the *only* doctrine which does so. I will try to explain why.

If we are, in our moral reasoning, required to prescribe universally for cases of a given sort, then these universal prescriptions will have to apply to all cases of that sort, including cases in which *we* are in the various situations resulting from possible alternative actions. The universality of the prescriptions prevents us from prescribing differently for cases in which we ourselves would be adversely affected. We have, in other words, to treat the preferences of any party in a given situation as of equal weight, strength for strength, whether that party is ourselves or somebody else. In a universal prescription, no mention can be made of individuals as such, and therefore in adopting such a prescription we cannot exclude the possibility that the individual affected by its carrying out might be ourselves. Only by giving equal positive weight to the equal preferences of all individuals can we find universal prescriptions which are the most acceptable to us.

This is simply utilitarianism put into other words. It is that variety of utilitarianism which says that we ought to choose that alternative, of those available to us, which maximizes the preference-satisfactions, in sum, of all those affected by our action, considered impartially. For this is the alternative which we shall choose if we give equal weight to equal preferences, whosoever preferences they are. Since there are a great many different varieties of utilitarianism, and some of them (for example, the naturalistic version mentioned earlier) are open to very obvious objections, it is necessary to be extremely careful which variety we are discussing. I shall be defending my own variety, which is not open to these objections.

Most of the common objections rely on finding discrepancies between what, it is said, a utilitarian would have to prescribe and what our common moral convictions tell us. The examples used always concern highly unusual sets of circumstances. The short answer to such objections is that our common moral convictions, and the strong moral feelings that go with them, are not designed to deal with such improbable cases. They are the result of our upbringing, which (if those who brought us up were wise) was intended to fit us for life in the world as it is, and cope with its common contingencies. In order to keep us in the path of virtue, we have, most of us, been imbued with very strong and deep convictions of this sort. A wise utilitarian educator would do his best to achieve this. But in unusual situations these deep convictions will conflict with one another, and are not able by themselves to resolve the conflict. This gives rise to the agonizing dilemmas so beloved of writers of fiction.

This short answer to these objections is capable of being developed into a complete account of the moral life with all its complex phenomena. The principal feature of such an account is the division of moral thinking into two levels. There is, first of all, the intuitive level, at which we apply to normal situations that confront us the moral principles and convictions that we have acquired through our upbringing. Intuitionist philosophers give, generally speaking, an adequate account of this level of thinking. In it, as they say, the morally well-educated person will know what he ought to do. Their fault is to think that this is a sufficient description of the whole of moral thinking. It is quite powerless to deal with two crucial questions that remain. First, how do we know which moral convictions are the right ones to cultivate, or what is the best kind of moral education? Secondly, what do we do when, as inevitably happens in unusual cases, these moral convictions conflict with one another?

To these questions the intuitionists have no answer, but utilitarians have one. The answer is to say that there is another level of moral thinking, which I call the critical level, at which we ask, first of all what are the best moral convictions and dispositions to cultivate, and secondly what to do when they conflict in difficult cases, as they inevitably will.

The virtue of this account is that it leaves intact that part of intuitionism which has the greatest intuitive appeal, its description of the moral thinking that we do in all normal cases, while at the same time enabling us to explain, as the intuitionists cannot, how to deal with out-of-the-way cases, and how to justify the convictions to which intuitionists appeal. Their justification is that it is best that we have them. Those are the convictions which a wise utilitarian educator would seek to cultivate. Religious people will say that God, who is a wise educator, has cultivated them in us under the name of 'conscience'. That was the view of Joseph Butler, whose remarks on this subject at the end of his *Sermons* and in his *Dissertation on Virtue* are very penetrating (see p. 58).

So then, the answer to the question in my title, 'How to decide moral questions rationally', is this. First of all, we are to realize that deciding a moral question is committing oneself to a universal prescription for all similar cases. Because the prescription has to be universal, we shall not be able in choosing it to give particular weight to our own interests, but shall have to choose in the interests of all those affected considered impartially. This means doing the best, in sum, for them all; and this in turn means that we have to give equal weight to the equal preferences of all.

If we were completely rational beings, and had unlimited information and superhuman powers of clear thinking, what we should do would be to find out all the facts and then determine what would be best in the particular case. This is what would be done by the being whom I call in *MT* ch. 3 'the archangel'. We may assume that it is what is done by God.

But since we humans are far from being completely rational beings, the best way of achieving the decisions that a completely rational being *would* make is to cultivate in ourselves, and in those whom we influence, dispositions which on the whole will make our decisions coincide with those of such a rational being. Because we are always incompletely informed and always subject to other human failings, we are more likely that way to make, over the course of our lives, the decisions that we ought to make than by doing a utilitarian calculation on each occasion. For this reason the utilitarian himself will bid us not to think in a simple utilitarian way in the normal case, but to use our intuitions; but he will add the warning that we should also cultivate the habit of critical moral thought, reviewing, when we are not subject to the stress of actual moral dilemmas, the intuitions that we have, in order to satisfy ourselves that they are the best ones. This will also prepare us for those rare occasions on which our intuitions do not give us clear or consistent guidance.

So, if I am asked how to decide moral questions rationally, my answer will vary according to the degree of rationality that we think we possess. A supremely rational being would decide all moral questions by critical thinking; that is, by asking what universal prescriptions to accept for cases just like the one before him; and his answer would be such as to maximize the satisfactions of preferences of all considered impartially. But for somebody who recognizes his own ir-rationality, it will be rational not to try to think all the time like this supremely rational being. He may get the reasoning wrong. However, to the extent that we are able, we have to cultivate our reasoning powers, for there is no other secure guide or authority. Even if God and archangels exist, we have no reliable line of communication with them, and have to use our reason in order to determine, if we can, what they would say. Our feeble human reason is better than no reason at all; when we are not able to rely on our intuitions, either because they conflict in a particular case, or because we are uncertain what are the right intuitions to cultivate, we have to do the best we can.

8
A *Reductio ad Absurdum* of Descriptivism

MOST moral philosophers are, I suppose, descriptivists of some sort; and most of those who become so (unlike John Mackie (1977), who was one of the few exceptions) do it because of a certain motivation. They have a deep desire to establish something that can be loosely described as the objectivity of moral judgements. And this desire in turn arises from a still deeper one, the desire to do one's moral thinking in a rational way. The route from the desire for rationality via the desire for objectivity to descriptivism is a well trodden one; but it is nevertheless a primrose path; for, as we shall see, it leads those who follow it into one or another form of relativism, which is precisely what these thinkers are trying to avoid. They can avoid it only by retracing their steps.

This primrose path starts from the assumption that the only way to achieve rationality is to secure objectivity. This assumption might be acceptable, if only the word 'objectivity' had a clear and unambiguous meaning. But it notoriously has not. The primrose path is followed by those who take it as obvious that the only kind of objectivity is that provided by descriptivism. What this kind is we shall see in a moment.

Luckily we now have available a very elegant illustration of how one may proceed down the primrose path, in Professor MacIntyre's presidential address to the American Philosophical Association at its Eastern Meeting in New York (1984). This is so well written and so larded with excellent examples that I shall be able to describe the route more briefly and clearly than if I had to take the reader through the more tortuous writings of some other primrose-fanciers.

I am sure that MacIntyre is a descriptivist, and that he has proceeded all the way down the primrose path to relativism;

From *Philosophy in Britain Today*, ed. S. Shanker (London, Croom Helm, 1986).

but I am not sure what motives have led him down it, or whether they are as I have been describing. His thesis is a quite general one. It applies not only to moral and other evaluative words, but to expressions used in science and even to proper names. He does not indeed claim that in any of these areas of discourse it affects all words; but he implies that it affects enough of them to establish his pessimistic conclusion. I shall in what follows largely confine myself to the bearing of his thesis on moral philosophy, partly because I am only an amateur in those other fields, and partly because, as MacIntyre rightly implies, it is in moral philosophy and in its close relation political philosophy that the thesis would, if true, have its greatest practical impact.

The thesis is this, if I may attempt a brief summary which does not do it too much injustice. A very large number of words in all languages are culture-bound in this sense, that their serious use in speech-acts to which the speaker subscribes is not available to those who are not participants in the culture. So much is familiar from other authors, and indeed from MacIntyre's own earlier writings. What is more peculiar to him is the political pessimism.

MacIntyre thinks we cannot use the words of a culture in which we are not participants, and therefore cannot by using them communicate with those who are, in order to discuss with them the moral and other disagreements between us. His reason is that the meaning of these words is tied to common beliefs and values and traditional texts, shared by the participants but not by others. For the same reason it is, he thinks, impossible for participants in one culture to use words which are tied to their own culture in order to discuss differences with members of other cultures. They will just not be understood. And so, if the differences are important ones with political consequences which the disputants think vital, their only recourse, MacIntyre implies, will be to violence and the struggle for power. MacIntyre's arguments for un-translatability are different from, and largely independent of, those of the Quine-Davidson school, so I shall not in this paper discuss the latter.

I agree that if the thesis is accepted, these consequences are likely to follow. But unlike MacIntyre I regard this as a *reductio ad absurdum* of the thesis. For although it must be admitted that there is too much violence in the world, not all disputes between people of different cultures are settled by violence or power struggles. It would have been worth MacIntyre's while to look more closely at how they are sometimes settled even by more or less rational discussion.

I explained the essentials of an understanding of how to bring this about a long time ago in *LM* 148 ff., but in terms of an example (missionary converting cannibals) which MacIntyre might not like, and which in any case introduces irrelevant factors. Perhaps there are those now who think that it is colonialistic and wrong to convert cannibals so that they no longer go scalp-hunting. And in most cases, unlike that which I described, force played a part in the suppression of cannibalism. And even where it did not, it is unlikely that rational discussion had much to do with the cannibals' conversion.

So let me take a different example; that of a discussion between, say, a Sudanese and an American of the practice of female circumcision. (I will use this familiar term, although to be accurate one should use the more specific terms 'clitoridectomy' and 'infibulation'.) While I was writing this paper and had already chosen the example, I was lucky enough to be lent a very illuminating as well as horrifying booklet on this subject (McLean 1980). The main author is a Westerner, but several of her collaborators were from cultures which practise female circumcision. The fact that they could jointly produce the booklet casts some doubt on MacIntyre's thesis. Evidently people from different cultures *can* discuss a question like this, because the contributors *had* discussed it, and reached the rational conclusion that the practice is wrong. Their reasons are in the booklet. The discussion is mainly factual, but it does make some use of value-words. The ones that occur most commonly are words like 'harmful'. This shows that such discussions can have a utilitarian basis. 'Rights', however, are also mentioned, so that is another possibility, although it would be a mistake to suppose that utilitarians cannot also use the term 'rights' (*MT* ch. 9; H 1984*a*, *b*, *d*).

I have read at least one article by a Western journalist

highly sympathetic to this practice as an element in an indigenous culture with which it would be wrong to interfere; so it is at any rate *possible* for Westerners to respect the values of other cultures. But let us suppose that our American is not so sympathetic, and thinks the practice wrong. The Sudanese, on the other hand, thinks it is obligatory upon young Sudanese women: they would be doing wrong if they did not follow the custom.

They will naturally use the word 'wrong' in discussing their difference (let us suppose that the Sudanese speaks English). One of them will say that it is wrong to circumcise girls, and the other that it is wrong not to circumcise them. Is it MacIntyre's view that communication must inevitably break down, because the word 'wrong' will have different meanings in their two mouths? I cannot answer this question, at least until I have drawn attention to a distinction, which ought to be already familiar (*LM* 121; *FR* 24 ff.), between two classes of evaluative words, in order to forestall an arrant piece of argument-rigging to which descriptivist philosophers often have recourse. They have repeatedly urged us to turn our attention away from the more 'general' evaluative words like 'wrong' and towards more 'specific' words like 'cruel'. Because 'general' and 'specific' have other uses (see p. 50), I prefer to use 'primarily evaluative words' or 'primary value-words' for the first class, whose evaluative meaning is primary, and 'secondarily evaluative words' or 'secondary value-words' for the second, whose evaluative meaning is secondary to an entrenched descriptive meaning. The object of this common descriptivist ploy is to suck the greatest possible advantage from the fact that the descriptive meaning of the second sort of words is entrenched. We *know*, they wish to argue, that to inflict pain just for fun is cruel.

I shall not now labour the obvious prescriptivist counter-argument that it is just as important to turn our attention in the opposite direction too, towards primary value-words like 'wrong', in order to get the whole picture. Secondarily evaluative words were not a new discovery, nor was their behaviour unexplored, when these writers pounced on them. My purpose in mentioning the distinction is that it plays an important part in showing why MacIntyre is too pessimistic.

The Sudanese and American, I am going to argue, *could* communicate if they had a primary value-word 'wrong' which meant the same in both their mouths. It would not make any difference if, instead of this, there were a primarily evaluative Arabic word which meant the same as the English word. In either case they could communicate about their difference, using the Arabic or the English word, once they were assured of their equivalence. The issue between MacIntyre and me concerns whether there can be this equivalence. We can readily grant him that, if they were confined to the use of secondarily evaluative words, it might well be the case that the appropriate Arabic word of this secondarily evaluative sort did *not* mean the same as its nearest American equivalent, because its use carried with it substantial evaluative commitments, necessary to the understanding of the word— commitments which the American could not accept. I do not disagree with MacIntyre about the limitations on the use of such words. The question is whether there are any words apt for use in their dispute which are not subject to these limitations.

Whether 'wrong' could be such a word, or whether it could have any serviceable Arabic equivalent, cannot be determined without some more ethical theory: it will depend on the answer to some important theoretical questions. Let us first make another concession, that *if* descriptivism were correct, and 'wrong' were a descriptive, that is, a purely descriptive, word, it could not serve their purpose of communication, because, for the reasons MacIntyre gives, it could not be univocal in their two mouths.

I say it *could* not be univocal; but this may have been to overstate MacIntyre's case. There are more ways than one in which it might be univocal without ceasing to be descriptive. First of all, there might be common values which the American and the Sudanese shared, and to which they could both appeal. In that case we should expect there to be common univocal words, or equivalent words in the two languages, for invoking these values, and these words could have a common descriptive meaning. This is what happens all the time between members of the same culture, and the Sudanese and the American might to this limited extent *share* a culture. However, though MacIntyre might well agree to this, it is not unrealistic to suppose that in our imaginary case it might not be so, but that nevertheless the way to a discussion of their dispute in a common language might still be open. Later we shall be exploring this way.

It must be added that it is not necessary, and is probably wrong, to give a descriptivist interpretation of this phenomenon. Moral philosophers of the sort that used to be called 'naturalists' (people now try to make us give up this useful expression) would say that the descriptive meaning of these words is the only meaning they have, and seek to give a definition or at least explanation of the words in terms of non-moral expressions. But a non-descriptivist like myself can give a better, because less vulnerable, explanation by saying that, although the words might indeed have such a common descriptive meaning, this might not be the only element in their meaning. They might have an evaluative or prescriptive meaning too, which might also be common to the two disputants. I shall later be giving an account of this common prescriptive meaning, which, as we shall see, offers the possibility of rational discussion between them even when they do *not* initially share any common values. I shall also be saying more about how the two kinds of meaning can combine and interact.

Another possibility is that, although they shared no values which could be appealed to in this dispute, they might have a common stock of value-words which were the names of 'non-natural qualities' of an intuitionistic sort, of which wrongness might be one. I put the suggestion in this Moorian way, not to caricature it, but to place it in its historical context. However, this manœuvre is not going to save the intuitionist from relativism of a different sort. For in cases where the disputants remained irreconcilable, as they might in this case, they would each be left relying on their own intuitions or convictions, and there would be no way of deciding which was right, as there should be if 'wrong' were a genuinely descriptive word. It would, indeed, be possible to say, Tarski-fashion, that the statement that the practice is wrong is true, and the person who makes it is right, if and only if the practice is wrong. But if this is all they can say, and each is left in complete liberty to go on maintaining that he is right, although both cannot be, the realist claim is empty, and no different from relativism. If there are no constraints on what we can attribute non-natural properties to, they are descriptive of nothing in particular.

However, if we grant to MacIntyre what he seems to want to say, that there are cases in which none of these expedients will serve (that is, cases in which there are no relevant common values to be appealed to, and in which their *intuitions* about the wrongness or obligatoriness of the practice of female circumcision remain irreconcilable) is there any way, in spite of what MacIntyre says, in which they might discuss their difference rationally and reach agreement (if necessary by questioning those irreconcilable intuitions)? Such a way could *ex hypothesi* not make use of intuitions. I shall argue that prescriptivism, unlike descriptivism of MacIntyre's or any other sort, does offer such a way.

Let us start with a very simple model, which, since I am not an ethical imperativist (see p. 20), I do not think to be an example of a moral dispute at all, though it is, like moral disputes, about a prescriptive question. The example is designed to show that there can be a common *prescriptive* element in language, even when there is no agreement about the truth of any descriptive statements about values. I say to someone 'Shut the door'; and a third party says to the same person 'Do not shut the door'. It cannot be denied that all three of us might understand what was being said. However, the two people making the requests might share no values, nor any factual opinions that are relevant to our present argument. They would have, of course, to agree on what it is to shut a door, and agree that there is a door, and perhaps that the addressee is able to shut it; but these presuppositions, as they are called, are immaterial to the present argument.

The example shows that there can be a common understanding of prescriptive expressions even where there is no agreement on the *reasons* for the requests or other prescriptions that they are used to express (see H 1987*c*: 75). This is important, because the whole drift of MacIntyre's argument is the following: No shared values; therefore no serviceable common language for discussing their dispute; therefore no reasons that either can adduce why the other should change his opinion. Notice how it is the underlying descriptivism that leads to this train of argument: since meaning on this view has to be descriptive meaning (there being no other kind of meaning for it to be), if two people do not have common descriptive rules for the use of expressions, those expressions cannot have a common meaning for them, and therefore cannot be parts of a common language. And since, on this view, the descriptive rules, specifying what words one can correctly apply to what, also specify the reasons for the application (analogously to 'You can call it a triangle because it has just three straight sides'), in the absence of shared descriptive rules there will be no shared reasons.

This is a good point at which to make clear what exactly *is* the descriptivism that I am attacking, before I go on to show why the imperative example I have just given should lead us to reject it. Descriptivism (or the descriptive fallacy as Austin called it—1961: 234, 1962: 3) is the belief that all words get their meaning in the same way as descriptive words and statements do, by having application-conditions or truth-conditions. The importance of imperatives for ethics is not that moral judgements *are* imperatives, but that imperatives are a standing counter-example to refute this mistaken view. To explain the point more fully: descriptivists think that for any sentence to have meaning is for there to be some condition under which statements expressed by it would be true; and this in turn would depend on the conditions for the correct application of the descriptive expressions in it. It will also depend on the reference of the referring-expressions in it, and perhaps on other things too; but that need not here concern us.

Descriptivism is tailored to fit the case of descriptive statements, and perhaps works all right for these, though doubt could be cast on this (Lewis 1985); but it is mistaken to extend the doctrine to all kinds of speech act. It obviously does not work for imperatives, which cannot be true (there are no *application*-rules for the imperative verb-form). To know the meaning of 'Shut the door' is not to know under what conditions we can truly say it, nor even under what conditions we can say it at all (*MT* 70). The Latin word '*esto*' ('let it be so'), which we may take as a pure imperative verb-form, does not get its meaning from rules which tell us when and what we can, when using it, command or request.

That MacIntyre is a descriptivist in this sense seems evident from what he says about communication between members of different cultures, and in particular about bilinguals, whose predicament I have myself discussed in *LM* 121. The problems of communication between cultures and the personal problems of the bilingual arise, in his view, because of divergence between different 'standards of truth and justification' (e.g. 1984: 10). His idea seems to be that the different cultures use different standards of truth, and that therefore they have 'rival conceptual schemes' (ibid.), and their words are mutually untranslatable, because a word in one language will lack any equivalent in the other. His thought is, evidently, that if there are different 'standards of truth' (truth-conditions), there must be different meanings, and untranslatability is the consequence.

MacIntyre intends this to apply not only to descriptive words but to evaluative and prescriptive ones too. This is clear from the fact that he includes, among the choices that confront people in such a conflict between cultures, the choice of a 'way of life' (ibid.). As he says earlier (1984: 81 f.), very different cultures may still share a common stock of expressions such as 'Snow is white'; and from this we may infer that it is, by contrast, the evaluative words in their languages that will create the trouble. And we may agree that *if*, as MacIntyre appears to think, all these evaluative words had their entire meaning determined for them by descriptive meaning-rules or truth-conditions, the trouble would indeed be unavoidable. For there would then be no evaluative words that were not culture-bound; when discussing questions of value, one could not open one's mouth without, by the use of some value-word, committing oneself to the values of one culture or the other. There would be no evaluative language available in which communication could take place *between* cultures.

But this is all on the assumption that descriptivism is correct, which our imperative example shows it not to be. The position is radically altered if, as in fact is the case, our languages contain, besides secondarily evaluative words which *are* culture-bound, primarily evaluative words which are not. The biggest contribution that moral philosophy can make to the resolution of conflicts between cultures and ways of life, and in general between adherents of conflicting values, is to explore the logic of these primarily evaluative words, in order to show how people who disagree can reason with one another. Is it not possible that these words, like 'ought' and 'wrong', are among the 'large parts of every language that are translatable into every other' (MacIntyre 1984: 8 f.)? The 'every' may be an exaggeration; for no doubt there are languages which do not contain equivalents of these words, any more than languages in tropical countries, perhaps, contain words for snow; but it would be surprising if evaluative words of this culture-independent kind were not available to the disputants in most intercultural disagreements.

I shall come later to a possible objection that MacIntyre might make, namely that even these primarily evaluative words like 'wrong' are culture-bound too, and therefore are not apt vehicles for communication between cultures. He might think this for two reasons, one of them obviously a bad one and the other more plausible. The more plausible one is that since, as I shall be arguing, the logic of these words does constrain us to reason in accordance with certain rules, and therefore in principle will lead us to certain conclusions, it is not neutral, and therefore must be culture-bound. To this form of the objection I shall return.

The bad reason is that the *descriptive* meanings attached to all value-words reflect the ways of life of different cultures (as they do) and that therefore by using even primarily evaluative words we bind ourselves to a culture. This is indeed true of secondarily evaluative words, as we have seen. But the primarily evaluative words are so classified just because their descriptive meaning is secondary, and is therefore more able to give way when attitudes change, the evaluative meaning remaining unaltered. It is possible, as we shall see, to argue in terms of these words without clinging to their existing descriptive meanings, because it is not the particular descriptive meanings that determine the logic of the argument, but the evaluative meaning. The latter, indeed, does carry with it the requirement that, because of universalizability, there has to be *some* descriptive meaning at any one time (*LM* 122; *FR* ch. 2); but it is not required that it remain unchanged through time.

That evaluative and descriptive meanings can thus vary independently of one another can be shown *a fortiori* by considering the case of secondarily evaluative words, of which we may take as a well-worn example 'cruel'. If people's attitude towards the treatment of animals changes, they will start to speak of 'cruelty to animals', where earlier the infliction of pain on animals for fun would not have been called cruel. The suffering inflicted in those earlier days was part of the fun, and was not condemned; so the pejorative word 'cruel' could not be used of it. But in these kinder times the descriptive meaning of 'cruel' has changed. Before, one could not call badger-baiting cruel; now one can. If I now say 'Tom is a cruel man', it will have become the case, as it was not before, that one possible confirmation of this statement is that Tom indulges in badger-baiting. But the word may not have altered its evaluative meaning at all. It may be no less, and no more, pejorative than before.

This possible independent variation of the evaluative and descriptive meanings might be denied by those, of whom MacIntyre seems to be one, who think that in principle no distinction can be made between these two elements in the meaning of value-words, or, less extremely, that the meanings cannot be detached from each other in the way I have been assuming. It seems hard to sustain this view in the light of the phenomena I have been describing. One argument used for it rests on a fact to which MacIntyre also draws attention, that we have (as indeed we have) 'a power to extrapolate from uses of expressions learned in certain types of situation to the making and understanding of new and newly illuminating uses' (1984: 9). It has been argued that we could not perform this extrapolation on the basis of the descriptive meaning alone, and that therefore the evaluative meaning must be part and parcel of the whole meaning of the word.

I cannot follow this argument. In the natural sense of the words, it can be readily agreed that both kinds of meaning are part and parcel of the whole meaning. But this does not prevent our distinguishing them. We can do so by specifying each separately (H 1963*b*: § ii; *MT* 74). The suggestion is that if we had just the descriptive meaning to go on, we should not *know* how to extend it to new uses. We need the evaluative meaning to show us what new sorts of thing we can apply the word to, and thus extend the adverse or favourable evaluation to a new kind of object. But I can see no difficulty here.

The matter may become clearer if we attend to a pervasive feature of language which was noticed a long time ago by the pragmatist F. C. S. Schiller, and called by him 'the plasticity of meaning' (1929: 56 ff.). Almost any use of any descriptive word can in principle (perhaps subtly and slightly) affect its accepted meaning. For example, whenever we use the word 'white' of some object, we do not merely rest on the basis of a convention about its use; we signify our subscription to the convention. It will be taken that we do accept that such objects can truly be called white. Often the effect is only to reinforce the convention, but sometimes, if the object in question was just outside the previous borderline, we thereby make a move towards altering it by extending the meaning of the word. If others follow us, the change will stick, and the convention will thereafter be different.

How, it may be asked, do we *know* when to extend meanings in this way? In the strict sense we do not know; we decide. Obviously, if we want to be followed in our extended use, we must not go too far beyond the existing use. We must not stretch the analogy further than other users of the word will tolerate. But subject to this constraint we are at liberty to extend our uses of words, and it is not a question of knowing what we may or may not do, but of what we can get away with.

If this is true of pure descriptive words, it is true all the more of the descriptive meanings of secondarily evaluative words. Here too we must not stretch analogies too far. Cruelty to animals has to be *like* cruelty to people in more or less obvious ways. But how do we *know* whether to call badger-baiting cruel? As before, we do not know; we decide. We decide on the basis of a changed sensibility which has made us feel about badgers some of the sentiments we feel about humans in analogous situations. I shall come later to arguments for extending our sympathies in this way, as it is very natural to do (see Singer 1981; H 1981 *b*); but nothing about the descriptive meaning of the word 'cruel' compelled us to, for that is not firmly attached; it does not determine our attitudes but follows them. A quite different sort of argument is needed to justify the change in attitude, which a deeper understanding of ethical theory and of the *prescriptivity* of moral judgements would explain (*MT* chs. 5, 6).

What happened in the badger-baiting case was that our evaluations changed (and whether or why they *should* have changed is another matter); and so we started to use this secondarily evaluative word with an extended descriptive meaning. That this can happen does nothing to show that the two elements in the meaning cannot be distinguished, nor even that they cannot be separately specified.

In the case of primarily evaluative words what happens is even clearer. I said earlier that the two kinds of value-words are distinguished by a difference in the firmness with which the two elements in their meaning are attached to them. In the case of the primary value-words, it is likely to be the descriptive meaning that gives way; in the case of the secondary value-words, the evaluative. But this is only a matter of probability and of degree. We have just been looking at a case in which it is the descriptive meaning of a secondary value-word that yields. In the case of such words, as we saw, it cannot yield too abruptly or too far, because the analogy cannot be stretched more than other people will tolerate, or we shall be misunderstood.

But in the case of primary value-words like 'ought' and 'wrong' the position is reversed. That is one of their most useful features, because it enables us to go on using them when our values have changed, and to use them to discuss value-disputes between cultures or between individuals who disagree; these words, unlike secondary value-words, are not tied so firmly to one value-system. We might, if our sensibilities and our attitudes changed in the way I have described, say 'One ought not to treat badgers like that; it is wrong.' If we said this, we should be *understood*, even if we had said something was wrong that nobody had seen anything wrong in before, nor in anything like it. People would understand us, though they would wonder why we said it. We must not confuse being unable to understand what somebody says with being unable to understand why he says it (see p. 192 and H 1963*b*: § vii). If we could not understand what he was saying, we could not even begin to wonder why he said it, because we should not know what *it* was. We would know what words he uttered, but not what he meant by them; and we have to do the latter if we are to be perplexed at his holding such an opinion. We have, that is, to know what the opinion is before we can be perplexed.

Because the descriptive meaning of primarily evaluative words like 'wrong' and 'ought' is relatively loosely tied to them, and they therefore have the useful feature just noticed, these are the words that our American and Sudanese are likely to use in talking about female circumcision. But before I show how, I must deal with two moves, both of them inspired by Wittgenstein, which are sometimes made in this argument. The first concerns *rules* for the uses of words (Wittgenstein 1953: 185, 1956: 1; McDowell 1981; Blackburn 1981). The model commonly used is that of extending a series in arithmetic. Suppose that somebody tells us to extend the series 2, 4, 6 . . . Do we know what to do? When we get to 200, do we know that we are not at liberty to go on '200, 204, 208'? The natural answer is that we do not, if *all* we have been told is to extend the series, 2, 4, 6. If that is all we have been told, we do not know whether, when we get even to 8, we are on the right lines in continuing '10, 12 . . .'. To know that, we should have to have been given the rule for extending the series, namely 'Add 2'.

There is a dilemma here: either we have the rule or we do not have it. If we have it, we can extend the series indefinitely. If we do not have it, we cannot extend it at all. I said, we have to have *been told* the rule. But it would do as well if we had caught on to it by ourselves (see Hesiod *ap.* Aristotle 1095^{b}10), provided that we were sure what it was. The important thing is that the rule should be definite in our minds. This does not, needless to say, require an ability to formulate the rule in words; we can have a rule in this sense if, as Ryle put it, we 'know how' to extend the series (1949: 29 ff.).

The same dilemma applies to word-use. Either we know the exact meaning of a word we are going to use, or we do not.

In the case of all ordinary words (exceptions being the precisely defined terms of some sciences and of mathematics) we most probably do not, since their meanings are not exact and do not need to be. To the extent that we do not, we are *at liberty* to extend the meaning in the way I have been illustrating. But, as we saw, it is not a question of *knowing* how to extend it; we can extend it in ways we can get away with, if we are so inclined. When using purely descriptive words, we may have reasons for being so inclined, though they have to be fairly obvious ones if communication is not to break down.

In the case of secondarily evaluative words, the reason will be a change in attitude or in sensibility; and here too, if we are to go on using a word *of this secondarily evaluative sort*, the change will have to be not too abrupt. There are even cases, like that of 'super apple', where we are not allowed to change the meaning at all without higher authority (Urmson 1950: 152). But with primarily evaluative words, the change can be much more abrupt. Prophets and moral reformers can preach against new sins; they may be thought crazy, but their words will be understood. Was not Pythagoras understood when he said that one ought on no account to eat beans? Or Govind Singh when he said that Sikhs ought never to cut their hair? Or Jesus when he taught that we ought to love our enemies?

The other Wittgensteinian move has become very fashionable in moral philosophy, though I should be surprised if the Master himself would have used it in this area. He said 'If language is to be a means of communication there must be agreement not only in definitions but, queer as this may sound, agreement in judgements also (1953: § 152). This may be true of descriptive words whose meanings are determined by truth-conditions. The 'paradigm case argument', which used to be more popular, even in ethics where it is clearly inapplicable, than it is now, has this much to be said for it, that if we do not agree, regarding some typically white things which are plainly visible to us, that they are white, we can hardly be said to understand the use of the word. It is a crass error to extend this argument to value-words; and the same error is committed by those who invoke this Wittgensteinian dictum in ethics. It has the highly conservative consequence, which it shares with most forms of naturalism, that we have, on penalty of failure of communication, to stick to the values which have given moral words their descriptive meanings hitherto. This will no doubt be palatable to those who do not want to have to think about whether to abandon their existing mores. It is more curious to see how at least one would-be revolutionary struggles to escape from this consequence, thereby landing herself in a kind of non-descriptivism hardly distinguishable from that which, without perhaps fully understanding it, she thought she had summarily discarded at the beginning of her book (Lovibond 1983). There could be no better illustration of how 'realists', starting from a desire to discipline their thought by attaching it to supposed moral 'facts', end up in a position which allows them to say whatever they feel like saying.

Because prescriptive words do not get their meanings from truth-conditions, neither the paradigm case argument nor this Wittgensteinian move applies to them. This is most clearly seen in the case of imperatives, which obviously can be used in communication between people who do not agree in the prescriptions they accept. But for the same reason they do not apply to the prescriptive meanings of evaluative words either. They therefore ought not to be used in ethics, and I hope will cease to be when the nature of moral words is better understood. What is extraordinary is that descriptivist philosophers should make such heavy weather of these familiar phenomena, which are easily explicable on lines quite consistent with the views of their opponents, and base arguments on them which, once the phenomena are understood, at once collapse.

Applying all this to MacIntyre's views, we see that the existence of secondarily evaluative words whose use is tied to the mores of particular cultures is no reason for pessimism about the possibility of changing these mores by rational discussion with members of other cultures. All that has to happen is for attitudes to change; and they can change *through* the rational discussion, *talking about* these culture-bound words and the mores they reflect, but *using* the more general words which the languages of the reasoners are likely to have in common. To use the example with which we began, they can discuss whether the practice of female circumcision *is wrong* and whether the mores which require it *ought* to be changed. In the course of the discussion, the descriptive meanings attached to the words by either party may change in the ways I have described, to reflect new attitudes.

The task of the moral philosopher is not (congenial as this may be) to mope about the violence and irrationality that there is in the world, but to do something as a philosopher to remedy it. There is indeed cause for pessimism, but the cause is not the inadequacies of our language, but the unreadiness of so many philosophers to explore and exploit its resources in a helpful way. This they will do, if they examine the logic of the primarily as well as the secondarily evaluative words, in order to determine what rules this logic imposes upon our reasoning in situations of moral dispute—even dispute between members of radically different cultures.

I have not much doubt that if our American and Sudanese were to consider at all deeply (perhaps with philosophical help) what they can say about the question of female circumcision, and in particular whether it is wrong, they would reach agreement on the basis of their understanding of the word 'wrong'. This is likely to have the same prescriptive or evaluative meaning in both their languages, although the descriptive meanings will be different. They will have to forget, for the purposes of their argument, these descriptive meanings. If descriptivists were right, this would leave the word with no meaning at all. But in fact it is fairly easy to throw open the descriptive meanings of such general value-words. What will guide their discussion will be the evaluative meaning and the logic determined by it. I have in *MT* discussed what this logic is, and it is not my purpose here to repeat that discussion. But briefly, when they become fully cognizant of the effect of the experience of female circumcision on the victims, and ask themselves whether they can prescribe universally (for all cases including their own) that such suffering be inflicted, they will at least start to ask what advantages it may bring to the victims or others that could compensate for the suffering. The inquiry will then take a factual turn; they will explore the consequences of the practice and of its abolition. If this factual inquiry discloses no consequences of the practice which they can evaluate highly enough to make them accept a universal prescription that people be made to suffer in that way, they may come to agree that it *is* wrong. The argument is a longer one than this, but I can do no more than summarize it.

A retort that is likely to be made is that the word 'wrong', as bound by these universal-prescriptivist rules, is itself tied to particular mores and therefore not available to disputants one of whom has the mores and the other does not. Even if this were true, it would not be so bad. For though there may be languages that do not contain a universal-prescriptive word equivalent (in its evaluative meaning) to 'wrong', I think it fairly certain that the disputants in our example would have such a word. MacIntyre disguises this fact by making so much play with the divergent *descriptive* meanings.

However, even if the disputants do not have any such word in common, it is possible for either of them to *learn* the word. They can do this without as yet unlearning any of their other words or the mores that go with them. In this sense the new word, and its attached logic, is neutral. *After* they have learnt the new word, they can reason, and they may come to think that it would be wrong not to abandon some of the old words and the mores that they reflect. But this is no different from the case where somebody learns how to count above ten for the first time, and thus becomes able to say 'I have fifteen sheep, and so I have more than so-and-so, who has fourteen.' Some people might not want to learn to count above ten, and they might not want to learn to use the word 'wrong'; but if they wanted to be able to talk and think about things which can only be talked and thought about by those who have these means, they will have to adopt them. It is my belief that many disputes that there are in the world might be peaceably ended if more people either adopted such words or, as is probably all that is necessary in nearly all cases, understood more fully the logic of similar words already available in their languages, and in particular learnt to distinguish their evaluative from their descriptive meanings, and to utilize the resources of the former in their reasoning. And to help people to do this is a main task for moral philosophers.

9

The Promising Game

ONE of the most fundamental questions about moral judgements is whether they, and other value-judgements, can be
logically derived from statements of empirical fact. Like most
important philosophical questions, this one has reached the
stage at which its discussion is bound to proceed piecemeal,
in terms of particular examples, arguments, and counter-
arguments. This article is intended as a contribution to one
such controversy. Professor J. R. Searle (1964) attempts a
feat which many before him have thought to perform. His
argument, though it seems to me unsound, is both more
plausible, and sets a higher moral tone, than that recently
supplied by Mr MacIntyre (1959: § v) and repeated in an
unimportantly different form by Professor Black (1964). While
Searle seeks to demonstrate logically that we ought to keep
our promises, Black and MacIntyre seek to demonstrate that
we ought to do whatever is the one and only means to
achieving *anything* that we happen to want, or avoiding *anything*
that we want to avoid (see H 1971*a*).

Searle asks us to consider the following series of statements:

(1) Jones uttered the words 'I hereby promise to pay
you, Smith, five dollars.'
(2) Jones promised to pay Smith five dollars.
(3) Jones placed himself under (undertook) an obligation
to pay Smith five dollars.
(4) Jones is under an obligation to pay Smith five dollars.
(5) Jones ought to pay Smith five dollars.

He then argues concerning this list that:

the relation between any statement and its successor, while not in
every case one of 'entailment', is nonetheless not just a contingent
relation; and the additional statements necessary to make the

From *Revue internationale de philosophie* 70 (1964).

relationship one of entailment do not need to involve any evaluative
statements, moral principles, or anything of the sort. (1964: 44)

Though there may be other steps in the argument that are
open to question, I shall concentrate on those from (1) to (2)
and from (2) to (3). One of the 'additional statements' which
Searle supplies between (1) and (2) is

> (1*a*) Under certain conditions *C* anyone who utters the
> words (sentence) 'I hereby promise to pay you, Smith,
> five dollars' promises to pay Smith five dollars.

This, he says, in conjunction with the further premiss,

> (1*b*) Conditions *C* obtain,

turns the step from (1) to (2) into an entailment. Next, he
similarly inserts between (2) and (3), in order to show that
that step is an entailment, what he calls the 'tautological'
premiss,

> (2*a*) All promises are acts of placing oneself under (under-
> taking) an obligation to do the thing promised.

This premiss is 'tautological' because 'No analysis of the
concept of promising will be complete which does not include
the feature of the promiser placing himself under an obligation'
(1964: 45).

Later, Searle puts what appears to be the same point in
terms of what he calls 'constitutive rules'. There are some
institutions which are not merely regulated but constituted by
the rules governing them. Thus 'the rules of chess, for example,
do not merely regulate an antecedently existing activity called
playing chess; they, as it were, create the possibility of or
define that activity' (1964: 55). The rules of chess and baseball
are examples of constitutive rules, and so is 'the constitutive
rule that to make a promise is to undertake an obligation'
(1964: 56).

I wish to consider the relations between (1*a*) and (2*a*). In
order to clarify them, I shall appeal to the 'baseball' analogy
with which Searle has helpfully provided us (ibid.). He
describes a set of empirical conditions such that, if they obtain,
a baseball-player is out, and is obliged to leave the field. I
will call these conditions '*E*', in order to conceal my ignorance
of the rules of baseball in which they are specified. What

correspond, in the 'promising' case, to conditions E in the baseball case, are conditions C *together with* the condition that the person in question should have uttered the words 'I promise etc.'. Let us number the propositions in the 'baseball' case to correspond with Searle's numbering in the 'promising' case, distinguishing them by the addition of a prime. There will then be a constitutive rule of baseball to the effect that:

($1a'$) Whenever a player satisfies conditions E, he is out.

And, since no analysis of the concept *out* will be complete which does not include the feature of the player who is out being obliged to leave the field, we can add the 'tautological' premiss,

($2a'$) All players who are out are obliged to leave the field.

We can simplify the argument by combining ($1a'$) and ($2a'$) into the single constitutive rule,

($1a'\text{*}$) Whenever a player satisfies conditions E, he is obliged to leave the field.

For, if the definition in virtue of which ($2a'$) is a tautology is applied direct to ($1a'$), it turns into ($1a'\text{*}$). And similarly in the 'promising' case, the argument will be simplified if we combine ($1a$) and ($2a$) into the single constitutive rule,

($1a\text{*}$) Under certain conditions C anyone who utters the words (sentence) 'I hereby promise to pay you, Smith, five dollars' places himself under (undertakes) an obligation to pay Smith five dollars.

The rule could be put in a general form, leaving out the reference to Smith; but we need not trouble with this.

What then is the status of ($1a\text{*}$)? Five answers seem plausible enough to merit discussion:

(a) It is a tautology;

(b) It is a synthetic empirical statement about English word-usage;

(c) It is a synthetic prescription about word-usage in English;

(d) It is a synthetic empirical statement about something other than word-usage;

(e) It is, or implicitly contains, a synthetic evaluation or prescription, not merely about word-usage.

Searle would appear to maintain (*b*). I shall argue for (*e*). Since the arguments which I shall use against (*a*), (*b*), and (*c*) are all the same, I shall not need to detail them separately for the three answers; (*d*) will require to be rebutted independently, but this will not take long.

Let us start by discussing the status of the analogous statement (1*a′**). Is it a tautology? There certainly is a tautology with which it can be easily confused, namely:

(1*a′**) = + *In* (*i.e. according to the rules of*) *baseball*, whenever a player satisfies conditions *E*, he is obliged to leave the field.

This is a tautology because a definition of 'baseball' would have to run 'a game with the following rules, viz. . . . .' followed by a list of rules, including (1*a′**) or its equivalent. But this does not make (1*a′**) itself, in which the italicized part is omitted, into a tautology. (1*a′**) is a summary of part of the rules of baseball; and, although it may be that some of the rules of a game are tautologies, it is impossible that they should all be. For if they were, what we should have would be, not the rules for playing a game, but rules (or, more strictly, exemplifications of rules) for speaking correctly about the game. To conform to the rules of a game it is necessary to act, not merely speak, in certain ways. Therefore the rules are not tautologies.

For the same reasons, as we shall see, the rules of baseball (and in particular (1*a′*) and (1*a′**)) cannot be treated as synthetic statements, or even as synthetic prescriptions, about word-usage. They are about how a game is, or is to be, played.

Let us now apply all this to the 'promising' case. By parity of reasoning it is clear that (1*a**) is not a tautology, although it is easy to confuse it with another proposition (1*a*^+), which *is* a tautology. (1*a*^+) will consist of (1*a**), preceded by the words 'In the institution of promising'—we might say, if it were not liable to misinterpretation, 'In the promising game'. This is a tautology, because it is expansible into 'According to the rules of an institution whose rules say "Under conditions *C* anyone who utters the words . . . (etc., as in (1*a**))", under conditions *C* anyone who utters the words . . . (etc., as in (1*a**)).' But (1*a**) itself is not a tautology. As before, the

constitutive rules of an institution may contain some tautologies, but they cannot all be tautologies, if they are going to
prescribe that people *act* in certain ways and not in others.
And, as before, we must not be misled into thinking that,
because it is a tautology that promising is an institution of
which (1*a**) is a constitutive rule, (1*a**) itself is a tautology.

As before, and for analogous reasons, (1*a**) is neither a
synthetic statement nor a synthetic prescription about how
English is, or is or ought to be, spoken. Just because it has
the consequences which Searle claims for it, it is more than
this.

There is one apparent disparity between the 'promising'
and 'baseball' cases which might be a source of confusion. In
the 'baseball' case the word 'baseball' does not occur in (1*a*′**);
and therefore, though (1*a*′**) is in a sense definitive of 'baseball',
it is not thereby made tautologous. But in the 'promising'
case, (1*a**) does contain the word 'promise'; and this makes
it much more plausible to suggest that (1*a**), since it is in a
sense explicative of the notion of promising, is a tautology.
This plausibility is even stronger in the case of (1*a*). The
answer to this objection may help to clarify the whole
procedure of introducing a word like 'promise' into the
language. The word is introduced by means of such a
proposition as (1*a**). But we must not be misled into thinking
that this makes (1*a**) a tautology, or a mere statement about
word-usage. For, as we shall see, it is a characteristic of words
like 'promise', which have meaning only within institutions,
that they can be introduced into language only when certain
synthetic propositions about how we should *act* are assented to.
(1*a**) is such a proposition. The word 'promise' depends for
its meaning upon the proposition, but the proposition is not
true solely in virtue of the meaning of 'promise'. Similarly, a
word like 'out' is dependent for its meaning upon the rules of
baseball or cricket; but those rules are not tautologies in virtue
of the meaning of 'out' and other such words.

However, this may not seem to go the root of the objection.
For Searle's argument could be stated without mentioning the
word 'promise' at all. He could simply, in (1*a*), substitute the
words 'place upon himself an obligation' for the word 'promise'
throughout. The proposition then becomes:

> Under certain conditions *C* anyone who utters the words
> (sentence) 'I hereby place upon myself an obligation to
> pay you, Smith, five dollars' places upon himself an
> obligation to pay Smith five dollars.

Surely, it might be said, I cannot deny that *this* is a tautology,
or, alternatively, a statement about word-usage. But this is
just what I do wish to deny. For, to begin with, if the mere
repetition of the words 'place . . . an obligation' in the
proposition made it into a tautology, it is hard to see what
the words 'Under certain conditions *C*' are doing; one might
think that under any conditions whatever a person who says
'I hereby place upon myself an obligation etc.' must necessarily
have thereby placed upon himself an obligation etc. But once
we have seen that this is not so (for example, the man might
be under duress or mad), we see that the appearance of
tautology is deceptive. It is not in general true (let alone
tautologous) that the man who says '*p*' makes it the case that
p. Something like this does happen in the case of what used
to be called performative verbs; it happens in our present case
with the verb 'promise'. The man who says 'I promise',
promises (under certain conditions). But it is not a tautology
that he does so, nor is it a tautology that the man who says
'I hereby place myself under an obligation' places himself
under an obligation, even under certain (empirical) conditions.
Nor are either of these merely remarks about word-usage. For
it is a necessary condition for the adoption of these performative
expressions that certain synthetic constitutive (and not merely
linguistic) rules be also adopted, thus creating the institution
within which the expressions have meaning.

To make this clearer, let us suppose that we have already
in our language the word 'obligation' (and kindred words like
'ought'), but that none of our obligations has been, as Searle
puts it, 'institutionalized' (1964: 56). That is to say, we can
speak of our having obligations (e.g. to feed our children) and
even of our placing upon ourselves obligations (e.g. by having
children we place upon ourselves the obligation to feed them);
but we cannot yet speak of placing upon ourselves an obligation
just by saying, merely, 'I place upon myself the obligation
etc.'. Then suppose that some inventive person suggests the

adoption of this useful expression (or rather its conversion to this new use). The other members of society may well stare at him and say 'But we don't see how you can place upon yourself an obligation just by saying these words.' What he will then have to say, in order to sell this device to them, and therewith the institution of which it is a part, is something like this: 'You have to adopt the constitutive rule or moral principle that one has an obligation to do those things of which one has said "I (hereby) place upon myself an obligation to do them." ' When they have adopted this principle, or in adopting it, they can introduce the new use for the expression. And the principle is a synthetic one. It is a new synthetic moral principle, and not merely a new way of speaking, that is being introduced; this shows up in the fact that, if they adopt the principle, they will have acquired obligations to do things that they have not done before, not merely to speak in ways that they have not spoken before.

There may be, indeed, an interpretation on which (1*a*), (1*a**), and their analogues could be said to be statements 'about' the English language. They could be treated as statements which say, or imply, that the English have in their language the performative expression 'I promise', or the performative expression 'I place myself under an obligation', whose use is tied to the institution of promising (or undertaking obligations); and which therefore imply also that the English (or sufficient of them) subscribe to the rules of this institution. The latter half of this would be an anthropological statement about the English. But it is obvious that such a statement cannot generate the entailments which Searle requires. For the conclusions which will then follow will be, at most, of the type: 'The English subscribe to the view that Jones is under an obligation', 'The English subscribe to the view that Jones ought', etc. For the required non-anthropological moral (or at least prescriptive) conclusions to follow, (1*a*) must, interpreted in the light of (2*a*), be taken as expressing the speaker's own subscription to the rules of the institution of promising, i.e. to moral principles. I do not wish to argue which is the most natural way to take these statements; all I need to say is that *unless* they are taken in this way, the derivation will not work.

It is often the case that performative expressions cannot be introduced without the adoption of synthetic constitutive rules. Thus it would be impossible to introduce the expression 'I stake a claim to this land' unless there were adopted, at the same time, a principle that by saying this, under the appropriate conditions, if the claimant has not been forestalled by somebody else, he acquires at least some claim to the land. In pioneering days in America one could do this; but try doing it in modern Siberia, where they do not have that principle.

Another way of showing that ($1a*$) is not a tautology, and is not made so by the fact that it is used for introducing the word 'promise' into the language, is the following. If ($1a*$) were true in virtue of the meaning of the word 'promise', and therefore tautologous, then both ($1a$) and ($2a$) would have to be tautologous. For ($1a*$) was arrived at by applying to ($1a$) the definition which made ($2a$) tautologous; and it is impossible to get a tautology out of a synthetic proposition by definitional substitution. But ($1a$) and ($2a$) cannot both be made tautologous without an equivocation on the word 'promise'. For ($2a$) is tautologous, if it is, in virtue of *one* definition of 'promise', and ($1a$) is tautologous, if it is , in virtue of *another* definition of 'promise' (or, on the alternative suggestion that ($1a$) is a statement about language, it can be so only in virtue of *another* definition of 'promise'). If we take ($1a$) as tautologous, or as a usage-statement, it will have to be in virtue of some such definition as the following:

> (D1) Promising is saying, under certain conditions C, 'I hereby promise etc.'.

But ($2a$), if it is tautologous, is so in virtue of a *different* definition, namely:

> Promising is placing oneself under an obligation . . .

How the definition is completed does not matter; it has at any rate to start like this. To make ($1a*$) tautologous, or a usage-statement, we have to take 'promise' simultaneously in these two different senses. And the trouble cannot be escaped by completing the last definition thus:

> (D2) Promising is placing oneself under an obligation by

saying, under certain conditions *C*, 'I hereby promise
etc.'

This definition sounds attractive, and may be more or less
correct; but it does not make (1*a*) a tautology, and would
make it into more than a statement about word-usage.
According to (D2), a man who says 'I hereby promise etc.'
has satisfied only one of the conditions of promising, but may
not have satisfied the other; he may have said the words, but
may not have thereby placed upon himself any obligation.
We can only say that he has succeeded in doing this if we
assent to the *synthetic* principle (1*a**). The necessity of assenting
to this synthetic principle before the trick works may be
concealed by taking (D2), not as a verbal definition of the
modern type, but as that old device of synthetic-a-priorists,
an 'essential' or 'real' definition of promising. But then it will
be synthetic.

I conclude, for these reasons, that (1*a**) cannot be tautologous or a statement about word-usage, but must be a synthetic constitutive rule of the institution of promising. If the
constitutive rules of the institution of promising are moral
principles, as I think they are, then (1*a**) is a synthetic moral
principle. It follows that, if Searle sticks to it that (2*a*) is
tautologous, he must allow that (1*a*) either is or implicitly
contains a synthetic moral principle. But this would destroy
his argument; and indeed he says that it is not; for, after
introducing it, he says 'As far as I can see, no moral premises
are lurking in the logical woodpile' (1964: 43). He says this,
in spite of the fact that he is going on immediately to make
(1*a*) by definition equivalent to (1*a**), which we have seen to
be a synthetic moral principle.

It might be suggested that (1*a*) is an empirical statement
of some non-linguistic sort. I have been assured by Searle that
he does not think this; but the suggestion is worth examining.
If it were true, it might save his argument, which is, essentially,
that no moral or other non-empirical, non-tautological, premisses have to be included. He spends some effort in showing
that conditions *C*, to which (1*a*) alludes, are empirical
conditions—and this may be granted for the sake of argument.
But, although this would make the proposition (1*b*), 'Conditions *C* obtain', into an empirical statement, it by no means

makes (1*a*) into one. For however empirical these conditions *C* may be, it is possible to construct non-empirical propositions, and even imperatives, of the form 'Under conditions *C*, *p*' — e.g., 'Under conditions *C*, switch off (*or* you ought to switch off) the motor'. Nevertheless, it is easy to be misled into thinking that, if the conditions under which a man who utters 'I hereby promise' can correctly be said to have made a promise are empirical conditions, this proves that (1*a*) is not a moral statement.

I said that I would concentrate my attack on steps (1)–(3) of Searle's argument. But I may mention here that an analogous attack could be made against steps (3)–(5). These too depend on a non-tautologous rule of the institution of promising, or in general of (performatively) placing onself under obligations. This non-tautologous rule is as follows:

> (3*a*) If anybody has placed himself under an obligation (in the past) he is (still) under an obligation, unless he has done already what he was obliged to do.

To find out whether this is a tautology , we should have, as before, to rewrite it with the aid of the definition or tautology which is required to make the step from (4) to (5) into an entailment, viz. the definition

> (D3) For one to be under an obligation to do a thing is for it to be the case that one ought to do that thing.

(I shall not enquire whether this definition is a sufficient one; it is probably not); or the tautology

> (4*a*) All people who are under obligations to do things ought to do them.

(3*a*) then turns into:

> (3*a**) If anybody has placed himself under an obligation (in the past), it is (still) the case that he ought to do the thing that he placed himself under an obligation to do, unless he has already done it.

That this is not a tautology (or for that matter a statement about word-usage) could be shown, if it is not plain already, by an argument analogous to the preceding.

I will conclude with some general remarks about the nature of the mistake that Searle seems to me to have made in this paper. There are many words which could not have a use unless certain propositions were assented to by the users or a sufficient number of them. The possibility of using a word can depend on assent to synthetic propositions. This will apply especially to many words whose use is dependent upon the existence of institutions, though not only to them.[1] Unless there were laws of property, we could not speak of 'mine' and 'thine'; yet the laws of property are not tautologies. Unless there were a readiness to accept currency in exchange for goods, words like 'dollar' and 'pound' would pass out of use; yet to be ready to accept currency in exchange for goods is not to assent to a tautology or to a statement about language. In a community which did not play, or accept the rules of, baseball, the word 'out', as it is used by umpires, would lack a use (though not as used by anthropologists, if they were discussing the ways of a community which did have the game); but this does not make the rules of baseball into tautologies or statements about word-usage.

In the case of promising we have a similar phenomenon. Unless a sufficient number of people were prepared to assent to the moral principles which are the constitutive rules of the institution of promising, the word 'promise' could not have a use. To take the extreme case: suppose that nobody thought that one ought to keep promises. It would then be impossible to make a promise; the word 'promise' would become a mere noise (except, as before, in the mouths of anthropologists), unless it acquired some new use. But it does not follow from this that the moral principles, assent to which by a sufficient number of people is a condition for the remaining in use of the word 'promise', are themselves analytic.

It is necessary, moreover, only that a sufficiently large number of people should assent to the constitutive rule. If they do so, and if the word in question comes into use, it is possible for people who do not assent to the rule to use the word comprehensibly. Thus an anarchist can use the word 'property'; a man who for reasons of his own has no confidence

---

[1] What Kant was driving at, without the synthetic-a-priorism, might possibly be hinted at by pointing out that many words that we use in physics and in everyday life, such as 'table', and in general 'material object', would lack a use unless we made certain assumptions about the regularity of the universe.

in paper money, and is therefore not prepared to exchange goods for it, can still use the word 'pound'; and a Machiavellian politician who recognizes no duty to keep promises can still use the word 'promise'. He can even use it to make promises, always provided that his moral opinions are not too well known.

Such people are, admittedly, parasites; but not all parasites are reprehensible. Let us suppose that somebody is opposed to fox-hunting. This does not stop him engaging in fox-hunting, in the sense of going to meets, following hounds, etc., and using all the terminology of the chase. He may think it his duty, whenever he can get away with it, to help the fox to escape (that may be why he goes fox-hunting); but this does not involve him in any self-contradiction. It may be that to try to help foxes to escape is contrary to the constitutive rules for fox-hunting;[2] for unless there were among these rules one which said that the object of the game was to kill the fox, it would not be fox-*hunting*. But this does not stop our opponent of blood sports masquerading as a person who accepts this rule; nor does it mean that, by so masquerading, he lays upon himself any obligation to abide by it. And in just the same way the Machiavellian politician can, without self-contradiction, think it is his duty to break some of the promises he makes (and think this even while he is making them). He could not have made them unless the word 'promise' were in use; and it could not be in use unless a sufficient number of people assented to the moral principles governing promising; but this does not mean that a person who, while making promises, dissents, silently, from the principles contradicts himself. In using the word 'promise' indeed, he is masquerading as one who thinks that one ought to keep promises, just as one who lies is masquerading as one who thinks that p, when he does not. But neither the liar nor the man who makes lying promises is contradicting himself. And when the lying promiser comes to break his promise, he is still not contradicting himself; he can say 'I pretended to think, when I made the promise, that

---

[2] It might be objected that the rules of fox-hunting are not constitutive but regulative. This would depend on establishing some relevant difference between the chasing of foxes and chasing of cricket balls—a question into which I shall not go, but whose investigation might cast doubt on this distinction.

one ought to keep promises; but I don't really think this and never have.'

Talking about 'institutional facts', though it can be illuminating, can also be a peculiarly insidious way of committing the 'naturalistic fallacy'. I do not think that Searle actually falls into this particular trap; but others perhaps have. There are moral and other principles, accepted by most of us, such that, if they were not generally accepted, certain institutions like property and promising could not exist. And if the institutions do exist, we are in a position to affirm certain 'institutional facts' (for example, that a certain piece of land is my property), on the ground that certain 'brute facts' are the case (for example, that my ancestors have occupied it from time immemorial). But from the 'institutional facts', certain obviously prescriptive conclusions can be drawn (for example, that nobody ought to deprive me of the land). Thus it looks as if there could be a straight deduction, in two steps, from brute facts to prescriptive conclusions via institutional facts. But the deduction is a fraud. For the brute fact is a ground for the prescriptive conclusion only if the prescriptive principle which is the constitutive rule of the institution be accepted; and this prescriptive principle is not a tautology. For someone (a communist for example) who does not accept this non-tautologous prescriptive principle, the deduction collapses like a house of cards—though this does not prevent him from continuing to use the word 'property' (with his tongue in his cheek).

Similarly with promising. It may seem as if the 'brute fact' that a person has uttered a certain phonetic sequence entails the 'institutional fact' that he has promised, and that this in turn entails that he ought to do a certain thing. But this conclusion can be drawn only by one who accepts, in addition, the non-tautologous principle that one ought to keep one's promises. For unless one accepts this principle, one is not a subscribing member of the institution which it constitutes, and therefore cannot be compelled logically to accept the institutional facts which it generates in such a sense that they entail the conclusion, though of course one must admit their truth, regarded purely as pieces of anthropology.

If I do not agree with Searle's reasons for maintaining that

we ought to keep our promises, what are my own reasons?
They are of a fundamentally different character, although
they take in parts of Searle's argument in passing. To break
a promise is, normally, a particularly gross form of deception.
It is grosser than the failure to fulfil a declaration of intention,
just because (if you wish) our society has, *pari passu* with the
introduction of the word 'promise', adopted the moral principle that one ought to keep promises, thus constituting the
institution called 'promising'. My reason for thinking that I
ought not to take parasitic advantage of this institution, but
ought to obey its rules, is the following. If I ask myself whether
I am willing that I myself should be deceived in this way,
I answer unhesitatingly that I am not. I therefore cannot
subscribe to any moral principle which permits people to
deceive other people in this way (any general principle which
says 'It is all right to break promises'). There may be more
specific principles which I could accept, of the form 'It is all
right to break promises in situations of type *S*'. Most people
accept some specific principles of this form. What anybody
can here substitute for '*S*' he will determine, if he follows my
sort of reasoning, by asking himself, for any proposed value
of '*S* ', whether he can subscribe to the principle when applied
to all cases, including cases in which he is the person to whom
the promise is made. Thus the morality of promise-keeping is
a fairly standard application of what I have called elsewhere
(*FR* 86–125) the 'golden-rule' type of moral argument; it
needs no 'is'–'ought' derivations to support it—derivations
whose validity will be believed in only by those who have
ruled out a priori any questioning of the existing institutions
on whose rules they are based.

10

Rawls's Theory of Justice

ANY philosopher who, like John Rawls (1971), writes on justice or on any other subject in moral philosophy is likely to propound, or to give evidence of, views on one or more of the following topics:

(1) *Philosophical methodology*—i.e. what philosophy is supposed to be doing and how it does it. Rawls expresses some views about this, which have determined the whole structure of his argument, and which therefore need careful inspection.

(2) *Ethical analysis*—i.e. the meanings of the moral words or the nature and logical properties of the moral concepts. Rawls says very little about these, and certainly does not treat them as fundamental to his inquiry (51/10).[1]

(3) *Moral methodology*—i.e. how moral thinking ought to proceed, or how moral arguments or reasonings have to be conducted if they are to be cogent.

(4) *Normative moral questions*—i.e. what we ought or ought not to do, what is just or unjust, and so on.

I shall argue that, through misconceptions about (1), Rawls has not paid enough attention to (2), and that therefore he has lacked the equipment necessary to handle (3) effectively; so that what he says about (4), however popular it may prove, is unsupported by any firm arguments.

(1) Rawls states quite explicitly how he thinks moral philosophy should be done: 'There is a definite if limited class of facts against which conjectured principles can be checked, namely our considered judgments in reflective equilibrium' (51/3). It is clear from the succeeding passage that Rawls does not conceive of moral philosophy as depending primarily on the analysis of concepts in order to establish their logical properties and thus the rules of valid moral argument. Rather, he thinks

From *Philosophical Quarterly* 23 (1983).

[1] References of this form are to pages/lines of Rawls's text.

of a theory of justice as analogous to a theory in empirical science. It has to square with what he calls 'facts', just like, for example, physiological theories. But what are these facts? They are what people will *say* when they have been thinking carefully. This suggestion is reminiscent of Sir David Ross (1930: 40 ff.). But sometimes (though not consistently) Rawls goes farther than Ross. Usually he is more cautious, and appeals to the reflections of *bien-pensants* generally, as Ross does (e.g. 18/9, 19/26). But at 50/34 he says, 'For the purposes of this book, the views of the reader and the author are the only ones that count.' It does not make much practical difference which way he puts it; for if (as will certainly be the case) he finds a large number of readers who can share with him a cosy unanimity in their considered judgements, he and they will think that they adequately represent 'people generally', and congratulate themselves on having attained the truth.[2] This is how phrases like 'reasonable and generally acceptable' (45/16) are often used by philosophers in lieu of argument.

Rawls, in short, is here advocating a kind of subjectivism, in the narrowest and most old-fashioned sense. He is making the answer to the question 'Am I right in what I say about moral questions?' depend on the answer to the question 'Do you, the reader, and I agree in what we say?' This must be his view, if the considered judgements of author and reader are to occupy the place in his theory which is occupied in an empirical science by the facts of observation. Yet at 516/15 he claims objectivity for his principles.

It might be thought that such a criticism can be made only by one who has rejected (as Rawls has apparently accepted) the arguments of Professor Quine and others about the analytic-synthetic distinction and the way in which science confronts the world. But this is not so. Even Quine would hardly say that scientific theories as a whole are to be tested by seeing what people say when they have thought about them (it would have been a good thing for medieval flat-earthers if

---

[2] See 104/3-14 for a 'considered judgment' with which many of us now would agree, but which differs from the views of most writers of other periods than the present, and is not argued for.

they could be); but that is what Rawls is proposing for moral principles.

In order not to be unfair to Rawls, it must be granted that *any* enquirer, in ethics as in any other subject, and whether he be a descriptivist or a prescriptivist, is looking for an answer to his questions which he can accept. I have myself implied this in *FR* 73 and elsewhere. The element of subjectivism enters only when a philosopher claims that he can 'check' his theory against his and other people's views, so that a disagreement between the theory and the views tells against the theory (see p. 19). To speak like this (as Rawls does constantly throughout the book) is to make the *truth* of the theory *depend on* agreement with people's opinions. I have myself been so often falsely accused of this sort of subjectivism that it is depressing to find a self-styled objectivist falling as deeply into it as Rawls does—depressing, because it makes one feel that this essentially simple distinction will never be understood: the distinction between the view that thinking something can make it so (which is in general false) and the view that if we are to say something sincerely, we must be able to accept it (which is a tautology).

Intuitionism is nearly always a form of disguised subjectivism. Rawls does not call himself an intuitionist; but he certainly is one in the usual sense. He says, 'There is no reason to suppose that we can avoid all appeals to intuition, of whatever kind, or that we should try to. The practical aim is to reach a reasonably reliable agreement in judgment in order to provide a common conception of justice' (44/34, cf. 124/38). It is clear that he is here referring mainly to moral intuitions; perhaps if he appealed only to linguistic intuitions it would be all right. He reserves the name 'intuitionist' for those (including no doubt Ross) who advocate a·*plurality* of moral principles, each established by intuition, and not related to one another in an ordered structure, but only weighed relatively to each other (also by intuition) when they conflict. The right name for this kind of intuitionism would be 'pluralistic intuitionism'. Rawls's theory is more systematic than this, but no more firmly grounded. There can also be another, non-pluralistic kind of intuitionist—one who intuits the validity of a single principle or ordered system of them, or of a single method, and erects his entire structure of moral thought on this. Sidgwick might come into this category—though if he were living today, it is unlikely that he would find it necessary to rely on moral intuition.

'Monistic intuitionism' would be a good description of this kind of view. It might apply to Rawls, did it not suggest falsely that he relies only on one great big intuition, and only at one point in his argument. Unfortunately he relies on scores of them. From 18/9 to 20/9 I have counted in two pages thirty expressions implying a reliance on intuitions: such expressions as 'I assume that there is a broad measure of agreement that'; 'commonly shared presumptions'; 'acceptable principles'; 'it seems reasonable to suppose'; 'is arrived at in a natural way'; 'match our considered convictions of justice or extend them in an acceptable way'; 'which we can affirm on reflection'; 'we are confident'; 'we think'; and so on. If, as I have done, the reader will underline the places in the book where crucial moves in the argument depend on such appeals, he may find himself recalling Plato's remark: 'If a man starts from something he knows not, and the end and middle of his argument are tangled together out of what he knows not, how can such a mere consensus ever turn into knowledge?' (*Rep.* 533c). Since the theoretical structure is tailored at every point to fit Rawls's intuitions, it is hardly surprising that its normative consequences fit them too—if they did not, he would alter the theory (19/26 ff., cf. 141/23); and the fact that Rawls is a fairly typical man of his times and society, and will therefore have many adherents, does not make this a good way of doing philosophy.

Rawls's answer to this objection (581/9) is that *any* justification of principles must proceed from some consensus. It is true that any justification which consists of a 'linear inference' (*FR* 87 f.) must so proceed; but Rawls's justification is not of this type. Why should it not *end* in consensus as a result of argument? There may have to be a prior consensus on matters of fact, including facts about the interests of the parties (though these themselves may conflict); and on matters of logic, established by analysis. But not on substantial moral questions, as Rawls seems to require. This is not the place for an exposition of my own views of how moral argument can succeed in reaching normative conclusions with only facts, *singular* prescriptions, and logic to go on; all that I wish to say here is that the matter will never be clarified unless these ingredients are kept meticulously distinct, and the logic carefully attended to.

(2) I shall mention only in passing Rawls's views about the meanings of the moral words or the natures, analyses, and logical properties of the moral concepts. It would be wrong to take up space on something which Rawls evidently thinks of little importance for his argument. He wishes to 'leave questions of meaning and definition aside and to get on with the task of developing a substantive theory of justice' (579/17). There is in fact a vast hole in his 600-page book which should be occupied by a thorough account of the meanings of these words, which is the only thing that can establish the logical rules that govern moral argument. If we do not have such an account, we shall never be able to distinguish between what we have to avoid saying if we are not to contradict ourselves or commit other *logical* errors, and what we have to avoid saying if we are to agree with Rawls and his coterie. So far as he does say anything about the meanings of the moral words, it is mostly derivative from recent descriptivist views, my arguments against which it would be tedious to rehearse. I found this reliance surprising, in view of the fact that what he says about justice, at any rate, clearly commits him to some form of prescriptivism: the principles of justice determine how we *are to* behave, not how we are to *describe* certain kinds of behaviour (61/7, 145/12, 14, 33, 149/16, 351/15). My quarrels with Rawls's main theory do not depend at all on the fact that I am a prescriptivist.

There are significant passages in which Rawls compares moral philosophy with mathematics (51/23) and linguistics (47/5, 49/8). The analogy with these sciences is vitiated by the fact that they do not yield substantial conclusions, as moral philosophy is supposed, on Rawls's view, to do, and in some sense clearly should. It is quite all right to test a linguistic theory (a grammar) against what people actually say when they are speaking carefully; people's *linguistic* 'intuitions' are indeed, in the end, authoritative for what is correct in their language. The kind of interplay between theory and data that occurs in all sciences can occur here, and it is perfectly proper for the data to be the utterances of native speakers. But the only 'moral' theories that can be checked against people's actual moral judgements are anthropological theories about what, in general, people *think* one ought to do, not moral principles about what one ought to do. That these latter can be so checked is not, indeed, what Rawls is suggesting in this passage; but do not the whole drift of his argument, and the passage quoted above (51/3), suggest it?

The case of mathematics is more controversial. Rawls seems to imply that if we had a 'moral system' analogous to the systems of logic and mathematics, then we could use such a system to elucidate the meanings of moral judgements, instead of the other way about, as I have suggested. There is no objection, so far as I can see, to such a claim in mathematics and logic, provided that we realize that the concepts used in the formal systems may be different from (perhaps more useful for certain purposes than) our natural ones. Such a procedure is all right in logic and mathematics, since the construction of artificial models can often illuminate the logic and the meaning of our ordinary speech; but whichever way the illumination goes (why not both ways?) it can work only if the system in question is purely formal. If what Rawls calls 'the substantive content of the moral conceptions' (52/7) is part of the system, then what will be revealed by it are not the meanings of moral judgements but the moral opinions of those who adhere to the system. And when he proposes (111/6) to *replace* our concept of right by the concept of being in accordance with the principles that would be acknowledged in the original position, he is in effect seeking to foist on us not a new meaning for a word, but a substantial set of moral views; for he thinks that he has tailored the original position so as to yield principles which fit his own considered judgements.

(3) Rawls's moral methodology takes the form of a picture or parable—and one which is even more difficult than most to interpret with any confidence. We are to imagine a set of people gathered together (hypothetically, not actually), to agree upon a set of 'principles of justice' to govern their

conduct.[3] The 'principles of justice' are those principles to which these 'people in the original position' (POPs) would agree for the conduct of all of them as 'people in ordinary life' (POLs), if, when making the agreement, they were subject to certain conditions.

It is obviously these conditions which determine the substance of the theory (indeed they *are* its substance, the rest being mere dramatization, useful for expository purposes, but also potentially misleading). Rawls's theory belongs to a class of theories which we may call 'hypothetical choice theories'— i.e. theories which say that the right answer to some question is the answer that a person or set of people *would* choose if subject to certain conditions. The best-known example of such a theory is the 'ideal observer' theory of ethics, about which Rawls says something, and which we shall find instructive to compare with his own. The important thing to notice about all such theories is that *what* this hypothetical person would choose, if it is determinate at all (which many such theories fail to make it) has to be determined by the conditions to which he is subject. If the conditions, once made explicit, do not deductively determine the choice, then the choice remains indeterminate, except in so far as it is covertly conditioned by the prejudices or intuitions of the philosopher whose theory it is. Thus intuition can enter at two points (and in Rawls's case enters at both; cf. 121/7–15). It enters in the choice of the

---

[3] It is tempting to say 'their *subsequent* conduct'; but the tenses in Rawls's account are one of its most baffling features. On the one hand, these 'people in the original position' (POPs) are to make a 'contract'; this, and terms like 'original position' and 'initial situation' (20/18), seem to indicate that this conclave is temporally prior to the time at which these same people are to enter the world as we know it, become 'people in ordinary life' (POLs) and carry out their contract. But on the other hand Rawls seems to speak commonly in the present tense (e.g. 520/27 ff.), as if they were somehow simultaneously POPs and POLs. Not surprisingly this, and other obscurities, make it often difficult, and sometimes (to me at any rate) impossible, to determine whether some particular remark is intended to refer to POPs or POLs. Who, for example, are 'they' in 206/5? And in 127/25, is it the POLs who are being said to be mutually disinterested, as the passage seems to imply, and as is suggested by the reference to 'circumstances of justice' on 128/5 (which seems usually, though not on 130/1–5, to mean circumstances of POLs, not POPs)? But if so, how are 129/14–18 or 148/2 ff. consistent? Again, do POLs lack envy, or only POPs? (see 151/22–4, 143–4, §§ 80–1). A book as long as Rawls's itself could be spent on such questions of interpretation; I was intending to set a few more of these exercises for the reader, but have not had time to compile them.

conditions to which the chooser is to be subject; and it enters to determine what he will choose in cases where the conditions, as made explicit, do not determine this (for examples see below).

The more important of the conditions to which Rawls's POPs are subject are the following (§§ 22–5):

1. They know certain facts about the world and the society in which POLs live, but have others concealed from them by a 'veil of ignorance'. It is obviously going to be crucial *which* facts they are allowed to know, and which they are not.

2. They are motivated in certain ways, especially in being selfish or mutually disinterested, and also in lacking envy and in being unwilling to use the principle of insufficient reason. They are also 'rational' (i.e. take the most effective means to given ends (14/5)).

3. They are subject to 'the formal constraints of the concept of right'. Rawls explicitly says that he does not 'claim that these conditions follow from the concept of right, much less from the meaning of morality' (130/16). Instead, he as usual says that it 'seems reasonable' to impose them (130/14). He does not tell us what he would say to somebody to whom they did not 'seem reasonable'.

4. There are also certain important procedural stipulations, such as that the POPs should all agree unanimously in their choice of principles. Later in the book, the procedure is very much elaborated, and takes the form of a series of stages in which the 'veil of ignorance' is progressively lifted; but I shall ignore this complication here.

In comparing Rawls's theory with other theories, it is most important to notice the roles played by these groups of conditions. If I may be allowed to mention my own theory, I would myself place almost the whole emphasis on (3), and would at the same time aim to establish the 'constraints' on the basis of a study of the logical properties of the moral words. This still seems to me the most rigorous and secure procedure, because it enables us to say that *if* this is how we are using the words (*if* this is what we mean by them), then we shall be debarred from saying so-and-so on pain of self-contradiction; and this gives moral arguments a cutting edge which in Rawls they lack. In a similar way, Achilles should have answered the Tortoise by saying, 'If you mean by "if" what we all mean, you have to accept *modus ponens*; for this is the rule that gives its meaning to "if".' It is of course in dispute how much we can do by this method; but I think, and have tried elsewhere to show, that we can do much more than Rawls allows.

The 'ideal observer' theory (in a typical form) differs from Rawls's theory in the following respects. Under (1), it allows the principle-chooser to know everything; there is no 'veil of ignorance'. On the other hand, under (2), he is differently motivated; instead of being concerned with his own interest only, he is impartially benevolent. Now it is possible to show that on a certain simple and natural 'rational contractor' theory of the Rawls type (though not, it is fairly safe to say, on Rawls's own version of this type of theory) these two changes exactly cancel one another, so that the normative consequences of the 'ideal observer' and 'rational contractor' theories would be identical. To see this, let us remember that the main object of these conditions is to secure impartiality. This is secured in the case of the rational contractor theory by not allowing the POPs to know what are to be their individual roles as POLs in the society in which the contract has to be observed; they therefore cannot choose the principles to suit their own selfish interests, although they are selfishly motivated. It is secured in the case of the ideal observer theory by express stipulation; he is required to be impartially benevolent. It looks, therefore, as if *these* versions of the two theories are, as I have said elsewhere (H 1972*b*: 166), practically equivalent.

We must next ask *how much* the POPs have to be ignorant of, in order to secure impartiality. It must be noticed that much of the work is already done by the 'formal constraint' that the principles have to be 'general'.[4] Rawls himself says that the formal constraints rule out egoism (136/13); it might therefore be asked what there is left for the 'veil of ignorance'

---

[4] Rawls's word; I have commented on his use, and given reasons for preferring the word 'universal', which *he* uses for something else, on p. 50.

to do, since to abandon egoism (and for the same formal reasons the pursuit of the interests of any other particular person or set of them) is *eo ipso* to become impartial. I do not think that this objection sticks; for a POP, if he had full knowledge of his own role as a POL, might adopt principles which were formally 'general' or universal but were rigged to suit his own interest. Rawls, however, thinks (wrongly[5]) that such rigged principles can be ruled out on the formal ground of lack of 'generality', and so is open to the objection *ad hominem*. That is to say, *he* has left nothing for the veil of ignorance to do as regards impartiality.

Be that as it may, however, we need to be clear how thick a veil of ignorance is required to achieve impartiality. To be frugal: all that the POPs need to be ignorant of are their roles as individuals in the world of POLs. That is to say, it would be possible to secure impartiality while allowing the POPs to know the entire history of the world—not only the general conditions governing it, but the actual course of history, and indeed the alternative courses of history which would be the result of different actions by individuals in it, and in particular to know that there would be in the world individuals *a*, *b* . . . *n* who would be affected in specific ways by these actions—*provided* that each of the POPs did not know which individual he was (i.e. whether he was *a* or *b*, etc.). Impartiality would be secured even by this very economical veil, because if a POP does not know whether he is *a* or *b*, he has, however selfish, no motive for choosing his principles so as to suit the interests of *a* rather than those of *b* when these interests are in conflict.

A superficial reading of Rawls's rather ambiguous language at 137/4, 12/12, and 198/20 might lead one to suppose that this 'economical veil' is what he has in mind. But this cannot be right, in view of 200/17 and other passages. We need to ask, therefore, why Rawls is not content with it, if it suffices to secure impartiality. The answer might just be that he is unclear as between two things: (1) the POPs' not knowing which of them is going to be *a* and which *b*; (2) their knowing

---

[5] I have hinted why on p. 52. For my own answer to the 'rigging' difficulty see p. 196 and *FR* 107.

this, but not knowing how *a* and *b* are going to fare. Much of his language could bear either interpretation. And 141/25 seems to imply that Rawls thinks that the 'economical veil' would allow the POPs to use threats against each other based on the power which as individual POLs they would have; but this is obviously not so if they do not know *which* individuals they are going to be, however many particular facts about individuals they may know.

Nevertheless, sooner than accuse Rawls of a mere muddle, let us look for other explanations. One is that he wants, not merely to secure impartiality, but to avoid an interpretation which would have normative consequences which he is committed to abjuring. With the 'economical veil', the rational contractor theory is practically equivalent in its normative consequences to the ideal observer theory and to my own theory (see above and below), and these normative consequences are of a utilitarian sort. Therefore Rawls may have reasoned that, since an 'economical veil' would make him into a utilitarian, he had better buy a more expensive one. We can, indeed, easily sympathize with the predicament of one who, having been working for the best part of his career on the construction of 'a viable alternative to the utilitarian tradition' (150/12), discovered that the type of theory he had embraced, in its simplest and most natural form, led direct to a kind of utilitarianism. It must in fairness be said, however, that Rawls does not regard this motive as disreputable; for he is not against tailoring his theory to suit the conclusions he wants to reach (see above, and 141/23 where he says, 'We want to define the original position so that we get the desired solution'). I shall be examining later the question of whether Rawls's thicker veil *does* help him to avoid utilitarianism; it is fairly clear from §28 that he *thinks* it does.

A further motive for the thicker veil is a desire for simplicity both in the reasoning and in the principles resulting from it (140/31, 142/8; but cf. 141/22). By letting the POPs know only the general facts about the world in which the POLs live, and also by other devices (e.g. 95/14, 96/6, 98/28), Rawls effectively prevents them from going into much detail about the facts. This means that his principles can and must be simple; but at the same time it raises the question of whether they can be adequate to the complexities of the actual world. Rawls is, in fact, faced with a dilemma. If he sticks to the 'economical veil', then there will be no difficulty of principle in doing justice even in highly specific and unusual cases in the actual world; but this will involve very complex calculations, in advance, on the part of his POPs. On the other hand, if, in order to avoid these complex calculations, he limits the POPs' knowledge to 'general' facts about the world, he is in danger of having his POPs choose principles which may, in particular cases, result in flagrant injustice, because the facts of these cases are peculiar.

This is merely the analogue, in Rawls's system, of the dilemma which afflicts utilitarians, and which I have tried to solve on p. 221 and in H 1972*b*: 166. The solution lies in distinguishing between two levels of moral thinking, in one of which (for use 'in a cool hour') we are allowed to go into all the details, and in the other of which (for normal use under conditions of ignorance of the future, stress, and temptation, and in moral education and self-education) we stick to firm and simple principles which are most likely in general to lead to right action—they are not, however, to be confused with 'rules of thumb', a term whose undiscriminating use has misled many. The first kind of thinking (let us call it *critical*) is used in order to select the principles to be adhered to in the second kind (the *intuitive*), choosing those principles which are best for situations likely to be actually encountered. If this kind of solution were applied to Rawls's system, he would allow his POPs to know everything but their individual roles as POLs (the 'economical veil'); but since their task would be to choose the best intuitive principles for the thinking of POLs, they could still, since these principles have to be simple and observed only in general, attend only to the general facts about the POL society and the general run of cases. The contract would then not be a contract to act universally in certain ways, but rather a contract to employ certain firm principles in the moral education of POLs themselves and their children, and to uphold such principles as the norm in their society. For unusual cases, and for those in which the principles conflicted, the POLs would be allowed (in

Aristotelian fashion) to do a bit of POP-thinking for themselves (1137ᵇ24; cf. 19/9, 138/20).

Rawls does not adopt this solution, although he shows some awareness of the distinction between intuitive and critical thinking on 28/19. Ross's different but related distinction between '*prima facie* duties' and 'duties all things considered' is referred to and indeed used on 340/15. On the whole Rawls's principles are treated as unbreakable ones for universal observance (e.g. 115/36); but they are supposed to have the simplicity which in fact only intuitive or prima-facie principles can, or need, have (132/17). Other passages which *might* be relevant to this question are 157/32, 159/16 ff., 161/17, 304/13, 337/11, 340/28, 341/14, 454/6; but I have been unable to divine exactly what Rawls's view is.

He has tried to meet the problems of conflicts between principles and of unusual cases in two ways. The first is by means of a rigid 'lexical' ordering of his principles (which could be guaranteed in unusual cases to yield absurd results); the second is by his 'four-stage sequence' (195 ff.), whereby the 'veil of ignorance' is progressively lifted, and at each 'lift' the knowledge of extra facts is absorbed and the principles expanded to deal with them. The sequence ends with the complete disappearance of the veil. Since Rawls can say this, he cannot have any objection on grounds of practicability to unrestricted knowledge from the start, and his reasons for forbidding it must be theoretical ones.

The four-stage sequence would only work if at each later stage the principles inherited from the stage before *determined*, in the light of the new information, what further principles were to be adopted. At least, this is so if the method is required to be rigorous; Rawls can perhaps escape this requirement by using intuitions all down the line. But if the principles chosen in the original position do *determine*, in conjunction with each new batch of facts, all the additional principles that are to be adopted at each stage, then the moral law is likely to turn out to be an ass. Some victim of the application of one of these lower-order principles may be found complaining that if the POPs had only *known* about him and his situation, likes and dislikes, then they would have complicated their principles a little to allow them to do justice to him (perhaps he does not give a fig for the 'priority of liberty'; or perhaps his preferences do not coincide with the POPs' ranking of the 'primary goods'). If it were rigidly applied, Rawls's system would be like a constitution having a legislature in which reading of the newspapers was forbidden, and lawcourts without any judicial discretion. But of course he does *not* apply it rigidly.

I will now explain why the ideal observer theory, the rational contractor theory, and my own theory must, on certain interpretations of each of them, yield the same results. As pointed out above, the 'economical veil' version of the rational contractor theory secures impartiality between the individuals in society. The ideal observer theory includes impartiality as an express stipulation. My own theory secures impartiality by a combination of the requirement that moral judgements be universalizable and the requirement to prescribe for hypothetical reversed-role situations as if they were actual (*FR* 108; *MT* 113). So, as regards impartiality, the theories are on all fours. Next, some degree of benevolence is required by all three theories; the ideal observer is expressly required to be impartially benevolent; my universal prescriber, since he has to treat everybody as one and nobody as more than one, and since one of the persons included in 'everybody' is himself, to whom he is benevolent, has to be positively and equally benevolent to everybody; the rational contractor, although he is selfish, does not know which individual POL it is whose interests he should favour (since he does not know which is himself) and so his selfish or partial benevolence has the same results as impartial benevolence. For the same kind of reason the ideal observer and the universal prescriber, though they have additional knowledge (viz., knowledge of their own individual roles, if any, in the situations for which they are prescribing) are prevented by the previous requirements from using it for selfish ends.

Rawls himself says that the ideal observer theory leads to utilitarianism (185/24); and—at least if it takes a certain form, if it involves what Rawls calls 'sympathetic identification' with all affected parties—this seems plausible. In stating this form of the theory, he echoes some phrases of my own, and later treats my theory and the ideal observer theory as equivalent (186/30, 34; see *FR* 123, 94 n.). So, then, the rational contractor theory, in the version I have been discussing (which is not Rawls's) should also lead to utilitarianism. Rawls is aware of this possibility (121/33). He even seems to imply on 149/3 that *his own* theory is practically equivalent to the ideal observer theory; but this is not his usual view. I shall leave until later the difficult task of deciding whether Rawls, by the departures he makes from this simple version of the rational contractor theory, succeeds in establishing a non-utilitarian conclusion.

Of the three theories that I have just shown to be practically equivalent, it is largely a matter of taste which one adopts. Philosophers will differ in the use they like to make of dramatizations of their theories, and in the particular scenarios chosen. Such dramatizations do not help the argument, though they may help to expound it; Rawls himself seems to agree (138/31). For myself, I think such devices useful (though they can also mislead), and I had much greater hopes of Rawls's enterprise than have in fact been realized. For, knowing that the simplest and most natural version of the rational contractor theory was practically equivalent to my own position, I was optimistic enough to hope that Rawls's elaborate exploration of the normative consequences of such a theory might illuminate those of my own, and thus enable me (in the most favourable outcome) simply to plug in to his results. Such good luck, however, seldom befalls philosophers; and in fact Rawls's constant appeal to intuition instead of argument, and his tailoring of his theory to suit his anti-utilitarian preconceptions, have deprived it of the value which it could have had as a tracing of the normative consequences of views about the logic of the moral concepts.

It is interesting that in his peroration (587) Rawls as good as drops into an ideal-observer way of speaking. I myself should be happy to use any of these images (including C. I. Lewis's 'all lives *seriatim*' picture (1946: 547; cf. 189/12 and *FR* 199). But the work needs to be done on the logic of the argument, which has to be shown to be valid by the procedures of philosophical logic, involving the analysis of concepts, natural or, if need be, artificial. Without this, a 'theory of justice' is nothing but a suggestive picture.

(4) I turn next to Rawls's normative views about justice, and in particular the question of whether he succeeds in establishing them by argument. Since my own argument will be for the most part destructive (though I shall give some hints as to how I think the job might be done better), I must start by making it clear that I am not criticizing the project of bringing philosophical argument to bear on practical questions, but only Rawls's attempted execution of it. It is my hope, as it is his, that philosophers can so clarify these matters that we shall be able to argue more cogently than we do at present about what is just or unjust. I differ from him in thinking that unless the philosophers who attempt this base themselves on a thorough understanding of the concepts used and their logical properties, which is their proper and peculiar philosophical contribution, they run the risk of doing no more for the topic of justice than journalists and politicians.

I have just argued that the simplest form of the rational contractor theory would have the same normative consequences as a certain version of the ideal observer theory and as my own theory, and that these consequences would be of a utilitarian sort. I suggested that that was why Rawls himself does not adopt this simple version. It remains, therefore, to ask whether his more complex version (if we can ever determine exactly what it is) can bring him to the non-utilitarian conclusions that he so earnestly desires.

The crucial questions are:

(i) Who are to be included among the parties in the original position, or POPs?

(ii) What are they to be allowed to know? This I have already discussed, but I shall have to return to it.

(iii) How, given these restrictions on membership and knowledge, will the POPs set about making their choice? Under this heading come questions about their use of the 'principle of insufficient reason', and of their motivation (especially their aversion to risk).

We have to ask whether the answers to these three questions suffice to determine, without appeal to Rawls's own preconceptions or intuitions, what principles of justice the POPs would choose.

The principles which Rawls says they would choose are summed up by him in their 'final statement' on 302/15, thus:

First Principle. Each person is to have an equal right to the most extensive total system of equal basic liberties compatible with a similar system of liberty for all.

Second Principle. Social and economic inequalities are to be arranged so that they are both: (*a*) to the greatest benefit of the least advantaged, consistent with the just savings principle, and (*b*) attached to offices and positions open to all under conditions of fair equality of opportunity.

He also has what he calls 'priority rules' determining the relative priority that we are to give to these principles and their parts, and to the principles of justice over other principles. I shall not have space to deal with these. The most important of them is that which gives priority to liberty over the other principles. All the principles of justice are said to rest on what he calls the same 'General Conception', which runs thus:

All social primary goods—liberty and opportunity, income and wealth, and the bases of self-respect—are to be distributed equally unless an unequal distribution of any or all of these goods is to the advantage of the least favoured. (303/7)

Thus Rawls founds his theory of justice (rightly, as I think) on an account (though I think it is the wrong account) of distributive justice. This in turn is founded on a view about procedural justice in the selection of principles.

(i) *The Membership of the POP Committee*

It might be thought that the simplest and safest membership-rule for the assembly of POPs would be to include everybody who might be affected by their choice of principles—i.e. 'everyone who could live at some time' (139/4). This simple rule Rawls rejects, on the ground that 'to conceive of the original position [thus] is to stretch fantasy too far; the conception would cease to be a natural guide to intuition'

(139/5). In a book which relies so much on fantasy, this is a surprisingly weak ground. The membership is restricted in several ways:

(*a*) Non-human animals are excluded, thus neatly removing them from the direct protection of principles of justice.

The discussion of this topic is full of expressions like 'presumably' (505/6, 506/19), 'the natural answer seems to be' (505/12), and 'seems necessary to match our considered judgments' (509/25). Rawls himself says, very frankly, 'Now of course none of this is literally argument' (509/32); and it would certainly not convince a determined vegetarian. It is of course difficult to include dumb animals among the POPs (they could not make speeches in the assembly); but that is an unfortunate effect of the dramatic scenario—which might perhaps be overcome if we could suppose that the POPs do not know whether they may not be, or be going to become, dumb animals.

(*b*) By adopting the 'present time of entry intrepretation' (140/11—an opaque phrase which I have nowhere found explained) he seems to exclude all but the members of just one generation in the world's history.

He thus lays up for himself, as he believes, troubles about justice between generations. These troubles are quite gratuitous, and could easily have been solved by allowing all generations to join the assembly. Rawls himself attempts to get over the difficulty by an obscure and contrived assumption that the POPs are to be 'thought of as representing continuing lines of claims, as being so to speak deputies for a kind of everlasting moral agent or institution' (128/25). 'Everlasting' is toned down, two lines further on, to 'over at least two generations'. It might be thought that there was an important difference between two generations and eternity, and that, for securing impartiality between all generations, only eternity would do. But in fact it is strictly unnecessary to make any such assumption to secure impartiality if, as Rawls also rightly stipulates, the POPs, though they all belong to one generation, are not to know which this is (137/14, 288/9). For in that case they will not favour a particular generation, any more than they will favour particular individuals, not knowing who they themselves are or when they are born (cf. 137/23).

It is not the restriction of membership to one generation, by itself, that gets Rawls into trouble at this point, but rather this, combined with another feature of his theory to which we must now attend. He writes as if the POPs were not prescribing universally (or, as he would put it, 'generally') in choosing their principles of justice, but only prescribing for their *own* behaviour (and possibly also for that of *subsequent* generations— 13/4). From this it follows that (in default of the *ad hoc* restriction which he imposes) they can happily say 'Let our generation, whichever it is, consume all the world's resources and leave none for succeeding generations'. If, on the contrary, they were prescribing universally for all men at whatever time, and did not know at what time *they* were to be in the world, they could not happily universalize this prescription; for they would then be prescribing equally for their own predecessors. Thus Rawls has (characteristically, and as a consequence of his contempt for such logical tools) failed to avail himself of one of the 'formal constraints of the concept of right' to which he himself has earlier drawn attention (131/14). If the POPs do not know to what generation they all belong, and are prescribing universally for the conduct of all generations, they will have (if they are rational) to adopt principles of justice which maintain impartiality between the interests of all generations. We can say that they are either prescribing for the past as well as the present and future, or choosing the principles by which they want society to be governed in the future, and hope that it has been governed in the past. I have heard rumours that Rawls himself is now attracted by this manœuvre. Alternatively, we might take a hint from Kant via Professor Richards (1970: 88 f., 310), and suppose that, when they make their choice, they are in a noumenal atemporal green-room, and do not know at what point they are to come upon the stage of time as POLs. Any difficulties which attend these modifications to the scene arise from the creak-ings of the stage-machinery and not from the logic of the argument, which could be set out in universal-prescriptive terms without any such machinery. That the POPs cannot *affect* the past (292/5) is strictly irrelevant; Rawls thinks it relevant only because he takes his machinery too seriously.

> (*c*) The principles of justice are to be chosen from the 'perspective' or 'point of view' of 'representative men in all relevant social positions' (96/1; cf. 64/9).

This is not strictly a membership-restriction, but it has a similar effect. Those who are on the committee are compelled to choose from the *point of view* of representatives of these rather gross classes (in defining which, for example, we are not allowed to differentiate between large and small farmers (96/4); this perhaps illustrates how prone Rawls is to iron out material differences between cases in the interests of 'a coherent and manageable theory' (96/7)).

Does any of these membership-restrictions enable Rawls to avoid utilitarianism? It seems not; what they can do is, not to establish or refute any particular principle of distributive justice, but only to confine or limit the class of those protected by it. They will do this if the POPs *know* that the membership is so limited (as, perhaps, in the case of the disfranchisement of dumb animals); if they do *not* know, then the membership-restriction can make no difference at all, since each POP will have to envisage the possibility of his being *any* person out of the set *a, b . . . n,* even though the person who is going to be, say, *b* or *m*, is not actually present at the meeting. It does not matter if some person is not present, provided that nobody knows that he is not; and for that reason a committee is strictly unnecessary; one POP would do, provided that he did not know which POL he was going to be (cf. 139/23).

However, there is one membership-restriction stipulated by Rawls that does seem to make a big difference:

> (*d*) Only people who actually do or will exist are allowed on the committee.

In a passage which I quoted earlier, it has been implicitly laid down, on rather slender grounds, that (merely) *possible* people, as opposed to actual people, are to be blackballed (139/4); later it is explicitly stated that the POPs 'know that they already hold a place in some particular society' (166/12)—though of course they do not know what place in which society. This means that in Rawls's system the interests of possible people are simply not going to be taken account of.

This would seem to be crucial for questions about population policy and abortion, for example. The person that the foetus *would* turn into if not aborted, and the people who *will* be born if contraception is not practised, get no say if they are not actual people—i.e., if it is actually the case that abortion and contraception *are* practised. This would seem to have the curious consequence that, simply by performing an abortion, I can make sure that my act does not contravene Rawlsian justice, because I shall thereby have disfranchised the abortee. Since POPs have to have reached 'the age of reason' (146/15), it looks as if the same would apply to infanticide (since merely possible adults are excluded). But 248/37 ff. and 509/19 ff. seem to support a different and more orthodox view (if we can swallow the assumption that the veil of ignorance could conceal from one of the contracting parties the fact that he is a babe in arms).

It is only this membership-restriction that enables Rawls to pronounce so easily that the average utility principle, which bids us maximize average utility, is superior to the classical utility principle, which bids us maximize total utility (166/3). To understand this, consider a possible person P whose birth would have lowered average utility but raised total utility, because his own happiness would have been less than the previous average, but more than the combined losses suffered by the others owing to his arrival. If a POP might, for all he knows, be P, he will find the classical principle more attractive; but if he knows that he cannot be P, he will prefer the average principle. This is because the classical principle would require population policies which allowed P to be born, whereas the average principle would require policies which debarred him from existence. By excluding P from the committee, and allowing this to be known, Rawls makes sure that it will disregard P's interests, and thus brings it about that, from the POPs' point of view, the average utility principle is a stronger candidate against which to pit his own principles of justice than the classical utility principle. If the exclusion is unjust, he is perhaps choosing the weaker and not the stronger opponent; but I do not think that in fact this gives him much advantage. In any case, it would not seem that this membership-restriction helps him much in his fight with utilitarianism in general.

We may note here an embarrassing consequence of the inclusion of possible people among the POPs, if Rawls's own normative principles are adopted, and if it is assumed that to have any life at all is better than not to be born. The unborn will then be his least-advantaged class; and so his difference or maximin principle (see below) will require him to say that before anything is done for the rest of us, we ought to secure the birth of all these possible people.[6] This would lead us to a duty of procreation on a vast scale; we could stop only when the earth would support no more people above the starvation level. But Rawls could reasonably escape this consequence by rejecting the assumption that any life is better than none; he does not need for this purpose to disfranchise merely possible people. The classical principle also has been thought by some to require a very expansive population policy; but this too will depend on what weight is put upon quality of life as opposed to mere life.

(ii) *The Thickness of the Veil*

We saw earlier that Rawls does not adopt the simplest and most economical version of the 'veil of ignorance' to which his POPs are to be subject—namely that which deprives them only of knowledge of which *individual* each of them is to be. He prefers to say that they are not to know what *properties* of various sorts they are to have, and that they know only the 'general' facts about society.[7] That is, besides, or instead of, being ignorant of what individual each of them is to be, the POPs are ignorant of everything that cannot be described in general terms. So, for example, they are allowed to understand 'political affairs and the principles of economic theory' (137/30) and 'the laws of moral psychology' (138/6). There is one

[6] I owe this point, and much else, to Mr Parfit.

[7] It will perhaps not be necessary to inquire precisely what he means by 'general' (let alone such minutiae as whether he means the same by 'general' on 197/9 as he does on 137/1, or whether, rather, as seems necessary in order to preserve consistency, what are called 'general facts' on 197/9 are what have been called 'particular circumstances' on 137/11).

exception to the ban on particular knowledge: the POPs are allowed to know the 'particular fact' that the POLs' society is subject to the 'circumstances of justice'—a phrase under which Rawls covers such facts as that human beings are vulnerable to attack and that natural resources are limited (127/3, 6), as are also people's powers of reasoning, memory, and attention (127/27).

I have also suggested that § 28 indicates that Rawls thinks that his thick veil of ignorance helps him to avoid utilitarianism. It is not easy to see why he thinks this; but the key to the understanding of the reasoning seems to lie in the relation between ignorance of particular facts and refusal to use the 'principle of insufficient reason' (IR, see below). Rawls says that the POPs 'discount estimates of likelihood that are not based on a knowledge of the particular facts' (173/6; cf. 155/25 ff.). This seems to imply that if they *did* have knowledge of particular facts (even if they did not know their individual places in the world constituted by those facts), they would be able to work out relative frequencies of sorts of events, and thus 'the objective probabilities' of occurrences in the POL society (cf. 168/15, 171/31). Thus they would have no need to use IR, but could base their predictions of how each individual POP-turned-POL was likely to fare, given the adoption of any one set of principles of justice, on 'objective probabilities'. And this, he may have thought, would lead to utilitarianism (see below). I am far from certain that this *is* Rawls's argument. But if it is, it is fallacious. For even if the POPs had knowledge of objective probabilities of sorts of occurrences in the world, they still might not have knowledge of the probability of each of them being a particular individual POL, and so might not know how likely it was that any individual POP-turned-POL would fare well, or ill. For *this*, they might have to rely on IR. In other words, if the sortition which results in this POP being this POL is not subject to objective probabilities, no amount of objective probability in the distribution of welfare among the POLs will help any individual POP to know how likely it is that *he* will get a certain degree of welfare, unless he is allowed to use IR. So, since the knowledge of particular facts would not by itself make the use of IR unnecessary, Rawls does not gain anything by refusing to allow knowledge of these particular facts. The upshot is that *everything* in his argument for the rejection of utilitarianism depends on his refusal to allow the POPs to use IR. To this, therefore, we must now turn.

(iii) *Insufficient Reason and Aversion to Risk*

The principle of insufficient reason (IR) requires us to assign equal probabilities to two or more outcomes when we have no reason to suppose that the probability of one is greater than that of another. In some forms it leads to paradox: if we are drawing blindfold from an urn containing black, red, and yellow balls in unknown proportions, it gives us different values for the probability of drawing a black ball according as we state the alternatives, which by IR will be equiprobable, as black, red, and yellow or as black and coloured. If, therefore, the situation of the POPs were such that they had no basis for listing the members of the set of outcomes uniquely, then it would be hard to quarrel with Rawls's insistence that rational POPs would not use IR. However, (to use a Rawlsish phrase) it seems reasonable to suppose that a POP, knowing that he will be one of n individuals, all in some respects faring differently, will say that there are, correspondingly, n different outcomes, and will, if he uses IR, conclude that the probability of getting any one of them is $1/n$. At any rate, we have at least as much reason to suppose this as Rawls has to suppose anything else.

He admits (165/35) that 'if the parties are viewed as rational individuals who have no aversion to risk and who follow the principle of insufficient reason in computing likelihoods . . . , then the idea of the initial situation leads naturally to the average [utility] principle'. It is interesting that in this passage he seems to imply that it is possible to have no aversion to risk and to use IR, without thereby ceasing to be rational; if so, it cannot be the rationality of the POPs that he relies on. But his more considered view seems to be that it is not rational to use IR (cf. 172/30).

It is not clear whether he thinks that the POPs have an aversion to risk. On 172/13, 26 he says, 'The essential thing is not to allow the principles chosen to depend on special attitudes towards risk. . . . What must be shown is that choosing *as if* one had such an aversion is rational given the unique features of that situation irrespective of any special attitudes towards risk' (my italics). This seems inconsistent with 169/15 ff., where he implies that the POPs *actually have*, and ought to have, a reluctance to take great risks, on the inadequate ground that their descendants may reproach them if they do (might not their descendants be just as likely to say 'Nothing venture, nothing win'?). It also seems inconsistent with 165/35, quoted above, if that implies that one who was not averse to risk and used IR would not be, on that score, irrational. In 172/16 he says 'the parties do not know whether or not they have a characteristic aversion to taking chances'; and the reader is not to know either, nor whether the referent of 'they' is the POPs or the POLs. For if it is the POPs, Rawls is saying that a veil of ignorance can conceal from someone an aversion which he presently has (a rather steep assumption); but if the POLs, how is this condition relevant to the present motivation of the POPs as regards risk-taking?

It looks, at any rate, as if the principal weight is being placed on the rejection of IR. I am sure that critics more competent than me in the theory of probability will have discussed this topic at length. But the important thing to notice is that the answer to the question of whether it would be rational for the POPs, in default of objective probabilities, to use IR *does not matter*. Suppose we grant that it would not. The important point would then be: Why are they denied knowledge of objective probabilities? Rawls says that each of his assumptions about the POPs 'should by itself be natural and plausible' (18/15), but this particular feature seems to be quite arbitrary. It is only there because it may help to lead by arguments which Rawls finds acceptable to conclusions which he finds acceptable (cf. again the remark on 141/23, 'We want to define the original position so that we get the desired solution'). It is obvious that, if Rawls had wished to reach utilitarian conclusions, he could have so arranged it that the POPs were going to have their place as POLs assigned to them by means of a well-conducted mechanical or electronic lottery of the usual kind. In that case, the POPs, knowing this, *would* have known the objective probabilities of their getting any particular POL-role, and would have known that they were equal, and utilitarianism would have resulted. So the very most that Rawls may have done towards setting up a non-utilitarian theory of justice is to show that it is possible, if one desires, so to rig the assumptions of the theory that it does not lead straight to a utilitarian conclusion.

We next have to examine the conclusions that Rawls thinks it does lead to. He thinks that the POPs would, in choosing their principles, 'maximin'—that is to say, choose the course which has the best worst outcome. They will seek to maximize the welfare of the least-advantaged representative members of their society. It is important to distinguish this strategy from another, which I will call the 'insurance' strategy; for Rawls uses arguments in favour of maximining which are really only arguments in favour of insuring against utter calamity (cf. 156/30, 163/18, 176/23). We insure our houses against fire because we think that a certain outcome, namely having one's house burnt down and having no money to buy another, is so calamitous that we should rule it out. This is not at all the same strategy as maximining. If the POL society were going to be affluent enough to provide a more than just acceptable standard of living for even the least advantaged, the insurance strategy would allow the POPs to purchase a very great gain for the more advantaged at the cost of a small loss for the least advantaged; but the maximin strategy would forbid this. Maximiners would end up refusing to let the man with, say, £100,000 a year have any more if the man with the minimum income of £90,000 received in consequence a pound or two less; but the follower of the insurance strategy would by that time have lost interest.

POPs following an insurance strategy would fix a minimum and frame their principles of justice to secure that. They would not have to know whether the minimum was feasible; all they would have to do would be to say that below it, the interests of the more advantaged were always to be sacrificed to those of the less (as in wartime rationing). Rawls has not actually given us anything to determine what minimum the POPs would fix (might they not differ on this?). But neither has he given us anything to determine the minimum which he himself requires for his argument. It is what they 'can be sure of by following the maximin rule' (154/30); but how do they know what this amounts to? And if they do not know, how can they tell that anything less is 'intolerable' (156/24)?

The POP game is in effect played by imagining ourselves in the original position and then choosing principles of justice. Rawls's POPs come to the decisions that they come to simply because they are replicas of Rawls himself with what altruism he has removed and a veil of ignorance clapped over his head. It is not surprising, therefore, that they reach conclusions which he can accept. If I myself play this game, I import into the original position *my* prejudices and inclinations, which in some respects are different from Rawls's. I have some inclination to insure against the worst calamities, in so far as this is possible.[8] But I have no inclination to maximin, once the acceptable minimum is assured; after that point I feel inclined to take chances in the hope of maximizing my expectation of welfare, as I do in actual life (for example, I do not entirely refrain from investing my spare cash because I might lose it). And in certain cases I do not feel inclined to maximin even in very reduced circumstances. If, when I was a prisoner of war, a benevolent and trustworthy Japanese officer had said that he would play poker with me and, if I won enough, allow me to buy myself a ticket home through neutral territory with a safe conduct, then I should have accepted the invitation, in order to give myself a chance, however small, of freedom (the priority of liberty!) rather than forgo this chance and husband my money to buy some sugar with as I languished on the Burma Railway.

---

[8] It is a difficult question (too difficult for discussion here) to what extent an insurance strategy on the part of the POPs is compatible with utilitarianism. Utilitarian POPs could insure against calamities if the premium were such as to maximize their expection of utility; and this is what many POLs try to do. To be willing to pay a high premium may simply be an indication that one attaches a high negative value to the calamity in question, and less value to the possible affluence one is sacrificing. The diminishing marginal utility of affluence is relevant here. So, on the other hand, is the sheer impossibility of insuring against some of the worst calamities (for example, that of being a person whose temperament simply prevents him being happy). A utilitarian POP might well achieve the results of an insurance strategy without the strategy, if he assigned a high acceptance-utility to an intuitive (prima-facie) principle enjoining *compassion*—a sentiment which is perhaps better able than 'justice as fairness' to make us look after the unfortunate.

Thus the maximin strategy does not appeal to me as *in general* a good one for choices under uncertainty. Even Rawls does not go so far as to claim that. He states three features of situations which give 'plausibility' to the maximin strategy (154/11). The first is the ignorance of objective probabilities; but we have seen that the imposition of this condition is entirely arbitrary. The second is that the chooser has to have 'a conception of the good such that he cares very little, if anything, for what he might gain above the minimum stipend' (154/28); but this condition is clearly inapplicable, for the POPs 'do not know their conception of the good' (155/15). They therefore make do with assumptions about 'primary goods' (which seem in this passage, though not always, all to have monetary values). The fate of a man who was made miserable because he lacked something which he valued very much, but which was not on Rawls's list of primary goods, is therefore not even insured against. The third feature is that some outcomes are 'intolerable' (156/24); but this justifies only insurance, not maximining. It looks, therefore, as if Rawls has not succeeded in making his choice of strategy even 'plausible'. But in spite of this he says 'the original position has been defined so that it is a situation in which the maximin rule applies' (155/22). We can only say 'Amen'.

I do not claim to have shown that the maximin strategy is a bad one for POPs, only that Rawls has given no good reason for holding that it is a good one. The truth is that it is a wide-open question how the POPs would choose; he has reduced the information available to them and about them so much that it is hard to say *what* they would choose, unless his own intuitions supply the lack. Rawls, however, has one recourse, and that is that the results of his theory have to tally with his 'considered judgments'. But they do not tally with mine. A maximin strategy would (and in Rawls does) yield principles of justice according to which it would always be just to impose any loss, however great, upon a better-off group in order to bring a gain, however small, to the least advantaged group, however affluent the latter's starting-point. If intuitions are to be used, this is surely counter-intuitive; at least, not many of us are as egalitarian as that.

It is to Rawls's credit that he does not avail himself of

some well-worn but fallacious polemical arguments against utilitarianism. It is true that on 156/24 he insinuates, without stating, that utilitarianism could justify 'if not slavery or serfdom, at least serious infractions of liberty for the sake of greater social benefits'. But he very fairly admits on 26/13 that 'certain common precepts of justice, particularly those which concern the protection of liberties and rights' *can* be accounted for in a utilitarian system as 'those precepts which experience shows should be strictly respected and departed from only under exceptional circumstances if the sum of advantages is to be maximized'. It would be unfair on our part to expect Rawls to explore more fully the possibilities of showing the place of common notions of justice in a utilitarian system—that is not his enterprise. But he has not shown that there are no such possibilities; and until this has been shown, philosophers would do well to go on looking for them. It may be that they could be found, without anything like so much intuitive scaffolding as Rawls needs for his own system; it may be that the world *is* so constituted that to fail to inculcate and strenuously pursue principles of justice fairly closely related to *some* of the commonly accepted ones will result in a diminution of utility. I am indeed inclined to think that this is so; but obviously the question calls for further investigation (H 1977; *MT* ch. 9).

In concluding this not very sympathetic appraisal, it must be said that a critic with more ample patience and leisure might possibly have done better for Rawls. I have taken a great deal of pains (and it really has been painful) trying to get hold of his ideas, but with the feeling all the time that they were slipping through my fingers. Very often, when I had found what looked like a statement of his opinion on some issue, I later found another remark which seemed to say something different. The book is extremely repetitious, and it is seldom clear whether the repetitions really are *repetitions*, or modifications of previously expressed views. I have drawn attention to some of these difficulties, and there are all too many others. Rawls is not to be blamed for failing to keep the whole of this huge book in his head at the same time (the only way to avoid inconsistencies when writing a book); and still less are his readers. He is to be blamed, if at all, for not attempting something more modest and doing it properly.

Many years ago he wrote some extremely promising articles, containing in germ, though without clarity, a most valuable suggestion about the form and nature of moral thought. It might have been possible to work this idea out with concision and rigour (Richards (1970) has made a tolerably good job of it which is much clearer than Rawls's own book as an exposition of this type of theory). If Rawls had limited himself to, say, 300 pages, and had resolved to get his main ideas straight and express them with absolute clarity, he could have made a valuable contribution to moral philosophy. The discussions of other topics (which contain much that is of interest) could have been published separately; and that would have given him more room and more time to tighten up the main argument, which is all I have been able to consider here. As it is, his book is likely to waste a great deal of a good many people's time—though they will also gain *some* insights, and will at any rate get some exercise. Over the years he has collected a mass of criticisms of his views, but has thought it possible to insulate himself from the effects of them by folding each in a little piece of cotton wool. If he had been more self-confident and less rigid, or even if he had had a greater sense of style, he would have either stated the criticisms clearly and answered them concisely, or else revised the views. What he has done instead is to try to incorporate the criticisms without changing the views; and that is what has made the views so hard to catch.

11

The Structure of Ethics and Morals

I MUST start by saying what I think is the object of the enterprise called moral philosophy. It is to find a way of thinking better—that is, more rationally—about moral questions. The first step towards this is: *Understand the questions you are asking*. That might seem obvious; but hardly anybody tries to do it. We have to understand what we mean by expressions like 'I ought'. And to understand the meaning of a word like this involves understanding its logical properties, or in other words what it implies or what saying it commits us to. Then, if we find that we cannot accept what it commits us to, we shall have to give up saying it. And that is what moral argument essentially is. Ethics, the study of moral argument, is thus a branch of logic. This is one of the levels of thinking that are the concern of the moral philosopher. The others are about more substantial questions; but this first one, the logical or, as it is sometimes called, metaethical level is the foundation of the others.

Since the kind of ethics we are doing is a kind of logic, it has to use the methods of logic. But what are these? How do we find out what follows from what, what implies what, or what saying, for example, 'I ought to join the Army' or 'I ought to join the Revolution' commits me to? That is partly a general question about logical method, into which I shall not have room to go at all deeply. I can only declare what side I am on as regards some crucial questions. First, I think it is useful and indeed essential, and I hope it will not be thought pedantic, to distinguish between two kinds of questions. I am going to call the first kind *formal* questions, and the second kind *substantial* questions. Formal questions are questions that can be answered solely by appeal to the form—that is, the purely logical properties—of proposed answers to them. That

Previously unpublished.

is the sort of question we are concerned with in meta-ethics. In this part of our work we are not allowed to bring in any substantial assumptions.

I will illustrate the distinction by an example which has nothing to do with ethics, because it is a clearer example and does not beg any ethical questions. It comes from a well-known paper by Professors Strawson and Grice (1956) refuting (in my view successfully) a claim made in an even better-known paper by Professor Quine (1951; some of Quine's claims may be all right, but it is pretty clear that Strawson and Grice have refuted this one). Suppose I say 'My three-year-old child understands Russell's Theory of Types'. Everyone will be sure that what I have said is false. But logically it could be true. On the other hand, suppose I say 'My three-year-old child is an adult'. We know that I cannot consistently say this, if we know what the words mean and nothing else; and this is obviously not the case with the first proposition.

This illustrates the distinction between what I am calling formal questions and what I am calling substantial questions. It applies equally to moral questions, which can also be divided into these two kinds. Suppose I say 'There is nothing wrong with flogging people for fun'. People's reasons for disagreeing with me (and I will come later to what these reasons might be) are of a quite different sort from what they would be if I had said 'There is nothing wrong in doing what one ought not to do'. We know that I cannot consistently say the latter if we just know the meanings of the words 'ought' and 'wrong'; whereas I could *consistently* utter the first proposition; we all think it is a dreadful thing to say—only a very wicked person would say it—but in saying it he would not be being *logically* inconsistent.

It is not necessary here to discuss Quine's rejection of the notion of analyticity and of that of synonymy. Strawson and Grice may be right in defending these notions; but even if they are not, the formal claims that I need to make about moral concepts do not have to be stated in terms of them, but only in terms of the notion of logical truth, which Quine in that paper accepts. This is because the moral concepts are formal in an even stricter sense than I have so far claimed. That is, they require for their explanation no material semantic stipulations but only reference to their purely logical properties. The semantic properties of moral words have to do with their particular descriptive meanings only, which are not part of their meaning in the narrow sense and do not affect their logic, though the fact that they have to have some descriptive meaning does affect it. On this see *MT* 2 f. and *LM* 122 ff.

It will be noticed that the example I have just given of a moral statement which we should all reject on logical grounds, 'There is nothing wrong in doing what we ought not to do', is one whose contradictory ('There is something wrong in doing what we ought not to do') is a logical truth. This is because 'ought' and 'wrong' are interdefinable in terms purely of their logical properties without bringing in their descriptive meanings or semantics, just as are 'all' and 'some' in most systems of quantificational logic.

Next, I must mention a point which will turn out to be of fundamental importance for moral argument. When we are settling questions of the second kind in each case (that is, formal questions) we are not allowed to appeal to any other kind of consideration except those which can be established on the basis of our understanding of the words or concepts used. To take our two examples: we know that we cannot say 'There is nothing wrong in doing what one ought not to do' because we know what 'wrong' and 'ought' mean; and we know that we cannot say 'My three-year-old child is an adult' because we know what 'child' and 'adult' mean. If, in order to establish that we could not say these things, we had to appeal to any other considerations than these, the questions of whether we could say them would not be formal questions.

In general, we establish theses in logic (or in the kind of logic I am speaking of, which includes the kind we use in ethics) by appeal to our understanding of the uses of words, and nothing else. It is because this logic is the foundation of moral argument that it is so important to understand the words. We must notice that this is a feature of the method I am advocating which distinguishes it quite radically from almost all the ethical theories which we find being proposed at the present time. All these theories appeal at some point or other, and often very frequently, to the substantial moral convictions which their proponents have, and which they hope their readers will share. Although I recognize that many people do not believe in the distinction that I have been making between formal and substantial moral questions, and therefore feel at liberty to use what I would call substantial convictions of theirs to support their theories, I still think that my way of proceeding provides a firmer basis for ethics.

Let me give very briefly my reasons for this confidence. If we are arguing about some moral question (for example about the question 'Ought I to join the Army?' or 'Ought I to join the Revolution?'), one of the things we have to get clear about at the beginning is what the *question* is. That is to say, if we are not to talk at cross purposes, we have to be meaning the same things by the words in which we are asking our question. But if we *are* meaning the same by the words, we have a solid basis of agreement (albeit formal and not substantial agreement) on which we can found our future arguments. If the distinction between formal and substantial holds, then we can have this formal agreement in spite of our substantial disagreement. We can then, as I hope to show, use the formal agreement to test the arguments either of us uses to support his views. We can ask, 'Can he consistently *say* this?', or 'Can he consistently say *this*, if he also says *that*?'.

On the other hand, if people import their own substantial convictions into the very foundations of their moral arguments, they will not be able to argue cogently against anybody who does not share those convictions. This is what the philosophers called *intuitionists* do; and I say with some confidence that my own position is much stronger than theirs, because I do not rely on anything except what everybody has to agree to who is asking the same questions as I am trying to answer. That was why I said that before an argument begins we have to agree on the meaning we attach to our questions. That is *all* I require to start off with.

So much, then, for the question of ethical method. I could say, and in order to plug all the holes would have to say, a great deal more about it, and have done this elsewhere (*MT* ch. 1); but now I wish to go on, and say what I hope to establish by this method and how it helps with real substantial questions. At the formal or meta-ethical level I need to establish just two theses; and for the sake of simplicity I shall formulate them as theses about the word 'ought' and its logic. I could have spoken instead about other words, such as 'right' and 'good'. But I prefer to talk about 'ought', because it is the simplest word that we use in our moral questionings.

Here, then, are two logical features of the word 'ought', as it occurs in the questions 'Ought I to join the Army?' and 'Ought I to join the Revolution?'. They are parts of what I commit myself to if I say 'Yes, I ought'. The first is sometimes called the *prescriptivity* of moral judgements. If I say 'Yes, I ought to join the Army', and mean it sincerely, and in its full sense—if I really think I ought—I shall join the Army. Of course there are plenty of less than full-blooded senses of 'ought', or of 'think that I ought', in which I could say 'I think that I ought, but I'm not going to', or 'I ought, but so what?'. But anyone who has been in this situation (as I have— it was one of the things that made me take up philosophy) will know that the whole point of asking 'Ought I?' is to help us decide the question 'Shall I?', and the answer to the first question, when asked in this sense, implies an answer to the second question. If it did not, what would have been the point of asking it?

The second feature of the word 'ought' that I shall be relying on is usually called *universalizability*. When I say that I ought, I commit myself to more than that *I* ought. Prescriptivity demands that the man who says 'I ought' should himself act accordingly, if the judgement applies to him and if he can so act. Universalizability means that, by saying 'I ought', he commits himself to agreeing that *anybody* ought who is in just those circumstances. If I say 'I ought, but there is someone else in exactly the same circumstances, doing it to someone who is just like the person I should be doing it to, but he ought not to do it', then logical eyebrows will be raised; it is *logically inconsistent* to say, of two exactly similar people in exactly similar situations, that the first ought to do something and the second ought not. I must explain that the similarity of the situations extends to the personal characteristics, and in particular to the likes and dislikes, of the people in them. If, for example, the person I was flogging actually liked being flogged (some people do) that would mean that the situation was not exactly similar to the normal case, and the difference might be relevant.

So, putting together these two features of prescriptivity and universalizability, we see that if I say 'I ought to do it to him', I commit myself to saying, not just that I should do it to him (and accordingly doing it), but that he should do it to me were our roles precisely reversed. That is, as we shall see, how moral argument gets its grip. I must repeat that it is not an essential part of my argument that *all* uses of 'ought' have these features. All I am maintaining now is that we do sometimes, when asking 'Ought I?', use the word in this way. I am addressing myself to those who are asking such questions, as I am sure many people do. If anybody wished to ask *different* questions, he might have to use a different logic. But I am quite sure that we do sometimes find ourselves asking, and disagreeing about, universal prescriptive questions—that is, about what to prescribe universally for all situations of a given kind, no matter who is the agent or the victim. I shall be content if I can show how we can validly argue about such questions, whose logical character is determined by their being *those* questions, i.e. universal prescriptive ones.

I might add that the whole point of having a moral language with these features—a language whose meaning is determined by its logical characteristics alone, and which can therefore be used in discussion by two people who have very different substantial moral convictions, is that then the words will mean the same to both of them, and they will be bound by the same logical rules in their argument. If their different moral convictions had somehow got written into the very meanings of their moral words (as does happen with *some* moral words, and as some philosophers mistakenly think happens with all of them—see p. 121) then they would be at cross purposes from the start; their moral argument would very quickly break down, and they would just have to fight it out. It is because of this formal character of my theory about the moral words that I think it more helpful than the theories of other philosophers who try to write their own moral convictions into the meanings of the words or the rules of argument. This is especially true when we come to deal with the kinds of moral problems about which people have radically different convictions. If the convictions have infected the words, they will not be able to communicate rationally with one another. That is indeed what we see happening all over the world (think of South Africa, for example, where I gave an earlier version of this paper). In this situation the theories I am criticizing are of no help at all, because people will appeal to their opposing convictions, and serious, fruitful argument cannot even begin.

The next thing that I have to make clear is the place in moral argument of appeal to *facts*. If I ask 'Ought I to join the Army?', the first thing, as I said, is to be clear about what I mean by 'ought'. But that is not enough. I have to be clear what I am asking; but another important part of this is what the words 'join the Army' imply. In other words, what should I be doing if I joined the Army? There are some philosophers who use the word 'consequentialist' as a term of abuse for their opponents. Now I readily agree that there may be a sense in which we ought to do what is right and damn the consequences. But these philosophers are really very confused if they think that in deciding what we ought to do we can ignore what we should be doing if we did one or other of the things we could do. If someone thinks he ought not to join the Army, or that it would be wrong to do it, his reason (what in his view makes it wrong), must have something to do with what he would be doing if he joined the Army. That is the act or series of acts about whose morality we are troubled. Joining the Army means, in his circumstances (if that is the sort of regime he lives in, as in South Africa), committing himself to shooting people in the streets if the Government tells him to. That is what becoming a soldier involves in his present situation. Anyone who thinks that in this sense consequences are irrelevant to moral decisions cannot have understood what morality is about: it is about actions; that is, about what we do; and that is, what we are bringing about—the difference we are making to the course of events. These are the facts we have to know.

There are some ethical theories, known generally as *naturalistic* theories, which make facts relevant to moral decisions in a very direct way. They do it by saying that what moral words *mean* is something factual. To give a very crude example:

if 'wrong' *meant* 'such as would endanger the State', then obviously it would be wrong to do anything that would endanger the State, and we ought not to do it. The trouble with such theories is the same, in effect, as with those I mentioned earlier. It makes a theory useless for the purposes of moral argument if its author writes his own moral convictions into the theory itself; and *one* of the ways of doing this is to write them into the meanings of the moral words. This makes communication and rational argument between people of different moral convictions impossible (see pp. 102, 121). If 'wrong' did mean what has just been suggested, somebody who thought that there were some things more important morally than the preservation of the State could not use the word to argue with a supporter of the regime. One of them would just have to join the Army and the other the Revolution; they would just have to fight.

I am not saying what naturalists say, because the account I have given of the meaning of 'ought' in terms of prescriptivity and universalizability does *not* incorporate any substantial moral convictions; it is *neutral* between the two participants in such a dispute, and both of them can therefore use the words, if I am right, in discussing their disagreement. I therefore have to give, and have already partly given, a different account of how facts are relevant to moral decisions. This goes via an account of rationality itself—of the notion of a reason.

It may be helpful if we start with something simpler than moral judgements: with plain imperatives. These two sorts of speech acts must not be confused, because there are important differences; but imperatives like 'Join the Army' do illustrate in a much simpler way the point I am trying to explain. They are the simplest kind of prescriptions (moral judgements are a much more complex kind because of universalizability). To take an even simpler example: suppose I say 'Give me tea' and not 'Give me coffee'. I say this because of *something about* drinking tea or drinking coffee just then. That is my reason for saying it. If drinking tea were of a different character, I might not have said it. I want, or choose, to drink tea not coffee because I believe that that is what drinking tea would be like, i.e. because of a (supposed) fact about it. I hope that, if it is clear that, even in the case of simple imperatives like this, facts can be reasons for uttering them, it will be equally clear that moral judgements too can be uttered for reasons, even though they are not *themselves* (or not just) statements of fact, but are prescriptive. It would be irrational to ask for tea in complete disregard of what, in fact, it would be like to drink tea (see p. 37). Note that what I have just said in no way depends on universalizability; I have deliberately taken the case of plain simple imperatives which are *not* universalizable. We shall later be making a move which depends on universalizability; but it is not necessary at this stage.

Now I wish to introduce another move, which does not depend on universalizability either, and indeed is independent of everything I have said so far. It too is a logical move, which depends on the meanings of words. It concerns the relation between *knowing* what it is to experience something, and experiencing it. The relevance of this to what I have been saying so far is that, if we are to know the facts about what we should be doing if we did something, one of the things we have to know is what we, or others, would experience if we did it. For example, if we are thinking of flogging somebody for fun, it is important that what we should be doing if we flogged him would be giving him *that* extremely unpleasant experience. If he did not mind it, or even liked it, our act would be different in a morally relevant respect. So it is important to consider what are the conditions for being said really to know what an experience (our own or somebody else's) which would be the result of our proposed act would be like.

Suppose that the experience in question is (as in this case) *suffering* of some kind. I wish to claim that we cannot suffer without knowing that we are suffering, nor know that we are suffering without suffering. The relation between having experiences and knowing that we are having them was noticed already by Aristotle (1120^a29). There are two distinct reasons for the last half of the thesis I have just put forward. The first is that we cannot know *anything* without its being the case (that is the sort of word that 'know' is). The second reason is a particular one, and more important for our argument: if we did not have the experience of suffering, there would be nothing to know, and no means of knowing it. The knowledge that we are having the experience of suffering is *direct* knowledge, not any kind of knowledge by inference, and so cannot exist without the object of knowledge (that is, the suffering) being present in our experience. That, indeed, is why it is so difficult to know what the sufferings of other people are like. As we shall see, imagination has to fill, in an inadequate way, the place of experience.

Next, we cannot be suffering without having the preference, *pro tanto*, so far as that goes, that we should not be. If we did not prefer, other things being equal, that it should stop, it is not suffering. The preference that it should stop is what would be expressed, if it were expressed in language, by means of a prescription that it should stop. So, putting all this together, if we are suffering, and therefore know that we are, we are bound to assent to the prescription that, other things being equal, it should stop. We must want it to stop, or it is not suffering.

So much for our own present sufferings. We have now to consider what is implied by the knowledge that we *shall*, or *would* under certain conditions, be suffering, or that *somebody else* is suffering. Let us take the last-mentioned case first. What am I committed to if I truly claim that I know how somebody else is suffering, or what it is like for him to suffer like that? The touchstone for this is, it seems to me, the question 'What are my preferences (or in other words, to what prescriptions do I assent) regarding a situation in which *I* was forthwith to be put into *his* exact situation, suffering just like that?' If he is suffering like that, he knows that he is, and has the preference that it should stop (a preference of a determinate strength, depending on how severe the suffering is). He thus assents, with a determinate strength of assent, to the prescription that it should stop. This preference and this assent are part of his situation, and therefore part of what I have to imagine myself experiencing, were I to be transferred forthwith into it.

I asked just now, 'What am I committed to if I truly claim that I know how he is suffering?' My thesis is going to be that I am committed to having myself a preference that, if I were myself to be transferred forthwith into his situation with his preferences, the suffering should stop; and the strength of this preference that I am committed to having is the same as the strength of his preference.

I said that that was going to be my thesis. But I have not yet argued for it, and the argument for it will be, I am sure, controversial. The move I am going to make is this: whether I am really thinking of the person who would be put forthwith into that situation as *myself* depends on whether I associate myself with, or take to myself, the preferences which that person (i.e. I myself) would have. Of course, as before, we have to add 'other things being equal'; there may well be other things which I prefer so strongly that they outweigh my preference that that person's preference (the person who I imagine myself being) should be satisfied (see p. 247). But *other things being equal* I have to be preferring that it be satisfied, with the same strength of preference as I should have were I in that situation with those preferences. If I am not, then either I do not really know what it is like to be in that situation with those preferences (I am not really fully representing it to myself), or I am not really thinking of the person who would be in that situation as myself.

Let me give an example to illustrate all this (cf. also p. 40). Suppose that somebody has been tied up and a tyre put round his neck, and the tyre ignited with petrol. He is suffering to a certain extreme degree, and therefore knows that he is suffering. What is it for *me* to know what it is like for him to suffer like that? Or, to put it in terms of preferences: he prefers very much that he should stop being burnt in that way; what it is for me to know what it is like to have a preference like that for that outcome, or of that strength (to be saying 'Oh, stop! Stop!' with that degree of anguish)? And suppose then that I claim to know just what it is like for him to have such a preference and to be suffering like that; and then suppose that somebody offers to do the same to me without further delay, and I say 'I don't mind; it's all the same to me'. That would surely show that I do not know what it is like for him. This presumes that if I had it done to me, I should have the same experiences and the same preferences as the person to whom it is being done. I think that the same could be shown in less dramatic examples, and that, when we have made due allowance for other things not being equal (that is, for

competing preferences), I could show convincingly that the
thesis stands up; but I am not going to go on defending it
now, because I want to draw conclusions from it for my main
argument.

Let me first sum up the theses that I have advanced so far.
We have the prescriptivity and the universalizability of moral
judgements, which, I claim, can be established by arguments
based on the meanings of words—logical arguments. Then we
have the necessity, if we are to assent rationally to prescriptions,
including prescriptions expressed with 'ought', of correct
factual information. Lastly we have the thesis that we are *not*
in possession of correct factual information about someone
else's suffering, or in general about his preferences, unless we
ourselves have preferences that, were *we* in his situation with
his preferences, those preferences should be satisfied. Note,
again, that although I claimed to be able to establish
universalizability, I have not yet used it in the argument.
That is what I am going to do now, in conjunction with the
other theses.

Let us suppose that it is I who am causing the victim to
suffer. He very much wants me to untie him. That is to say,
he assents with a certain very high strength of assent to the
prescription that I should untie him. Already, without bringing
in universalizability, we can say, on the strength of our
previous theses, that I, if I know what it is like, for him, to
be in that state (and if I do not know that, my moral
judgement is faulted for lack of information)—I must myself
have a preference that if I were in that state they should untie
me. That is, I must be prescribing that they should, in those
hypothetical circumstances, untie me. Now suppose that I ask
myself what *universal* prescription I am prepared to assent
to with regard to my present conduct which is causing him
to suffer; that is, what I am prepared to say that I *ought*
now to do to him. The 'ought' here expresses a universal
prescription, so that, if I say 'I ought not to untie him', I am
committed to the prescription that they should not untie me
in similar circumstances.

I can of course say that I am not prepared to assent to *any*
universal prescription. That is the position of the person whom
I have elsewhere called the *amoralist*, and indicated how I

would deal with him (*MT* 182 ff.). But suppose I am not an amoralist, and am therefore prepared to assent to some universal prescription for people in precisely the present situation. The question is what this is going to be. If I universalize the prescription to go on making him suffer, then this entails prescribing that, if anybody were making me suffer in a precisely analogous situation, he should carry on doing it. But this runs counter to a prescription which, as we have seen, I already must be assenting to if I know what it is like to be in the situation of my victim: the prescription that if I were in that situation they should *not* carry on doing it, but should untie me. Thus I am in the predicament that Kant called a contradiction in the will (1785: § 2).

How is the contradiction to be resolved? The answer becomes obvious if we notice that what is happening (what has to happen if I am trying to universalize my prescriptions) is that I am being constrained to treat other people's preferences as if they were my own. This is just another way of putting the requirement to universalize my prescriptions. But if in this situation the two preferences which have come into contradiction were both my own, what I would do would be to let the stronger of them override the weaker. And that is what I am constrained to do in the present case, where, as a result of the attempt to universalize, I have landed myself with two mutually contradictory preferences or prescriptions as to what should be done to me in the hypothetical situation in which I was in the other person's shoes. So the answer is that if my victim's preference that I should desist from tormenting him is stronger than my own preference that I should not desist (as it certainly will be), I should desist.

We have thus, in this simple bilateral case involving only two people, arrived at what is essentially a utilitarian answer to our moral problem; and we have arrived at it by a Kantian route. People talk as if Kant and the utilitarians were at opposite poles in moral philosophy; but this just shows how little they have understood either the utilitarians or Kant (see H 1989a *s.f.*). We are led to give weight to the preferences of all the affected parties (in this case, two) in proportion to their strengths, and to say that we ought to act on the stronger. I could, if there were room, show how, by generalizing this argument to cover multilateral situations in which the preferences of many parties are affected, we should also adopt utilitarian answers, namely that we ought in each case so to act as to maximize the satisfactions of the preferences of all affected parties, treated impartially. But I am not going to attempt this now; I have done it elsewhere (*MT* 115 ff.), and I have to go on to explain how this way of thinking is going to work out in the course of our actual moral lives, when we have to decide practical issues. I shall be able to do this only in very general terms.

It might be thought that what we have arrived at is a kind of act-utilitarianism; and this is in fact true. But it is not the kind of act-utilitarianism to which all beginner philosophy students are taught the standard objections. I will now try to explain how the kind of act-utilitarianism that I am advocating differs from the crude kind. The difference is not, strictly speaking, a theoretical one. It derives rather from a consideration of our actual human predicament when we are doing our moral thinking. To see this, let us think what it would be like if we had no human limitations. Suppose, that is to say, that we had infinite knowledge and clarity of thought and no partiality to self or other human weaknesses. Elsewhere I have called a being who has these superhuman powers the *archangel* (*MT* ch. 3). He really could think in an act-utilitarian way. But it would often be disastrous if we humans tried to do it, for obvious reasons. First of all, we lack the necessary information nearly always; in particular, we are very bad at putting ourselves in other people's shoes and imagining what it is like to be them. Secondly, we lack the time for acquiring and thinking about this information; and then we lack the ability to think clearly. These three handicaps make it all too easy for us to pretend to ourselves that some act is likely to be for the best (to satisfy preferences maximally and impartially) when in fact what commends it to us is our own self-interest. One sees this kind of special pleading going on all the time.

Suppose that, conscious of these handicaps, we went to an archangel for advice, not about a particular situation (for we shall not always have access to him, and therefore want him to give us advice for the future) but about how in general to minimize their bad effects. People think that they can appeal to God in this way; though what they say he tells them varies from one person to another. But let us suppose that we *had* immediate access to some supreme or at least superior being who could advise us. He would point out that the best we can do is on each occasion to make as great as possible the expectation of preference-satisfaction resulting from our actions. I am sure that this is what God would do, because he loves his creatures, and he wants us to do the best we can for them.

The expectation of preference-satisfaction (of utility, for short) is the sum of the products of the utility and the probability of the outcome for all the alternative possible outcomes of the action. This is what I mean by 'Acting for the best'. The question is, How shall we achieve this? Given our limitations, we shall not achieve it by doing a utilitarian calculation or a cost-benefit analysis on each occasion. The archangel will tell us, rather, to cultivate in ourselves a set of dispositions or principles, together with the attitudes or feelings or, if anybody wishes to use the word, intuitions that go with them: a set such that the cultivation of them is most likely on the whole to lead to the maximization of preference-satisfaction. The archangel, who can get the right answer on every single occasion, can do better than us; but that is the best that we can do.

It will be noticed that this, although in a sense it is a form of rule-utilitarianism, is a form which is not incompatible with act-utilitarianism. For what the archangel is advising us to do is to perform certain acts, namely acts of cultivating dispositions; and his reason for advising this is that these acts are the most likely to be for the best—which is exactly what an act-utilitarian would advise. However, this version of utilitarianism secures the advantages which older forms of rule-utilitarianism claimed, in particular the advantage of making our proposed system immune to objections based on the counter-intuitiveness of its consequences. For the intuitions which the act-utilitarian archangel will bid us cultivate are the *same* intuitions as those to which the objectors are appealing.

The effect of this move is to divide moral thinking into two levels (in addition to the third or meta-ethical level which is concerned, not with substantial moral thinking, but with the form of moral thinking (that is, with the logic of the moral language). I call these two levels the *intuitive* level and the *critical* level. If we follow the archangel's advice, we shall do nearly all our moral thinking at the intuitive level; in fact, for nearly all the time, we shall behave just as the intuitionists say we do and should. The difference, however, will be that because, as everyone realizes, the good dispositions and principles and attitudes that we rightly cultivate are to some degree general and simple and unspecific (if they were not, they would be unmanageable and unhelpful and unteachable), they will come into conflict in particular hard cases; and then, unlike intuitionists, we shall know what we have to try to do, difficult and dangerous as it is. Since we do not in fact have archangels on call, we have to do the best we can to think critically like archangels on those problematic occasions. But when our intuitions give us clear guidance, we shall follow them—at least that is what our utilitarian archangel will advise us during our once-for-all counselling session with him.

But, it will be said, this presumes that our intuitions are the right ones. Indeed it does. This gives us another reason for using critical thinking. It is dangerous to use it in crises; but when they are over, or in anticipation of them, it may be essential. Otherwise how shall we have any confidence that the intuitions we happen to have grown up with are the best ones? Intuitions about how Whites should treat Blacks, for example, or men women? So what the wise archangel will advise, and what wise human educators and self-educators will practise, will be a judicious admixture of intuitive and critical thinking, each employed on appropriate occasions. And this is what wise people do already.

12

Relevance

In the mouths of many radicals, a piece of philosophical or other academic work is said to be relevant if it lends support to the speaker's own political opinions. I shall not be using the word in that sense; nor even in the sense in which I used it in the title of my inaugural lecture 'The Practical Relevance of Philosophy' (H 1971b: 98), although I do think that what I am going to say has that kind of relevance, because it helps to sort out some practical issues of great importance. The problem I have in mind to discuss is the following: How, when we are confronted with a situation or an action, do we decide what features of it are relevant to its moral appraisal?

The claim that certain features are morally irrelevant can play a crucial part in moral argument. To give two examples: if I am being blamed for missing an appointment, the fact that there was a flight at such-and-such a time which would have enabled me to keep the appointment if I had caught it is irrelevant, if I could not have caught it; and it is generally held that it is irrelevant to moral appraisals of my actions that it was I, that individual, who did them (it is said that morally relevant features of situations or actions have to be specifiable without using individual constants, and that, instead, universally quantified individual variables have to be used in stating the moral principle which gives a feature its relevance). The use made of this thesis in moral argument, though it has given rise to controversy about the details, is too well known to need exposition.

Some have sought to extend this imputation of irrelevance to descriptions in universal terms which include features of situations that *in fact* serve to pick out particular individuals, although formally speaking the descriptions are universal. Thus Professor John Rawls, in the section of his book (1971:

From *Values and Morals*, ed. A. I. Goldman and J. Kim (Dordrecht, Reidel, 1978).

131) called 'The Formal Constraints of the Concept of Right', says of his principles that 'it must be possible to formulate them without the use of what would be intuitively recognized as proper names, *or rigged definite descriptions*' (my italics); and Marcus Singer attempts a somewhat similar manœuvre in his book *Generalization in Ethics* (1961; see p. 154 and H 1962). The essence of the manœuvre is to adapt an argumentative move, which is legitimate in the case of individual references, to cover features which are, formally speaking, described in universal terms, but look as if they were selected to pick out just one favoured individual. Some people want to go even further, and claim that the same kind of manœuvre can be used to rule out, as morally relevant features of, e.g. people, their black skin or even their sex.

Others again have wanted to say that there are quite narrow *material* restrictions on what features can be morally relevant. For example, that a man clasps and unclasps his hands cannot be relevant (Foot 1959); and the production of benefits and harms to human beings is paradigmatically relevant (Warnock 1967: 67). I have already in many places said what is wrong with this view: it confuses our extreme surprise that anybody should *hold* a certain view with an inability to understand what he is saying (see p. 125 and H 1963*b*: § vii). If a man said that another man was a good man because he clasped and unclasped his hands, I should *understand* what he was saying, and might even, if he said 'morally good man' understand that it was a moral judgement; indeed, if I did not understand it in this way, there might be no occasion for my surprise. The surprise is occasioned by an inability to understand, not what the view is, but why anybody should think that. As well as being based on this confusion, the position in question is practically futile as a way of achieving what seems to be the aim of its propounders; if they tried to use this kind of argument to constrain somebody to accept or reject some moral opinion, he would be likely to reply 'If that is how you interpret the expression "morally good", I am just not interested in being morally good' (H 1968). This is always the result of trying to write material stipulations into our explanations of the meanings of moral words or of the word 'moral'.

All these extensions of the restriction are illegitimate; there are indeed reasons for thinking the features in question irrelevant to moral appraisal, but the philosophers I am attacking have taken much too short a way with them (H 1972*a*: 92 ff.). A very much deeper understanding of the whole question is needed before we can see why they are irrelevant, in cases in which they are. What we seem to require, as a basis for this understanding, is a general account of what makes features of situations etc. morally relevant. This paper is intended as a prolegomenon to such an account, though I shall also be trying to shed light on some vexing subsidiary problems.

The first thing that must be said is that the decision to treat certain features of a situation as morally relevant is not independent of the decision to apply certain moral principles to it, i.e. to make certain moral judgements about it. It is a great mistake to think that there can be a morally or evaluatively neutral process of picking out the relevant features of a situation, which can then be followed by the job of appraising or evaluating the situation morally. We can indeed *describe* a situation without committing ourselves to any moral judgements about it (that this is not so has become a dogma in some circles, but I know of no good reasons for accepting the dogma); nevertheless, when we decide what features of the description are morally relevant, we are already in the moral business. There are certain exceptions to this rule; some features of situations can be ruled out as irrelevant on purely formal grounds, as we have seen. But in the main to call a feature morally relevant is already to imply that it is a reason for or against making some moral judgement; and to say this is already to invoke a moral principle. That the act resulted in the death of a patient is relevant because of the principle that one ought not, in these circumstances, to cause the death of a patient; abandon the principle, and *that* reason for thinking the feature relevant goes by the board, though others may survive.

The question, therefore, of what features can be relevant to moral appraisal is the same question as that of what features can figure in moral principles. Even the formal restrictions that I mentioned just now are covered by this general statement of the position. The reason why the fact that it was that individual who did the act cannot be relevant is that individual references are formally excluded from moral principles. The reason why it could not be relevant that there was a flight at that time if the man could not have caught the flight is that, for formal reasons connected with the prescriptivity of moral judgements, there cannot be a moral principle which bids us catch flights that we cannot catch (*FR* ch. 4; H 1978).

The question of what features of a situation are morally relevant thus collapses into the question of what moral principles apply to the situation; any feature which figures in one of these principles is relevant. And the question of what features *can* be morally relevant collapses into the question of what restrictions there are on the form or the content of moral principles. I have given some examples of such restrictions and suggested restrictions already.

I will now try to explain why we do not treat skin colour as a morally relevant feature of people, except in unusual cases (for example, when I have a duty to take a faithful photograph of somebody's face and therefore must get the exposure right). I shall assume without argument that merely individual references cannot figure uneliminably in moral principles; and also that the proposed extension of this restriction to 'rigged definite descriptions' cannot stand unsupported.

Two other illegitimate extensions, not yet mentioned, may be taken in on the way. It is sometimes thought that, besides individual references, all references are ruled out which logically must be unique. For example, it is thought that this is why the expression 'the only man with fifteen toes' could not figure in a moral principle, because there logically cannot be more than one 'only man with' a certain feature. There are intuitively obvious counter-examples to this thesis: e.g., 'The first man past the post ought to be given the prize'; it is logically impossible for more than one runner to be 'the first man past the post', but nevertheless most of us accept this moral principle. The intuition which acquits this principle of deviance is a linguistic one, and therefore not subject to the strictures which I would make against substantial moral intuitions as a basis of argument; but we do not need in any case to rely on it, because it is not hard to spell out what has gone wrong. A term does not stop being a universal term just because it logically can apply only to one thing. The thesis of universalizability, therefore, rules out only individual references, not all unique (even logically unique) references. Put more informally, that it was I who did it could not be a reason for a moral judgement about an act; but any universal property of the act could be a reason, even though his possession of it rules out anybody else's possession of it.

The second illegitimate extension of this restriction that I must mention here is one which I have dealt with elsewhere (H 1955*a*) but which keeps on cropping up. It is thought that if there is some individual who is related to me by a relation which logically can tie an individual to one other individual and one only, the relation in question cannot figure in a moral principle. For example, it is thought that I cannot have duties to my mother as such, because it is logically impossible for a man to have more than one mother, and because of the occurrence of the individual reference 'my' in the expression 'my mother'. These are actually two separate reasons, both of them bad ones. The first (uniqueness) falls to the same objection as was raised in the preceding paragraph against an essentially similar mistake: uniqueness in a universal term (this time a relation) is not the same thing as individual reference. The second reason is ambiguous. It is true that I cannot have duties to my mother just because she is *my* mother (duties which other people in similar circumstances do not have to *their* mothers). The thesis of universalizability establishes that much. But it is not true that I cannot have duties to my mother just because she is my *mother* (duties which *any* son has to *his* mother in circumstances just like mine). If anybody stands in just this relation to any woman, then he ought to treat her in such-and-such a way. Sentences of this form:

$$(x)(y)(R_1x,y \rightarrow OR_2x,y)$$

(where '*O*' is the obligation sign of deontic logic) are properly universal and contain no individual references. Another even more obvious example, intuitively, is the duty to fulfil *one's own* promises, but not other people's.

Having got these two false moves out of the way, let us ask why we do not treat skin colour as morally relevant. It is a properly universal property which any individual man might have. It has been alleged that if I, a white man, became just like some black man, I should stop being me (the person that I now am). This is a difficult question into which I shall not enter in this paper; the point is effectively answered in a paper by Professor Zeno Vendler (1976; see *MT* 119 ff.), as are similar points arising from Professor Kripke's views about proper names. Briefly, I can well conceive of *my* being in precisely the situation of that black man, black skin and all, even though I could not conceive of Richard Hare being in that precise situation, because then it would not be Richard Hare (at least not *this* Richard Hare; there might be a totally dissimilar black of the same name). But we do not need to go into this, because the question is whether skin colour by itself could be morally relevant; and it is certainly the case that my skin might turn black without my ceasing to be me *or* Richard Hare.

So why do we not treat skin colour as morally relevant? For great periods of history people did. The reason is that we have been through a process of moral reasoning (briefly described in *FR* 108 f.) which, though indeed based on universalizability, is more complex than the simple move so far considered. And the move involves more than universalizability alone; it involves prescriptivity; i.e. it involves asking whether we are prepared to *prescribe* universally that, e.g. black people should be at a legal disadvantage compared with white people. We could without formal or logical offence prescribe this, but are we prepared to? The reason why we are not is that, since black skin is a universal property, it is logically possible that we might ourselves have it. If, therefore, we are asked what we are prepared to prescribe for all logically possible situations (in other words what we want to happen in them all), we have to prescribe that in situations in which we have a black skin we should be treated in one way or another. And we are unlikely to prescribe that in such situations we should be disadvantaged in the way proposed. So we cannot prescribe universally that this should be done, and therefore, because of universalizability, cannot prescribe that we ought to do it now.

So far, so good; but there are grave difficulties in this golden-rule argument which I shall be trying to overcome in the rest of this paper. First of all, it might be alleged that the racist could easily defeat the argument by the following manœuvre. He is confident that he and his white friends are not in fact ever going to have black skins. So why should he not happily prescribe that those with black skins should be disadvantaged? Or consider the man with fifteen toes or with a spot on his face in just that position: he knows that he will never lose his distinguishing mark, so why should he not adopt and subscribe to a prescriptive principle which says that people with this distinguishing mark should be privileged in some way? The essence of this objection is that we have not justified our claim that we have, in adopting moral principles, to be prescribing for all logically possible situations. There are two variant interpretations of this, but they come in practice to the same: either it is being objected that a man could prescribe happily that he be himself disadvantaged in some logically possible situation, knowing that in fact he would never be in that situation; or it is being objected that in adopting moral principles we do not have to be prescribing for all logically possible situations, but only for all situations which will actually occur.

Let us take these two interpretations of the objection in turn. On the first interpretation the answer to the objection hinges on a requirement of sincerity. If a person is sincerely prescribing something, he *wants* it to happen. Now there is no restriction on the concept of wanting which prevents our wanting something to happen in a hypothetical situation—a situation which is not in fact going ever to obtain. This is clear at any rate in cases where we do not know whether the situation is going to obtain or not. I can want to have money to rebuild my house if it burns down (that is why I insure it against fire); the fact that it never does burn down does not entail that I never really had the desire. More difficult are cases where I know that a situation is not going to obtain: can I then want something to happen in that situation?

When reading novels or watching plays, we certainly want

the hero to succeed in his enterprises, although we know that neither he nor his enterprises exist in real life. We want this because we *imagine* him existing. And we can also imagine a situation existing even though nobody is acting the situation for us in a play or describing it in a book; we can be our own playwrights. Nor can anything hang on how much a particular person can imagine; for the reach of people's imaginations is variable. The fact that I cannot imagine what it is like to be submitted to a certain torture does not entail that I could not, logically or even in fact, be submitted to it. And if I am contemplating inflicting that torture on somebody else, I cannot defend myself against golden-rule arguments on the ground that, since I cannot imagine the torture being inflicted on me, I cannot want it not to be inflicted on me. If a person has previously been unable to imagine himself in the situation of some victim of his, but then, through an increase in sensitivity, becomes able to do so, this fortunate change may indeed make him more *receptive* to golden-rule arguments, but can hardly make them into better arguments than they were before. His previous insensitivity was a defect in his moral thinking (for reasons which we shall be exploring), and even before the change we could have legitimately asked him to try to overcome it, with the object of making himself better able to do his moral thinking with a full appreciation of the facts of the situation, including facts about the experiences of his victim. Until he can imagine what those experiences are, he does not in the required sense know what they are.

Let us now put together these two points: first the point that we can want things to happen in situations which we imagine (including situations in which we ourselves would be the victims); and secondly the point that if we are to do our moral thinking in knowledge of the facts, we have to be able to imagine what it is like to be our victim, and therefore what it would be like for us if we were subjected to the same treatment. It then becomes easy to see that it is both possible (provided that we have the necessary sensitivity) and a requirement of moral thinking, that we should, in doing it, imagine ourselves, not only in situations which are actually going to happen, but in ones which logically might obtain, and in particular in the situation of our proposed victim, even though we are never actually going to be in it, and know this. We then have to ask whether the man who says that he wants to be tortured (i.e. desires that he should be tortured) if he should ever be in that situation, but says this only because he knows that he will never be in it, is doing anything that is logically at fault, or in other ways ruled out from moral thinking.

We can, as we have already seen, require of such a man that he should imagine himself being in the situation of his victim (with, of course, the victim's desires and other experiences). Can he then fail to desire that he should not be treated in that way (i.e. in a way which, he now knows, the victim very much dislikes)? Certainly he can have *other* desires and, in general, motives which outweigh the desire in question (see p. 247); for example, he may desire things for himself or for other affected parties which, taken in sum, outweigh the suffering of the victim. But that would introduce complications which are irrelevant to the present argument; so let us assume that it is a simple bilateral situation in which the agent has a desire of strength m to torture his victim, and the victim has a desire of strength n not to be tortured, and that n greatly exceeds m; and that these are all the desires that we need take into account. The agent then says that, in spite of n being greater than m, he desires and prescribes that he should torture his victim, and is prepared to universalize this prescription to apply to all logically possible similar cases, including that in which the roles are reversed; and he is able to say this because he knows that they will not be reversed, so that he will never have actually to suffer the effects of the carrying out of his universal prescription.

Such a man is guilty of insincerity. He cannot really think what he says he thinks and want what he says he wants. Suppose that he were watching a play and were imagining vividly (as moral thought requires) the experiences of the characters. And suppose that he were doing this, as the impartiality of moral thinking demands, equally for all the characters. Suppose, further, that the situation in the play is just the same as that of himself and his proposed victim in real life. Can he, having imagined vividly the experiences of all the characters equally, sincerely say that he wants the person in the play who corresponds to himself to torture the person who corresponds to his victim, although the victim's desire not to be tortured greatly exceeds the desire of the other person to torture him? I do not think so. And if not, then neither can a person sincerely prescribe this who has been through the same thought-processes in the actual situation.

The objection may be made that it is possible to imagine vividly the sufferings of another real or fictional person without wanting him not to have to suffer them. This is true; no doubt any talented torturer can do as much. But can he do this if he is wanting universally (i.e. accepting a universal pre-scription) that something should happen whoever is at the receiving end? The manœuvre which he is attempting is to want the victim to be tortured, though he is imagining himself in the victim's place with the victim's desires, relying on the fact that he knows that he is not actually ever going to be in that situation.

The answer to this objection is that, if he is not treating the victim, in his thought, as if he himself were the victim, he is not really imagining what it would be like to be the victim. If we are to make an informed moral judgement, we have to make it in full knowledge and awareness of the available facts; and the agent does not have this full knowledge and awareness of one of the available facts, namely the sufferings of his victim, unless he is aware of what it is like to be that person; and this he cannot be aware of unless he puts himself in thought in that person's position. But if he does this, he will be having the same desires [for the hypothetical case in which he was in that position with those desires] as that person has [for the actual case]. If he does not have them, he lacks the necessary awareness, because the desires are what he has to be aware of, and one can be aware of desires, in the required sense, only by having them. The objection rests on the supposition that we can be fully aware of the desires and feelings of others without imaginatively sharing them; but this is not so. Complete sympathy, not mere empathy, is a requirement of moral thought.[1]

---

[1] I have here and below made additions and corrections in square brackets to bring out a distinction put more clearly on *MT* 99. As the 'torturer' example just used shows, it is possible to imagine vividly another's predicament without desiring

If the objection be now made that it is possible to know the *intensity* of another's desire, though not its precise experiential quality, by ascertaining that it has the same intensity as some past or present desire of our own, though having a different object (e.g. that he wants not to be tortured as much as we want not to be bankrupted), the answer is that the argument can be quickly reconstructed even if this objection be a sound one. For in order to know that the desires have the same intensity, it would be necessary to know the intensity of the other's desire; so we are back where we were before.

We must now turn to consider the other possible interpretation of the objection mooted on p. 197. The first interpretation said that a man might happily prescribe that he himself be disadvantaged in some logically possible situation, knowing that in fact he would never be in that situation; we have answered that form of the objection by claiming that such a man would be guilty either of insincerity, because he did not really want what he was prescribing, or of lack of knowledge of a material fact, namely what it was like for his victim to desire not to be treated in a certain way. The second interpretation was in form different. It said that it is not a requirement of moral thought that we should prescribe for all logically possible situations, but only for those which are going to be actual.

To this second form of the objection we have to reply by showing that moral thought does require us to prescribe, not perhaps for *all* logically possible situations, but at any rate for all logically possible situations which differ from actual ones only in that different individuals are playing the several roles in them. But here we have to be very careful. In other places

it to be alleviated *for him*. What is impossible is to imagine it with full representation without desiring that, were *I* in that exact position with those desires, it should be alleviated. We can get thus far without appealing to universalizability (see *MT* 108). When it is brought in, however, a conflict appears between my newly acquired desire for the hypothetical situation in which I imagine *myself*, and my original desire to keep my victim in his predicament. For, given that the situations are identical in their universal properties, it is inconsistent to universalize both prescriptions (see *MT* 109). Impartiality is thus secured, not by the requirement of full representation alone, nor by universalizability alone, but by both in conjunction with prescriptivity. For a possible objection to this view, see Gibbard in H 1988 and my comments.

I have urged that we should distinguish two different levels of moral thinking: one of them, which I have called the intuitive, for practical use in most situations, in which we simply apply to the situations sound general prima-facie or intuitive principles; and the other, called the critical, which we employ when we have to select these general principles, or adjudicate between them in cases of conflict, or even override them when in a most unusual case we judge them to be inapposite (see pp. 110, 221). This suggestion is not in the least original; it goes back in origin to Plato's distinction between the level of thought required in his auxiliaries and that required in his rulers, which was refined by Aristotle when he distinguished the roles of the moral and intellectual virtues in practical thinking. It has reappeared in the controversies between the utilitarians and their opponents; but it has never to my knowledge been formulated with sufficient clarity, and so we must go on trying.

It will be evident already from what I have said that critical moral thinking, which is what we have been considering, is in practice an unrealizable ideal to which we can only try to approximate. We could not consider all logically possible cases; and there are other hazards which I have described elsewhere (p. 222; *MT* 35 ff.). In most of our actual moral thinking we are compelled to estimate what the results of critical thinking would be if we were able to pursue it; and we base on these estimates a set of fairly simple general principles and motivational dispositions (our prima-facie principles and the intuitions and character traits that go with them) which we try, so far as we can, to inculcate into ourselves and others. A reflective and articulate person will, however, never take his prima-facie principles for granted; when he is free from stress and from temptations to special pleading, he will examine them by engaging in critical thinking so far as he is able. It is this critical thinking to which nearly all that I have been saying so far applies.

When we are using critical thinking in order to scrutinize our prima-facie principles, and select the best ones, I have said that we ought to give weight to the cases we consider in proportion to the probability of their occurring (p. 223). People who know that I have said this are likely to hold it against me in the present argument unless I make some careful distinctions. Critical thinking proceeds in two stages. It first considers cases (and can in principle consider *any* logically possible cases) and comes to a decision about what ideally ought to be done in them, after ascertaining or positing all the detailed facts about the situations which might be claimed to be relevant. This is the stage with which we are concerned in the present argument. In the second stage it estimates the probability of these cases occurring, and on the basis of this estimate selects the best prima-facie principles in the way just mentioned. This second stage we can ignore in the present argument, because all that I am now trying to establish is that at the first stage the manœuvre attempted by our objector is illegitimate. Once our moral thought has finished with the first stage, it then has to make estimates of probability and concentrate on the cases which are likely to be actual when selecting the prima-facie principles. But we have to ask, for the present, only whether the manœuvre is legitimate at the first stage. Could an objector claim that even at the first stage only cases likely to occur need to be considered?

He could not, because what are being subscribed to at the first stage are properly universal principles not containing individual references. The cases are put up for consideration in universal terms, and must be so put up because of the logical character of the moral words. At this stage, the moral thinker has to judge that such and such should be done in a case *of a certain kind*. He is therefore forbidden to rule out the consideration of a certain case (that in which he himself will suffer from the application of a principle) merely because that case is not going to be actual. At this point we are in danger of getting engulfed in the complexities of possible-world modal logic; but I will resist the temptation to explore more of that jungle (which indeed I am hardly competent to do) than is required for the present argument. Let us simply suppose (*pace* Leibniz) that there are two possible world-histories which are identical in all their universal properties and differ solely in the roles occupied in them by different individuals. It is clear that one of these world-histories can be distinguished from the other only by referring to those individuals and saying that in one of the world-histories the individuals occupy one set of roles, in the other another. If, then, one of these possible world-histories is the history of the *actual* world in which our agent occupies a certain role and his victim another, it can be distinguished from a possible world-history in which the roles are reversed only by referring to those individuals and saying that in the first of them individual *A* tortures individual *B*, whereas in the second it is the other way round. It follows, if we accept the universalizability of moral judgements, that no moral distinction can be drawn between the two world-histories, and that therefore our objector cannot, if he is prescribing morally and universally, prescribe differently for them. It is therefore not possible for him to prescribe morally solely for the actual world in which he is safely ensconced in his privileged position; for any universal prescription which he accepts for this actual world will automatically apply to the other hypothetical world in which he occupies the less comfortable seat. So at this stage and level the objection cannot get a grip.

Can it then get a grip at the next stage, at which we are selecting the best prima-facie principles for use at the intuitive level? I do not think so. For what we are then selecting are still universal principles, having at that second stage the added feature of greater generality (see p. 50); and we are selecting them on the basis of the answers given in all cases reviewed at stage 1. The new feature of stage 2 is that cases are to be excluded if they are unlikely to occur. But that is of no use to the objector if the cases (*all* the cases) that were reviewed at stage 1 were specifiable without individual references. But we have seen that this is so; for individual references make no difference at stage 1, and are necessarily ignored; the two qualitatively identical world-histories considered in the last paragraph will come on to stage 2 as one case, not two. If special pleading cannot get in at the first stage, it cannot get in at all. All the cases to be considered at stage 2, and to be weighted for probability of occurrence, will be stated in the form 'a case in which a person of a certain kind does a thing of a certain kind in circumstances of a certain kind to another person of a certain kind'. Granted, at stage 2 the moral thinker has then to assign probabilities to the occurrence of cases of this kind. But since he is not mentioned, *qua* that individual, in the description of the cases, the probability of a case of this kind occurring will be the same whichever role in it he as an individual plays. Probability is relative to evidence, and evidence as to the role which he as an individual plays is denied him. He has, in assigning probabilities, to lump together all cases of this kind; he has no way of distinguishing those in which *he* plays a certain role.

It might be objected that, although the individual is not mentioned as such in the specification of the cases at stage 1, our moral thinker might make a private mental note that such-and-such were cases in which he would occupy the role of victim in the actual world, and so select his prima-facie principles in such a way as to favour his own interest. But if he did this, he would be selecting between the candidate principles on grounds other than the probability of the universally specified cases considered at stage 1 actually occurring. And this would be to frustrate the purpose of the entire procedure. It must be remembered that it is critical thinking which is ultimate, in the sense that if we were able to pursue it with the omniscience and the freedom from self-deception and special pleading of the archangel Gabriel, the highly specific principles which it arrived at for all logically possible cases would be the ones which we ought to follow. It is only because of our human limitations that we have to have recourse to simple general prima-facie principles. They help us approximate to the answers which we should give were we to apply critical thinking to every case. Although the expression 'mere rules of thumb', which is sometimes used of these prima-facie principles, is highly misleading, for reasons which I have given elsewhere (see pp. 64, 223), they are not ultimate. The manœuvre which is now being suggested by our objector will obviously frustrate the whole purpose of having these prima-facie principles; they will no longer help us approximate to the results of critical moral thinking, but at best to those of self-interested prudential thinking.

Rejecting, therefore, this manœuvre, let us suppose that, as in our example, the cases whose probability we have to assess are qualitatively identical ones in which somebody tortures somebody else in an identical manner in all the cases. The moral thinker is not able to rule out from consideration cases in which he occupies a certain role, in favour of cases in which *he* occupies some other role. The reason for this is that the cases do not come to him from stage 1 distinguished in this way. (We may notice that this is why we are able to distinguish moral from prudential thinking; I am not relying on an argument of the form 'It would not be *moral* thinking if we proceeded in a certain manner', since nothing hangs on the word 'moral'; I mention the point only because of its interest.)

I hope I have now shown that special pleading cannot enter in at stage 1, and therefore cannot at stage 2 either. It follows that the principles which get selected for use at the intuitive level will be, not merely universal in form, but impartially selected. We may notice that by this means we have achieved one of the purposes for which, I surmise, Professor Rawls's 'veil of ignorance' was introduced, but without employing that questionable device. Our moral thinker does not have to be ignorant of his own role in the situation for which he is legislating; the logical nature of the thinking in which he is engaging prevents him from making use of this knowledge even if he has it.

If it be objected that the clever man we are considering might observe all these logical restrictions with his tongue in his cheek (i.e., with the intention all the time of getting at the end prima-facie principles which suited him in his actual situation) he will be open to the charge of insincerity as already levelled against his colleague. For he is claiming to subscribe to prescriptive principles (i.e., 'to want things) to which he cannot really be subscribing. The above argument has put him into a position in which he has to prescribe for logically possible qualitatively identical cases, and not merely for actual ones; we are back to the first interpretation, and the argument against that form of the objection suffices.

It will next be asked whether all these requirements of moral thought that I have mentioned are *logical* requirements, as I have claimed, in the sense that they can be seen to be requirements by looking at the logical properties of the moral concepts. I should like to maintain that this is indeed so. Let us take the requirements one by one. First, the moral thinker has to know what someone would be doing (himself for example) if he did the act under discussion. This knowledge of the facts includes, as we have just seen, an awareness of its impact on the persons affected, which cannot be had without sharing, in imagination, the desires of those persons. This is a logical requirement, not in the sense that to break it would be self-contradictory, but in the sense in which it is a logical requirement that we should ascertain that the cat *is* on the mat before we state that the cat is on the mat. Statements, in the proper sense of that word, are by definition truth-claims; and therefore the person who makes one is obliged by this logical property of the statement-making form of speech to satisfy himself that what he is saying is true. This *logical* requirement is to be distinguished from the *moral* duty to tell the truth, and cannot be used as the sole ground of that moral duty; there may be cases where there is a moral duty to make a false statement, but even in those cases the person who makes it is committing a logical (semantical, dialectical, conversational) fault.

Moral judgements share with factual statements the feature called universalizability (*FR* ch. 2), and this brings with it an analogue of the requirement, when making statements, to speak the truth. Moral judgements are *about* situations, acts, people, etc.; they have subjects, just as factual statements have, and attach predicates to them, but the predicates are in this case moral ones.[2] However, because moral predicates are governed by this requirement of universalizability, they have what has been called descriptive meaning. The effect of this is that if I apply a moral predicate to something (an act, for example), I am committed to applying the same predicate to any precisely similar thing, if I am to be consistent, just as, when in a factual statement I apply a predicate to a thing, I am committed to applying the same predicate to any precisely similar thing. This has the consequence that when I am considering *what* predicates to apply to things, I have to consider, in both cases, what universal properties the things possess. For if I did not do this, I should be committing myself logically to I knew not what; in other words, I should not know what I was saying in either case.

[2] It would be tedious to complicate this remark in order to cover moral and other statements which are not of subject-predicate form; but it could be done.

This obscure point can also be put (at the cost of a certain undue rigidity) in terms of rules for the use of words. In using either descriptive or moral predicates we have to follow rules (i.e. we have to be consistent). And these rules have to be rules which prescribe the application of certain predicates to certain *kinds* of subjects and not others. In the case of factual statements, or of purely descriptive predicates, the rules are merely semantical ones; in the case of moral statements and predicates, they are moral rules. But in both cases we cannot observe such a rule without ascertaining what universal properties a subject possesses; if we could make statements without doing this, we could state without knowing what we were stating; for what we are stating is determined by the rules we are following in our use of expressions. Even in the moral case, we must know what the moral rule is, in the sense of knowing what it is about the subject that makes it appropriate to apply the moral predicate to it (*FR* ch. 2).

In the factual case, when I say 'That thing is red', I am stating what I am stating only because 'red' has a certain meaning, i.e. is governed by a rule confining its use to the description of a certain kind of thing. If it were not for this rule, nobody would know (not even myself) what I was stating. In the moral case, the restriction is not so severe; moral predicates are not (*pace* the naturalists) restricted as to the universal descriptive properties which things have to have before the moral predicates are applied to them.[3] But even from this less severe restriction it follows that, unless I am consistent in my moral judgements, applying moral predicates consistently to similar things, nobody will know (not even myself) what *moral* principles I am using in my judgements. And so the main function of moral judgements, to teach moral principles by instantiation, will be unfulfilled. The person who makes moral judgements without ascertaining the relevant facts about the subjects of them cannot have any principle in mind according to which he is making the judgements. The requirement to ascertain the facts is therefore a logical one. And, as we have seen, this extends to facts about the desires

---

[3] For this reason I must not be taken as withdrawing here the caution expressed on p. 127 and *MT* 70 against the misuse in ethics of Wittgenstein's famous dictum. It applies at most to *descriptive* speech and the *descriptive* meaning of value-judgements.

etc. of those affected, which can only be ascertained by somebody who puts himself imaginatively in their places.

Next, let us consider the requirement of impartiality. It is impossible for a person without logical offence to make different moral judgements about cases which, after observing the requirement just mentioned of knowledge of the facts, he knows to be exactly similar. So much, at least, follows from the logical requirement of universalizability. Moreover, we can always adduce a case (a hypothetical one) which *is* exactly similar (in its universal properties) to the actual case in which, say, a person is contemplating torturing somebody. In this hypothetical case the universal properties will remain the same, but the individuals will change places. The agent in question has to be prepared to prescribe (as the prescriptivity of evaluative judgements, another of their logical features, requires) that the same thing be done in both cases. If he has satisfied the requirement of the preceding paragraph, he knows what it is like to be that person, and in order to have that knowledge must, as we have seen, also have the desires [for the hypothetical case] that his prospective victim has [for the actual][4] (for if he did not have them he would not really know what they were). So these two applications of universalizability, coupled with prescriptivity, compel him to give weight to the desires of the parties (himself and his victim) solely in proportion to their intensity, not giving his own desires in his actual situation extra weight. Thus impartiality also is shown to be a logical requirement.

Applying all this to the case of skin colour, we can perhaps, by illustrating the requirements involved, make them less obscure. Let us imagine, as before, a simple bilateral situation in which a white man is trying to justify some discriminatory act against a black man solely on the ground of his skin colour. The act will have effects to which the black man has an aversion greater than the desire of the white man to do the act. The white man proposes the principle that whites ought to do this sort of thing to blacks but not vice versa, relying on his knowledge that his own skin will never be black and that therefore he will never suffer the effects of the

[4] See note 1 above.

application of his proposed principle. The principle is formally universal, and therefore, so far, logically unobjectionable. But can he *embrace* this prescriptive principle? To do so, he has, because it is prescriptive, to desire that it be observed; and, because it is universal, that it be observed universally in all cases to which it applies, including the hypothetical case in which he occupies the position of his proposed victim.

He says that he does desire this; but he says it only because he knows that he will never in fact occupy that position. We then ask him whether he really knows what the position is. In order to know this, he has to put himself in the position imaginatively, and in his imagination experience the desires which a person has in that situation, which entails himself having them [for the imagined case]. When he is doing this, we ask him whether he still wants the act to be done to him in that situation. He cannot answer, as he was previously disposed to answer, 'Yes', because if he did he would be being insincere; he would be claiming not to have a desire which he actually has: the desire not to be treated in that way if he were in that situation. If he did not have that desire, he would, as we have seen, not have full knowledge of the situation, which is a logical requirement for moral thinking, and itself requires the thinker to have [for the imagined case] the desires which are an integral part of the situation. Having this desire, which *ex hypothesi* is greater than his original desire to do the act, he cannot, if he is to make the same judgement about the actual situation as about this hypothetical similar one (another logical requirement), give greater weight to his own original desire than to his victim's; for to do so would be to give greater weight to the lesser desire among desires *which he himself has* (one of them originally, and one of them latterly [for the imagined case]). That is why he cannot really and sincerely assent to the principle on which he claims to be relying, that whites ought to do this to blacks in such a situation.

In order to see why skin colour is not morally relevant in such a case, we have had to go very deep into the requirements for moral thought. A superficial application of the universalizability-requirement such as is made by some writers will not do the trick, because the principles to which racists might appeal could be strictly universal ones. We have to ask whether they can go on appealing to them when they have understood (1) that moral principles are prescriptive; (2) that their universalizability requires knowledge of all the relevant facts; and (3) that these facts include one, namely the desire of their victim, whose full intensity cannot be known to them unless they have in imagination shared it. The answer is that, if the relative strengths of the desires are as we have supposed, they cannot then go on appealing to these racist principles, because they cannot desire, and therefore cannot sincerely prescribe, that greater present desires of theirs should be subordinate to lesser.

This does not dispose of by any means all the difficulties and objections which can be raised against golden-rule arguments. There is, for example, the objection that our opponent might claim, not that whites *ought* to treat blacks in the way proposed, but only that it is *all right* for them to do it (Gauthier 1968). To answer this objection would require another very deep examination of the requirements of moral thinking, and in particular of the logical properties of permissions (of which there are several diverse kinds, not always carefully enough distinguished), and also of the escape route from moral thinking known as amoralism. The too brief remarks about this in *FR* 100 f. would have to be expanded to at least the same length as in this paper I have expanded another paragraph in that book, in order fully to answer that objection (see *MT* 182 ff.).

13
Ethical Theory and Utilitarianism

MORAL philosophy is now in a phase which must seem curious to anybody who has observed its course since, say, the 1940s. During all that time moral philosophers of the analytic tradition have devoted most of their work to fundamental questions about the analysis or the meaning of the moral words and the types of reasoning that are valid on moral questions. It may be that some of them were attracted by the intrinsic theoretical interest of this branch of philosophical logic; and indeed it is interesting. But it may surely be said that the greater part, like myself, studied these questions with an ulterior motive: they saw this study as the philosopher's main contribution to the solution of practical moral problems such as trouble most of us. For if we do not understand the very terms in which the problems are posed, how shall we ever get to the root of them? I, at least, gave evidence of this motive in my writings and am publishing many papers on practical questions. But, now that philosophers in greater numbers have woken up to the need for such a contribution, and whole new journals are devoted to the practical applications of philosophy, what do we find the philosophers doing? In the main they proceed as if nothing had been learnt in the course of all that analytical enquiry—as if we had become no clearer now than in, say, 1936, or even 1903, how good moral arguments are to be distinguished from bad.

I cannot believe that we need be so pessimistic; nor that I am alone in thinking that logic can help with moral argument. But surprisingly many philosophers, as soon as they turn their hands to a practical question, forget all about their peculiar art, and think that the questions of the market-place can be solved only by the methods of the market-place—i.e. by a combination of prejudice (called intuition) and rhetoric. The

From *Contemporary British Philosophy 4*, ed. H. D. Lewis (Allen and Unwin, 1976).

philosopher's special contribution to such discussions lies in the ability that he ought to possess to clarify the concepts that are being employed (above all the moral concepts themselves) and thus, by revealing their logical properties, to expose fallacies and put valid arguments in their stead. This he cannot do unless he has an understanding (dare I say a theory?) of the moral concepts; and that is what we have been looking for all these years. And yet we find philosophers writing in such a way that it is entirely unclear what understanding they have of the moral concepts or of the rules of moral reasoning. It is often hard to tell whether they are naturalists, relying on supposed equivalences between moral and non-moral concepts, or intuitionists, whose only appeal is to whatever moral sentiments they can get their readers to share with them. Most of them seem to be some sort of descriptivists; but as they retreat through an ever vaguer naturalism into a hardly avowed intuitionism, it becomes more and more obscure what, in their view, moral statements say, and therefore how we could decide whether to accept them or not. Philosophy, as a rational discipline, has been left behind.

It is the object of this paper to show how a theory about the meanings of the moral words can be the foundation for a theory of normative moral reasoning. The conceptual theory is of a non-descriptivist but nevertheless rationalist sort. That this sort of theory could claim to provide the basis of an account of moral reasoning will seem paradoxical only to the prejudiced and to those who have not read Kant. It is precisely that sort of prejudice which has led to the troubles I have been complaining of: the belief that only a descriptivist theory can provide a rational basis for morality, and that therefore it is better to explore any blind alley than expose onself to the imputation of irrationalism and subjectivism by becoming a non-descriptivist (see p. 99).

The normative theory that I shall advocate has close analogies with utilitarianism, and I should not hesitate to call it utilitarian, were it not that this name covers a wide variety of views, all of which have been the victims of prejudices rightly excited by the cruder among them. In calling my own normative theory utilitarian, I beg the reader to look at the theory itself, and ask whether it cannot avoid the objections that have been made against other kinds of utilitarianism. I hope to show in this paper that it can avoid at least some of them. But if I escape calumny while remaining both a non-descriptivist and a utilitarian, it will be a marvel.

On p. 153 I said that there were close formal similarities between rational contractor theories such as Rawls's, ideal observer theories such as have been advocated by many writers (e.g., Brandt 1952, 1955; Haslett 1974), and my own universal prescriptivist theory. I also said that theories of this form can be made to lead very naturally to a kind of utilitarianism, and that Rawls avoided this outcome only by a very liberal use of intuitions to make his rational contractors come to a non-utilitarian contract. Rawls advocates his theory as an alternative to utilitarianism. Whether the system which I shall sketch is to be regarded as utilitarian or not is largely a matter of terminology. The form of argument which it employs is, as I have already said, formally extremely similar to Rawls's; the substantive conclusions are, however, markedly different. I should like to think of my view as, in Professor Brandt's expression, 'a credible form of utilitarianism' (1963); no doubt Rawls would classify it as an incredible form of utilitarianism; others might say that it is a compromise between his views and more ordinary kinds of utilitarianism. This does not much matter.

I try to base myself, unlike Rawls, entirely on the formal properties of the moral concepts as revealed by the logical study of moral language; and in particular on the features of prescriptivity and universalizability which I think moral judgements, in the central uses which we shall be considering, all have. These two features provide a framework for moral reasoning which is formally similar to Rawls's own more dramatic machinery. But, rather than put the argument in his way, I will do overtly what he does covertly—that is to say, I do not speculate about what some fictitious rational contractors *would* judge if they were put in a certain position subject to certain restrictions; rather, I subject myself to certain (formally analogous) restrictions and put myself (imaginatively) in this position, as Rawls in effect does, and *do* some judging (see p. 217). Since the position and the restrictions are formally analogous, this ought to make no difference.

In this position, I am prescribing universally for all situations just like the one I am considering; and thus for all such situations, *whatever* role, among those in the situations, I might myself occupy. I shall therefore give equal weight to the equal interests of the occupants of all the roles in the situation; and, since any of these occupants might be myself, this weight will be positive. Thus the impartiality which is the purpose of Rawls's 'veil of ignorance' is achieved by purely formal means; and so is the purpose of his insistence that his contractors be rational, i.e. prudent. We have therefore, by consideration of the logic of the moral concepts alone, put ourselves in as strong a position as Rawls hopes to put himself by his more elaborate, but at the same time, as I have claimed, less firmly based apparatus.

Let us now use these tools. Rawls himself says that an ideal observer theory leads to utilitarianism; and the same ought to be true of the formal apparatus which I have just sketched. How does giving equal weight to the equal interests of all the parties lead to utilitarianism? And to what kind of util-itarianism does it lead? If I am trying to give equal weight to the equal interests of all the parties in a situation, I must, it seems, regard a benefit or harm done to one party as of equal value or disvalue to an equal benefit or harm done to any other party. This seems to mean that I shall promote the interests of the parties most, while giving equal weight to them all, if I maximize the total benefits over the entire population; and this is the classical principle of utility. For fixed populations it is practically equivalent to the average utility principle which bids us maximize not total but average utility; when the size of the population is itself affected by a decision, the two principles diverge, and I have given reasons (on p. 165) for preferring the classical or total utility principle. In these calculations, benefits are to be taken to include the reduction of harms.

I am not, however, going to put my theory in terms of benefits and the reduction of harms, because this leads to difficulties that I wish to avoid. Let us say, rather, that what the principle of utility requires of me is to do for each man affected by my actions what I wish were done for me in the hypothetical circumstances that I were in precisely his situation; and, if my actions affect more than one man (as they nearly always will) to do what I wish, all in all, to be done for me in the hypothetical circumstances that I occupied all their situations (not of course at the same time but, shall we say, in random order). This way of putting the matter, which is due to C. I. Lewis (1946: 547), emphasizes that I have to give the same weight to everybody's equal interests; and we must remember that, in so far as I am one of the people affected (as in nearly all cases I am) my own interests have to be given the same, and no more, weight—that is to say, my own actual situation is one of those that I have to suppose myself occupying in this random order.

Some further notes on this suggestion will be in place here. First, it is sometimes alleged that justice has to be at odds with utility. But if we ask how we are to be just between the competing interests of different people, it seems hard to give any other answer than that it is by giving equal weight, impartially, to the equal interests of everybody. And this is precisely what yields the utility principle. It does not necessarily yield equality in the resulting distribution. There are, certainly, very good utilitarian reasons for seeking equality in distribution too (see H 1977); but justice is something distinct. The utilitarian is sometimes said to be indifferent between equal and unequal distributions, provided that total utility is equal. This is so; but it conceals two important utilitarian grounds for a fairly high degree of equality of actual goods (tempered, of course, as in most systems including Rawls's, by various advantages that are secured by moderate inequalities). The first is the diminishing marginal utility of all commodities and of money, which means that approaches towards equality will tend to increase total utility. The second is that inequalities tend to produce, at any rate in educated societies, envy, hatred, and malice, whose disutility needs no emphasizing. I am convinced that, when these two factors are taken into account, utilitarians have no need to fear the accusation that they could favour extreme inequalities of distribution in actual modern societies. Fantastic hypothetical cases can no doubt be invented in which they would have to favour them; but, as we shall see, this is an illegitimate form of argument.

Secondly, the transition from a formulation in terms of interests to one in terms of desires or prescriptions, or vice versa, is far from plain sailing. Both formulations raise problems which are beyond the scope of this paper. If we formulate utilitarianism in terms of interests, we have the problem of determining what are someone's true interests. Even if we do not confuse the issue, as some do (following Plato, *Rep.* 335), by introducing moral considerations into this prudential question (i.e. by alleging that becoming morally better, or worse, in itself affects a man's interests), we still have to find a way of cashing statements about interests in terms of such states of mind as likings, desires, etc., both actual and hypothetical. For this reason a formulation directly in terms of these states of mind ought to be more perspicuous. But two difficult problems remain: the first is that of how present desires and likings are to be balanced against future ones, and actual desires and likings against those which would be experienced if certain alternative actions were taken; the second is whether desires need to be mentioned at all in a formulation of utilitarianism, or whether likings by themselves will do. It would seem that if we arrive at utilitarianism via universal prescriptivism, as I am trying to do, we shall favour the former of the last pair of alternatives; for desires, in the required sense, are assents to prescriptions. All these are questions within the theory of prudence, with which, although it is an essential adjunct to normative moral theory, I do not hope to deal in this paper.

I must mention, however, that when I said above that I have to do for each man affected by my actions what I wish were done for me, etc., I was speaking inaccurately. When I do the judging referred to on p. 214, I have to do it as rationally as possible. This, if I am making a moral judgement, involves prescribing universally; but in prescribing (albeit universally) I cannot, if rational, ignore prudence altogether, but have to universalize this prudence. Put more clearly, this means that, whether I am prescribing in my own interest or in someone else's (see the next paragraph), I must ask, not what we do actually at present wish, but what, prudentially speaking, we should wish. It is from this rational point of view (in the prudential sense of 'rational') that I have to give my universal prescriptions. In other words, it is *qua* rational that I have to judge; and this involves at least judging with a clear and unconfused idea of what I am saying and what the actual consequences of the prescription that I am issuing would be, for myself and others. It also involves, when I am considering the desires of others, considering what they would be if those others were perfectly prudent—i.e. desired what they would desire if they were fully informed and unconfused. Thus morality, at least for the utilitarian, can only be founded on prudence, which has then to be universalized. All this we shall have to leave undiscussed, remembering, however, that when in what follows I say 'desire', 'prescribe', etc., I mean 'desire, prescribe, etc., from the point of view of one who is prudent so far as his own interest goes'. It is important always to supply this qualification whether I am speaking of our own desires or those of others; but I shall omit it from now on because it would make my sentences intolerably cumbrous, and signalize the omission, in the next paragraph only, by adding the subscript 'p' to the words 'desire' etc. as required, omitting even this subscript thereafter. I hope that one paragraph will suffice to familiarize the reader with this point.

Thirdly, when we speak of the 'situations' of the various parties, we have to include in the situations all the desires$p$, likings$p$, etc., that the people have in them—that is to say, I am to do for the others what I wish$p$ to be done for me were I to have their likings$p$ etc., and not those which I now have. And, similarly, I am not to take into account (when I ask what I wish$p$ should be done to me in a certain situation) my own present desires$p$, likings$p$, etc. There is one exception to this: I have said that one of the situations that I have to consider is my own present situation; I have to love$p$ my neighbour *as*, but *no more than* and *no less than*, myself, and likewise to do to others *as* I wish$p$ them to do to me. Therefore just as, when I am considering what I wish$p$ to be done to me where I in X's situation, where X is somebody else, I have to think of the situation as including *his* desires$p$, likings$p$, etc., and discount my own, so, in the single case where X is myself, I have to take into account *my* desires$p$, likings$p$, etc. In other words, *qua* author of the moral decision I have to discount my own desires$p$ etc., and consider only the desires$p$, etc. of the affected party; but where (as normally) I am one of the affected parties, I have to consider my own desires*p* etc., *qua* affected party, on equal terms with those of all the other affected parties.[1]

It will be asked: if we strip me, *qua* author of the moral decision, of all desires and likings, how is it determined what decision I shall come to? The answer is that it is determined by the desires and likings of those whom I take into account as affected parties (including, as I said, myself, but only *qua* affected party and not *qua* author). I am to ask, indeed, what I do wish should be done for me, were I in their situations; but were I in their situations, I should have their desires etc., so I must forget about my own present desires (with the exception just made) and consider only the desires which *they* have; and if I do this, what I *do* wish for will be the satisfaction of *those* desires; that, therefore, is what I shall prescribe, so far as is possible.

I wish to point out that my present formulation enables me to deal in an agreeably clear way with the problem of the fanatic, who has given me so much trouble in the past (*FR* ch. 9; cf. *MT* ch. 10). In so far as, in order to prescribe universally, I have to strip away (*qua* author of the moral decision) all my present desires etc., I shall have to strip away, among them, all the ideals that I have; for an ideal is a kind of desire or liking (in the generic sense in which I am using those terms); it is, to use Aristotle's word, an *orexis* (*De An.* 433ª9 ff.). This does not mean that I have to give up having ideals, nor even that I must stop giving any consideration to my ideals when I make my moral decisions; it means only that I am not allowed to take them into account *qua* author of the moral decision. I am, however, allowed to take them into account, along with the ideals of all the other parties

---

[1] Professor Bernard Williams says, 'It is absurd to demand of such a man, when the sums come in from the utility network which the projects of others have in part determined, that he should just step aside from his own project and decision and acknowledge the decision which utilitarian calculation requires' (1973: 116; cf. 117 n.). Christian humility and *agape* and their humanist counterparts are, then, according to Williams's standards, an absurd demand (which is hardly remarkable). What is more remarkable is the boldness of the persuasive definition by which he labels the self-centred pursuit of one's own projects 'integrity' and accounts it a fault in utilitarianism that it could conflict with this.

affected, when I consider my own position, among others, as an affected party. This means that for the purposes of the moral decision it makes no difference *who has* the ideal. It means that we have to give impartial consideration to the ideals of ourselves and others. In cases, however, where the pursuit of our own ideals does not affect the ideals or the interests of others, we are allowed and indeed encouraged to pursue them.

All this being so, the only sort of fanatic that is going to bother us is the person whose ideals are so intensely pursued that the weight that has to be given to them, considered impartially, outbalances the combined weights of all the ideals, desires, likings, etc. that have to be frustrated in order to achieve them. For example, if the Nazi's desire not to have Jews around is intense enough to outweigh all the sufferings caused to Jews by arranging not to have them around, then, on this version of utilitarianism, as on any theory with the same formal structure, it ought to be satisfied. The problem is to be overcome by, first, pointing out that fanatics of this heroic stature are never likely to be encountered (that no *actual* Nazis had such intense desires is, I think, obvious); secondly, by remembering that, as I shall be showing in a moment, cases that are never likely to be actually encountered do not have to be squared with the thinking of the ordinary man, whose principles are not designed to cope with such cases. It is therefore illegitimate to attack such a theory as I have sketched by saying 'You can't ask us to believe that it would be right to give this fantastic fanatical Nazi what he wanted'; this argument depends on appealing to the ordinary man's judgement about a case with which, as we shall see, his intuitions were not designed to deal.

A similar move enables us to deal with another alleged difficulty (even if we do not, as we legitimately might, make use of the fact that all desires that come into our reasoning are desires*p*, i.e. desires that a man will have after he has become perfectly prudent). It is sometimes said to be a fault in utilitarianism that it makes us give weight to bad desires (such as the desire of a sadist to torture his victim) solely in proportion to their intensity; received opinion, it is claimed, gives no weight at all, or even a negative weight, to such desires. But received opinion has grown up to deal with cases likely to be encountered; and we are most *un*likely, even if we give sadistic desires weight in accordance with their intensity, to encounter a case in which utility will be maximized by letting the sadist have his way. For first, the suffering of the victim will normally be more intense than the pleasure of the sadist. And, secondly, sadists can often be given substitute pleasures or even actually cured. And, thirdly, the side-effects of allowing the sadist to have what he wants are enormous. So it will be clear, when I have explained in more detail why fantastic cases in which these disutilities do not occur cannot legitimately be used in this kind of argument, why it is perfectly all right to allow weight to bad desires.

We have now, therefore, to make an important distinction between two kinds or 'levels' of moral thinking. It has some affinities with a distinction made by Rawls (1955, in which he seemed to be defending utilitarianism), though it is not the same; it also owes something to Sir David Ross (1930: 19 ff.), and indeed to others. I call it the difference between the intuitive and critical levels of moral thinking, or between the principles employed at these two levels (pp. 110, 237). Intuitive principles are for use in practical moral thinking, especially under conditions of stress. They have to be general enough to be impartable by education (including self-education), and to be 'of ready application in the emergency' (Burke 1815, cited in *FR* 45), but are not to be confused with rules of thumb (whose breach excites no compunction). Critical principles are what would be arrived at by leisured moral thought in completely adequate knowledge of the facts, as the right answer in a specific case. They are universal but can be as specific (the opposite of 'general', not of 'universal' (see p. 50)) as needs be. Intuitive (or, as I have elsewhere called them, prima-facie) principles are inculcated in moral education; but the selection of the intuitive principles for this purpose should be guided by leisured thought, resulting in critical principles for specific considered situations, the object being to have those intuitive principles whose cultivation and general acceptance will lead to actions in accord with the best critical principles in most situations that are actually encountered.

Fantastic and highly unusual situations, therefore, need not be considered for this purpose.

I have set out this distinction in detail on pp. 60 ff. and in *MT*; here we only need to go into some particular points which are relevant. The thinking that I have been talking about so far in this paper, until the preceding paragraph, and indeed in most of my philosophical writings until recently, is the critical. It results in a kind of act-utilitarianism which, because of the universalizability of moral judgements, is practically equivalent to a rule-utilitarianism whose rules are allowed to be of any required degree of specificity. Such thinking is appropriate only to 'a cool hour', in which there is time for unlimited investigation of the facts, and there is no temptation to special pleading. It can use hypothetical cases, even fantastic ones. In principle it can, given superhuman knowledge of the facts, yield answers as to what should be done in any cases one cares to describe.

The commonest trick of the opponents of utilitarianism is to take examples of such thinking, usually addressed to fantastic cases, and confront them with what the ordinary man would think. It makes the utilitarian look like a moral monster. The anti-utilitarians have usually confined their own thought about moral reasoning (with fairly infrequent lapses which often go unnoticed) to the intuitive level, the level of everyday moral thinking on ordinary, often stressful, occasions in which information is sparse. So they find it natural to take the side of the ordinary man in a supposed fight with the utilitarian whose views lead him to say, if put at the disconcertingly unfamiliar standpoint of the archangel Gabriel, such extraordinary things about these carefully contrived examples.

To argue in this way is entirely to neglect the importance for moral philosophy of a study of moral education. Let us suppose that a fully-informed archangelic act-utilitarian is thinking about how to bring up his children. He will obviously not bring them up to practise on every occasion on which they are confronted with a moral question the kind of archangelic thinking that he himself is capable of; if they are ordinary children, he knows that they will get it wrong. They will not have the time, nor the information, nor the self-mastery to avoid self-deception prompted by self-interest; this is the real, as opposed to the imagined, veil of ignorance which determines our moral principles.

So he will do two things. First, he will try to implant in them a set of good general principles. I advisedly use the word 'implant'; these are not rules of thumb, but principles which they will not be able to break without the greatest repugnance, and whose breach by others will arouse in them the highest indignation. These will be the principles they will use in their ordinary intuitive moral thinking, especially in situations of stress. Secondly, since he is not always going to be with them, and since they will have to educate *their* children, and indeed continue to educate themselves, he will teach them, as far as they are able, to do the kind of thinking that he has been doing himself. This thinking will have three functions. First of all, it will be used when the good general principles conflict in particular cases. If the principles have been well chosen, this will happen rarely; but it will happen. Secondly, there will be cases (even rarer) in which, though there is no conflict between general principles, there is something highly unusual about the case which prompts the question whether the general principles are really fitted to deal with it. But thirdly, and much the most important, this critical thinking will be used to *select* the general principles to be taught both to this and to succeeding generations. The general principles may change, and should change (because the environment changes). And note that, if the educator were not (as we have supposed him to be) archangelic, we could not even assume that the best intuitive principles were imparted in the first place; perhaps they might be improved.

How will the selection be done? It will be done by using critical thinking to consider cases, both actual and hypothetical, which crucially illustrate, and help to adjudicate, disputes between rival general principles. But, because the general principles are being selected for use in actual situations, there will have to be a careful proportioning of the weight to be put upon a particular case to the probability of its actually occurring in the lives of the people who are to use the principles. So the fantastic cases that are so beloved of anti-utilitarians will have very little employment in this kind of thinking (except as a diversion for philosophers or to illustrate purely logical points, which is sometimes necessary). Fantastic unlikely cases will never be used to turn the scales as between rival general principles for practical use. The result will be a set of general principles, constantly evolving, but on the whole stable, such that their use in moral education, including self-education, and their consequent acceptance by the society at large, will lead to the nearest possible approximation to the prescriptions of archangelic thinking. They will be the set of principles with the highest acceptance-utility. They are likely to include principles of justice (for further discussion see H 1988, Frankena's paper and my comments).

It is now necessary to introduce some further distinctions, all of which, fortunately, have already been made on pp. 60 ff. and can therefore be merely summarized. The first, alluded to already, is that between specific rule-utilitarianism (which is practically equivalent to universalistic act-utilitarianism) and general rule-utilitarianism. Both are compatible with act-utilitarianism if their roles are carefully distinguished. Specific rule-utilitarianism is appropriate to critical thinking, general rule-utilitarianism to intuitive thinking; and therefore the rules of specific rule-utilitarianism can be of unlimited specificity, but those of general rule-utilitarianism have to be general enough for their role. The thinking of our archangel will thus be of a specific rule-utilitarian sort; and the thinking of the ordinary people whom he has educated will be for the most part of a general rule-utilitarian sort, though they will supplement this, when they have to and when they dare, with such archangelic thinking as they are capable of.

The second distinction is that between what Professor Smart (1973: 46 f.) calls (morally) 'right' actions and (morally) 'rational' actions. Although Smart's way of putting the distinction is not quite adequate, as he himself recognizes, I shall, as he does, adopt it for the sake of brevity. Both here, and in connection with the 'acceptance-utility' mentioned above, somewhat more sophisticated calculations of probability are required than might at first be thought. But for simplicity let us say that an action is rational if it is the action most likely to be right, even if, when all the facts are known, as they were not when it was done, it turns out not to have been right. In such a society as we have described, the (morally) rational action will nearly always be that in accordance with the good general intuitive principles, because they have been selected precisely in order to make this the case. Such actions may not always turn out to have been (morally) right in Smart's sense when the cards are turned face upwards; but the agent is not to be blamed for this (see further p. 63).

It is a difficult question, just how simple and general these intuitive principles ought to be. If we are speaking of the principles to be inculcated throughout the society, the answer will obviously vary with the extent to which the members of it are sophisticated and morally self-disciplined enough to grasp and apply relatively complex principles without running into the dangers we have mentioned. We might distinguish subgroups within the society, and individuals within these subgroups, and even the same individual at different stages, according to their ability to handle complex principles. Most people's intuitive principles become somewhat more complex as they gain experience of handling different situations, and they may well become so complex as to defy verbal formulation; but the value of the old simple maxims may also come to be appreciated. In any case, intuitive principles can never, because of the exigencies of their role, become as complex as critical principles are allowed to be.

A third distinction is that between good actions and the right action (*LM* 186). The latter is the action in accordance with critical principles arrived at by exhaustive, fully informed, and clear thinking about specific cases. A good action is what a good man would do, even if not right. In general this is the same as the morally rational action, but there may be complications, in that the motivation of the man has to be taken into account. The good (i.e. the morally well-educated) man, while he is sometimes able and willing to question and even to amend the principles he has been taught, will have acquired in his upbringing a set of motives and dispositions such that breaking these principles goes very much against the grain for him. The very goodness of his character will make him sometimes do actions which do not conform to archangelic prescriptions. This may be for one of at least two reasons. The first is that when he did them he was not fully informed and perhaps knew it, and knew also his own moral and intellectual weaknesses, and therefore (humbly and correctly) thought it morally rational to abide by his intuitive principles, and thus did something which turned out in the event not to be morally right. The second is that, although he could have known that the morally rational action was on this unusual occasion one in breach of his ingrained principles (it required him, say, to let down his closest friend), he found it so much against the grain that he just could not bring himself to do it. In the first case what he did was both rational and a morally good action. In the second case it was morally good but misguided—a wrong and indeed irrational act done from the best of motives. And no doubt there are other possibilities.

The situation I have been describing is a somewhat stylized model of our own, except that we have no archangel to educate us, but rely on the deliverances, not even of philosopher kings, but of Aristotelian *phronimoi* of very varying degrees of excellence. What will happen if a lot of moral philosophers are let loose on this situation? Intuitive thinking forms the greater part of the moral thinking of good men, and perhaps the whole of the moral thinking of good men who have nothing of the philosopher in them, including some of our philosophical colleagues. Such are the intuitionists, to whom their good ingrained principles seem to be sources of unquestionable knowledge. Others of a more enquiring bent will ask why they should accept these intuitions, and, getting no satisfactory answer, will come to the conclusion that the received principles have no ground at all and that the only way to decide what you ought to do is to reason it out on each occasion. Such people will at best become a crude kind of act-utilitarians. Between these two sets of philosophers there will be the sort of ludicrous battles that we have been witnessing so much of. The philosopher who understands the situation better will see that both are right about a great deal and that they really ought to make up their quarrel. They are talking about different levels of thought, both of which are necessary on appropriate occasions

What kind of philosopher will this understanding person

be? Will he be any kind of utilitarian? I see no reason why he should not be. For, first of all, critical thinking, which is necessary, is not only utilitarian but act-utilitarian (for, as we have seen, the specific rule-utilitarian thinking of this level and universalistic act-utilitarianism are practically equivalent). And there are excellent act-utilitarian reasons for an educator to bring up his charges to think intuitively on most occasions on the basis of a set of principles selected by high-quality critical thinking. This applies equally to self-education. So at any rate all acts that could be called educative or self-educative can have a solid act-utilitarian foundation. To educate oneself and other people in intuitive principles *is* for the best, and only the crudest of act-utilitarians fails to see this. There will also be good act-utilitarian reasons for *following* the good general principles in nearly all cases; for to do so will be rational, or most likely to be right; and even an act-utilitarian, when he comes to tell us how we should proceed when choosing what to do, can only tell us to do what is *most probably* right, because we do not know, when choosing, what *is* right.

There will be occasions, as I have said, when a man brought up (on good general principles) by a consistent act-utilitarian will do a rational act which turns out not to be right; and there will even be occasions on which he will do a good action which is neither rational nor right, because, although he could have known that it would be right on this unusual occasion to do an act contrary to the good general principles, he could not bring himself to contemplate it, because it went so much against the grain. And since one cannot pretune human nature all that finely, it may well be that the act-utilitarian educator will have to put up with the possibility of such cases, in the assurance that, if his principles are well chosen, they will be rare. For if he attempted to educate people so that they would do the rational thing in these cases, it could only be by incorporating into their principles clauses which might lead them, in other more numerous cases, to do acts most likely to be wrong. Moral upbringing is a compromise imposed by the coarseness of the pupil's discrimination and the inability of his human educators to predict with any accuracy the scrapes he will get into.

The exclusion from the argument of highly unusual cases,

which I hope I have now achieved, is the main move in my defence of this sort of utilitarianism. There are also some subsidiary moves, some of which I have already mentioned, and all of which will be familiar. It is no argument against act-utiliarianism that in some unusual cases it would take a bad man to do what according to the utilitarian is the morally right or even the morally rational thing; good men are those who are firmly wedded to the principles which *on nearly all actual occasions* will lead them to do the right thing, and it is inescapable that on unusual occasions moderately good men will do the wrong thing. The nearer they approach archangelic status, the more, on unusual occasions, they will be able to chance their arm and do what they think will be the right act in defiance of their principles; but most of us ordinary mortals will be wise to be fairly cautious. As Aristotle said, we have to incline towards the vice which is the lesser danger for *us*, and away from that extreme which is to *us* the greater temptation (1109^b1). For some, in the present context, the greater danger may be too much rigidity in the application of intuitive principles; but perhaps for more (and I think that I am one of them) it is a too great readiness to let them slip. It is a matter of temperament; we have to know ourselves (empirically); the philosopher cannot tell each of us which is the greater danger for him.

The moves that I have already made will, I think, deal with some other cases which are well known from the literature. Such are the case of the man who is tempted, on utilitarian grounds, to use electricity during a power crisis, contrary to the government's instructions; and the case of the voter who abstains in the belief that enough others will vote. In both these cases it is alleged that some utility would be gained, and none lost, by these dastardly actions. These are not, on the face of it, fantastic or unusual cases, although the degree of knowledge stipulated as to what others will do is perhaps unusual. Yet it would be impolitic, in moral education, to bring up people to behave like this, if we were seeking intuitive principles with the highest acceptance-utility; if we tried, the result would be that nearly everyone would consume electricity under those conditions, and hardly anybody would vote. However, the chief answer to these cases is that which I have used elsewhere (H 1971*b*: 128 ff.; *FR* 132 ff.) to deal with the car-pushing and deathbed promise cases which are also well canvassed. It is best approached by going back to the logical beginning and asking whether I am prepared to prescribe, or even permit, that others should (*a*) use electricity, thus taking advantage of my law-abidingness, when I am going without it; (*b*) abstain from voting when I do so at inconvenience to myself, thereby taking advantage of my public spirit; (*c*) only pretend to push the car when I am rupturing myself in the effort to get it started; (*d*) make deathbed promises to me (for example, to look after my children) and then treat them as of no weight. I unhesitatingly answer 'No' to all these questions; and I think that I should give the same answer even if I were perfectly prudent and were universalizing my prescriptions to cover other perfectly prudent affected parties (see above, p. 218). For it is not imprudent, but prudent rather, to seek the satisfaction of desires which are important to me, even if I am not going to know whether they have been satisfied or not. There is nothing in principle to prevent a fully informed and clear-headed person wanting above all that his children should not starve after his death; and if that is what he wants above all, it is prudent for him to seek what will achieve it, and therefore prescribe this.

Since the logical machinery on which my brand of utilitarianism is based yields these answers, so should the utilitarianism that is based on it; and it is worth while to ask, How? The clue lies in the observation that to frustrate a desire of mine is against my interest even if I do not know that it is being frustrated, or if I am dead. If anybody does not agree, I ask him to apply the logical apparatus direct and forget about interests. Here is a point at which, perhaps, some people will want to say that my Kantian or Christian variety of utilitarianism, based on giving equal weight to the prudent prescriptions or desires of all, diverges from the usual varieties so much that it does not deserve to be called a kind of utilitarianism at all. I am not much interested in that terminological question; but for what it is worth I will record my opinion that the dying man's interests *are* harmed if promises are made to him and then broken, and even more that mine are harmed if people are cheating me without my knowing it. In the latter case, they are harmed because I very much want this not to happen; and my desire that it should not happen is boosted by my intuitive sense of justice, which the utilitarian educators who brought me up wisely inculcated in me (for further discussion see H 1988, Gibbard's paper and my comments).

Whichever way we put it, whether in terms of what I am prepared to prescribe or permit universally (and therefore also for when I am the victim) or in terms of how to be fair as between the interests of all the affected parties, I conclude that the acts I have listed will come out wrong on the act-utilitarian calculation, because of the harms done to the interests of those who are cheated, or the non-fulfilment of prescriptions to which, we may assume, they attach high importance. If we add to this move the preceding one which rules out fantastic cases, and are clear about the distinction between judgements about the character of the agent, judgements about the moral rationality of the action, and judgements about its moral rightness as shown by the outcome, I think that this form of utilitarianism can answer the objections I have mentioned. Much more needs to be said; the present paper is only a beginning, and is not very original. I publish it only to give some indication of the way in which ethical theory can help with normative moral questions, and to try to get the discussion of utilitarianism centred round credible forms of it, rather than forms which we all know will not do.

14
Utilitarianism and the Vicarious Affects

WHEN Professor Rescher was kind enough to dedicate his excellent book *Unselfishness* (1975) to me, he intended it, I am sure, not just as a kindness but also at least in part as the friendliest possible reproach, first for my neglect of the theory of games and its relevance to moral philosophy, and secondly for my remaining a utilitarian in spite of all the well-known arguments against that doctrine. The first fault I can readily acknowledge, and the book has helped me to begin to amend it. But in this essay I shall try to defend myself against the second reproach by showing that at any rate Professor Rescher's arguments in chapter 5 of his book do nothing to impugn utilitarianism, provided that this is carefully formulated (see also *MT* ch. 8).

I hope that I may without misrepresentation summarize his argument as follows. There are certain attitudes or feelings or motives (the word does not matter) which he calls the *vicarious affects*: those excited by good or harm occurring to other people. For example, I may experience distress because a child of mine is in pain, or fear because my wife is in danger, though I myself am in no danger or pain. These are examples of *positive* vicarious affects. There are also *negative* vicarious affects, when our own affect is the opposite of that appropriate to the other in his situation; examples of these are *Schadenfreude*, when we are pleased at the distress of another, and envy, when we are distressed at another's happiness.

The positive vicarious affects, Rescher thinks, have an important role to play in moral thinking and in thinking about morals, because they help to extricate us from various prisoners' dilemmas in which we should be caught if we were not endowed with such motives for co-operation and

From *The Philosophy of Nicholas Rescher*, ed. E. Sosa (Dordrecht, Reidel, 1979).

beneficence. Thus two people, who, if they were concerned only for their own selfish interests, would, if prudent, follow courses whose combination would lead to an outcome less than optimal for both of them, may, if the positive vicarious affects are added to their motivations, be led to co-operate and so achieve an optimal outcome for both.

Rescher does not claim that this will always be the case, nor that the positive vicarious affects are uniformly beneficial; only that they are so in some important and otherwise difficult cases, and thus explain how people can come to behave morally better and more beneficially than they would if not so motivated. I shall not enquire whether this part of Rescher's argument is correct; it certainly seems to be an important part of the truth, though not a complete solution to all difficulties in this area.

Rescher uses the vicarious affects to generate two main arguments against utilitarianism. I will summarize first that concerned with the positive vicarious affects. Since their existence and inculcation is generally beneficial and generally approved, any theory of moral reasoning which requires us to disregard them stands condemned. But utilitarianism does require us to do just this. For it is a characteristic of some of the most beneficial and approved positive vicarious affects that they are not directed impartially towards the good or harm of all people equally, but are selective in their scope. Thus a mother feels fear when her own child is in danger, but not, or not so much, when somebody else's child is. This partiality of the vicarious affects is built into a great area of our popular morality. We think it right and proper for parents to care especially for their own children, for example. But utilitarianism, it is argued, requires us to seek the good of all impartially, in accordance with Bentham's dictum 'Everybody to count for one, nobody for more than one' (Mill 1861 *s.f.*). So a consistent utilitarian would seek to suppress in himself, and at any rate not act on, these partial positive vicarious affects; and so, not only would he act differently from the way that received morality requires, but, since the partiality which it requires is productive of good, he would be committed by his utilitarianism to acting in a way that was less than optimific. Thus utilitarianism is shown (or so it is claimed) to be both contrary to received opinion and self-defeating.

The hardened utilitarian might seek to defend himself against the first of these charges, at a cost, by unashamedly flouting received opinion. If received opinion requires me to be partial in my benevolence and beneficence, he might say, so much the worse for received opinion. Utilitarianism, which requires impartial benevolence, is the correct morality, and it is only begging the question to *assume* that received opinion is right in order to impugn utilitarianism for conflicting with it. This area of argument is sufficiently charted, and I have explored it in greater depth elsewhere (H 1971*b* :117 ff.). The second charge, that utilitarianism is self-defeating because a consistent practice of it would be less than optimific, is of a sort which Dr Hodgson (1967) has made familiar, and is, if it can be pressed home, more damaging than the first; although it is only an argument *ad hominem*, it is none the worse for that (see, however, criticism in Singer 1972 and Mackie 1972).

I hope before long to show that neither of these forms of the objection to utilitarianism based on the positive vicarious affects can be sustained; but first I must summarize Rescher's other argument, that based on the negative vicarious affects. This is much simpler and can be stated briefly. It is characteristic of utilitarianism of the Benthamite variety to give equal weight to desires, pleasures, etc. of equal intensity, whatever their object or nature. 'Prejudice apart, the game of push-pin is of equal value with the arts and sciences of music and poetry' (1825: 206). Mill rebelled against this doctrine (1861: ch. 2), but is generally held to have thereby introduced a fatal inconsistency into his theory. It is commonly objected to utilitarianism that it would require us to give the same weight to desires and pleasures which everybody acknowledges to be disreputable as to those which we all think noble. This objection falls into the class of objections to utilitarianism by appeal to received opinion; I have dealt with the class of objections in general, and with this particular objection, elsewhere (pp. 222 ff.; *MT* ch. 8). Rescher is sufficiently well acquainted with this terrain to be aware of the arguments I shall be bringing against him; but I do not think that he has fully appreciated their force.

An example of the objection we are considering would be the pleasures of the sadist (see p. 220 and *MT* 141 ff.). Surely, it is claimed, we are not required in our calculation of utilities to give to these equal weight with the sufferings of his victim? To take other examples, utilitarianism 'gives envy, jealousy and ill-will a weight they do not deserve in ethical analysis' (1975: 82). From the frequency with which I have encountered this objection, it would appear that many people think it a cogent one; and this is not surprising, because in order to see its weakness one has to have an understanding of its target, utilitarianism, greater than most anti-utilitarians have allowed themselves to acquire.

In order to promote this understanding, I shall now make some general remarks, although I have made them before (pp. 57, 223), in the hope that some deep-seated causes of confusion will thereby be exposed. The first thing to understand is that utilitarianism is intended, like any moral view which has practical application, for use in the world as it is. Almost any doctrine in normative ethics can be divided into two parts. There is first the abstract or theoretical part, which is intended to hold for any logically possible world; and then there is the concrete or practical part which is applicable to the world as it is, but would have to be abandoned if the world were to change drastically. Opponents of such doctrines take too short a way with them if they insist that the practical part of them be shown to make sense not merely in the world as it is, but in artificially devised cases which are very different from those normally encountered.

Utilitarianism has frequently been the victim of such attacks. Its theoretical part is simply the requirement of impartial benevolence—a purely formal requirement which is, if my own view is correct, no more than a restatement of the logical properties of universalizability and prescriptivity which characterize evaluative judgements (see p. 179). It is one of the strengths of utilitarianism that its formal component is, if true, analytically true. However, this strength carries with it what might seem to be a disadvantage: that by itself the formal part of the doctrine has no implications whatever for practical moral questions. In default of information about the world, and in particular about what people actually desire and find to their liking, this formal component is consistent with a huge variety of substantial moral views.

The formal component has therefore to be supplemented by a substantial component, which can direct our conduct in the world as it actually is; and the connection between the components has to be explained. Whatever the connection, it should be clear already why the kind of attack which I have been considering is going to miss the target. The substantial component of utilitarianism, and in particular its contribution to the selection of intuitive or prima-facie principles (see *MT* 133–5) is grounded in the facts as they are; if the world were different, it too would have to be different. It is legitimate to demand of the formal component that it should hold for all logically possible worlds. But if this demand is made of the substantial component (which is what anti-utilitarians are doing when they complain that in certain fantastic examples devised by them utilitarianism yields counter-intuitive results) the point is entirely missed. The substantial component of a utilitarian system is framed to serve well, on the whole, in the world as it is; therefore it is obviously likely to yield bizarre results when applied to fantastic and unusual cases.

Rescher is ready to accept similar considerations to these when he is discussing another issue, that of whether 'the dictates of self-oriented prudence and other-concerned morality *must* yield concordant rather than divergent results' (1975: 69). He says that 'while this [divergence] remains true at the theoretical level, the actual, empirically given (rather than theoretically inevitable) circumstances of the case represented by the conditions prevailing here and now are in fact such that a convergence is forthcoming' (ibid.). But when he is attacking utilitarianism he is much more demanding. He says 'Even if one could justify on utilitarian principles the *practice* of treating people differently [sc. according to the nearness of their relation to us] (supposedly because this is maximally efficient in conducing to the good of all), this defense leaves us with an essentially contingent justification: "As things tend to work in the world, this *modus operandi* leads to the goal of . . . ". No moralist who regards differential obligations as a feature non-contingently inherent in the ethical ramifications of human relationships could accept this approach' (1975: 78).

Here he is in effect demanding that the practical moral system which utilitarianism generates for use in, and based partly upon, the conditions to be found in the actual world, should be equally applicable to all logically possible worlds. But why should it?

It may help to make the issue clearer if we take this particular case of the supposed duty to favour those most closely related to us, and ask, first, whether and to what extent it is really acknowledged as a duty; secondly, whether it ought to be so acknowledged and why; and thirdly, how a utilitarian could justify these findings.

The answer to the first question is not at all clear cut. On the one hand most people would hold it to be a duty of parents to feed their own children, but only in special circumstances to feed other people's children. On the other hand there is a difference of opinion (sometimes reflecting political, sometimes cultural differences) as to the extent to which we ought to seek to obtain for our own children (necessarily at the expense of other people's children with whom they are competing) the best education, the best jobs, and our own wealth after we die. In certain cultures nepotism is accounted a virtue, in others a malpractice. Rescher thinks that the more judicial roles, in which impartiality is required, can be separated from those in which partial vicarious affects are to be commended (1975: 72). But even if this is so, the line is drawn in very different places by different societies.

If we ask for the rationale of such distinctions, the utilitarian at least can provide an answer, and it is not clear that Rescher or anybody else can provide any substantially different answer that is at all convincing. The reason why parents are generally encouraged to feed their own children in preference to other people's children is that, if we inculcated a feeling of obligation to feed all children impartially, children would on the whole be less well fed and many more of them would starve. This is partly because the removal from parents of the responsibility for feeding their own children would remove, at the same time, the incentive to limit the number of one's children to what one thinks one can feed. But even given a determinate birth rate, it is plain that the vast, but at the same time universally shared and therefore indefinitely diluted, responsibility for feeding all human children (and why not animals too?) is less likely to spur me actually to do something about feeding them than the limited responsibility for feeding these two or four or even fifteen hungry brats. And so popular morality has very wisely limited people's main responsibility to something which, if not too idle and not too unfortunate, they are likely to be able to shoulder; and so, on the whole, children get fed, though not well enough fed in too many cases.

However, when we come to the questions of education, jobs, and inherited wealth, it is easy to see how people can have different opinions. Conservatives will give one answer, egalitarian radicals another. Utilitarians have a consistent and coherent way of answering such questions. They will say that the best attitudes to adopt and inculcate in these matters are those whose general cultivation and acceptance conduces most to the good, in sum, of those affected. Rival doctrines, usually based on intuitions about rights and justice which vary with the politics of their exponents, lack any ground besides appeals to these intuitions themselves, unless perhaps highly selective utilitarian considerations are brought in for want of other rational support.

It is impossible to understand the issue between utilitarians and their opponents without distinguishing the different levels of moral thinking, as I have tried to do in several papers (see Index: 'levels' and *MT* chs. 2, 3). Briefly, three levels of thinking have to be distinguished. The highest of these levels is the metaethical, by which a normative doctrine's formal component, which I distinguished just now, is established. Below this are two levels of moral thinking proper, i.e. substantial moral thinking. Let us then distinguish between the *intuitive* level of moral thinking and the *critical* level. The intuitive level is that at which nearly all of us do nearly all of our moral thinking. It consists in the application to particular cases of habits of mind, dispositions, intuitions, principles, rules, or whatever one cares to call them, which we take as given and do not question. Because this kind of thinking preponderates in the moral life of most people, a great many moral philosophers have paid exclusive attention to it. But other moral philosophers who are not so blinkered (starting at least with Plato) have seen that this level of moral thinking cannot be self-supporting; the principles etc. of intuitive thinking will conflict in difficult cases, and, even if they do not, the question may arise of whether a case is unusual enough to demand a departure from an accepted principle. Other acute difficulties emerge when we ask ourselves whether the principles on which we ourselves were brought up, and which have for us the force of moral intuitions, are the best principles for our children to adopt.

To resolve such questions by appeal to the intuited principles themselves is a laughably circular procedure—as may be seen by watching any rebellious child arguing with his respectably brought up parents about sex. A higher, critical level of thinking is required. The central part of utilitarianism is an account of this level. I say 'the central part' because a fully developed utilitarian system includes accounts of the other two levels. On the one hand, as I have said, the formal component of utilitarianism is grounded in a metaethical account of the logical properties of the moral concepts. On the other, the utilitarian can readily accept what intuitionists and the ordinary man have to say about intuitive moral thinking, and it is very boring how intuitionists and de-ontologists go on making points which they think are objections to utilitarianism, based, on alleged divergences between utilitarian moral thinking and our ordinary intuitive thinking, when in fact they arise out of the distinction (which is by no means a conflict) between intuitive and critical thinking. When the act-utilitarian is thinking intuitively, as his own doctrine will require him, in the interests of optimificity, to do for most of the time, there will be no divergence; the divergence will occur only when critical thinking is required, and intuitionist philosophers, in company with the less reflect-ive, but by no means all, ordinary men, are unable to perform it.

Before I set out the account which the utilitarian can give of intuitive moral thinking, I must first remove a source of misunderstanding by relating what I have said to the com-monly made distinction between act- and rule-utilitarianism (of both of which there are numerous kinds). I am not advocating any of the usual kinds of rule-utilitarianism (which is why at the end of the last paragraph I specifically and deliberately said 'the act-utilitarian'). I agree with most of what Professor David Lyons has said about the reducibility of rule- to act-utilitarianism (1965), and have said much the same more briefly myself (*FR* 130 ff.). The doctrine which I am advocating is a sophisticated form of *act*-utilitarianism which incorporates the defences that rule-utilitarianism was designed to provide against the vulgar objections to the doctrines of the earlier utilitarians. It is based on an understanding of what moral thinking, and in particular moral education, is like in real life, and it is not in the least original, having been anticipated in different forms by, among others, Butler and Moore, though they did not develop it sufficiently (see pp. 58 ff.).

We must start by acknowledging that we are human beings and not archangels, and that we need a sound moral education to fit us to make, in the course of our lives, the moral decisions which will best suit the varied and difficult situations in which we shall find ourselves, and which neither we nor our educators can foresee. If we *were* archangels, both omniscient and clear-headed and free from temptations to special pleading, then, perhaps, we should be able to carry on in the way that the stock straw act-utilitarian is supposed to: that is to say, we should on every occasion examine all the consequences of all alternative actions open to us and choose that yielding the greatest utility. But since we are not archangels, we need dispositions which will make us most likely, all in all, to hit off the decisions which archangels would make in the same situations. These dispositions came to us from our earlier experience, and from the experience of those who have influenced us. If we are lucky, we have a good set of moral dispositions; if not, not.

The dispositions, as I have said, express themselves in the intuitions which are the sole diet of many moral philosophers. This account of the origin of our moral intuitions is of course too bare: there are other influences that shape them, some beneficial and some the reverse. It is a contingent matter what moral intuitions we come to have; and therefore it is strange to find intuitionists (that is, the majority of moral philosophers)

appealing to them as sacrosanct and unquestionable—rather
as if they were the precepts of God; but do most contemporary
anti-utilitarians believe in him?

Because they do not criticize their own intuitions, they never
raise the question of how we would determine *what* intuitions
we ought to have—a question which is crucial for anybody
who is concerned with moral education and development, his
own and other people's. But as soon as we raise this question,
we have ascended to the critical level, and can no longer
without circularity appeal to intuitions to justify intuitions.
For the moment, however, in order to complete our account
of the intuitive level, let us ask what a rational *act*-utilitarian,
conscious of his human limitations, will do when faced with
moral decisions. Given these limitations, his aim must be to
act in the way which will *most probably* be in accord with the
act-utilitarian ideal—i.e. be what the act-utilitarian archangel,
with no human limitations, would choose. It is precisely in
order to fit himself to make such decisions wisely and overcome
his human limitations and temptations that he has equipped
himself with moral attitudes and intuitions; and therefore,
unless the case is a most unusual one, his best chance of acting
for the best is to be guided by them. If this were not so, the
attitudes and dispositions themselves would be at fault; and
this may be so in many cases. Whether it is so is determinable
only by a *critical* examination of the attitudes in a cool hour
(for the dangers of doing it *in mediis rebus* are well known).

The rational act-utilitarian, therefore, will proceed, in his
intuitive moral thinking, exactly as his intuitionist opponents
would themselves proceed, with one exception: if, owing to
'conflict of duties' or some other cause, the intuitions themselves
get called in question, he has a way of dealing with the
difficulty and they have not. This way we must now examine.

We can do so by asking what *other* way is being suggested
of determining whether the intuitions we have are those which
we ought to have, besides the utilitarian way (namely that of
asking what intuitions it is *best* that people inculcate and
encourage in themselves and others). We have already ruled
out as circular the appeal to intuitions in support of intuitions.
I do not think that most anti-utilitarians are really wanting
to appeal to God. But what else are they going to appeal to?

The act-utilitarian is here concerned with a particular and very crucial kind of act: the act of inculcating, and in general encouraging and supporting, or the reverse, moral attitudes and dispositions. His guide in doing this is the same as for all other acts: he is to encourage etc. those dispositions etc. whose encouragement, and therefore whose general acceptance in society, will be optimific. Any attempt here to draw a distinction between rule- and act-utilitarianism will founder on the fact that the observance of and the propagation of and the support of a rule are themselves acts or series of acts. We have to notice here that there are close links, partly logical and partly psychological, between holding a rule and acting on it. On the logical side, if one does not act on a rule when an occasion for acting on it arises, doubt at least is cast on the genuineness of one's conviction; and the same is true if one does not prescribe that others so act, and so, in the natural course of events, encourage them to do so. So the man who purports to hold a certain rule but does none of these things is at the best a logical oddity and at the worst a fraud. On the psychological side, it is beyond the power of most human beings to develop consistent ways of acting without acting in these ways consistently (cf. Aristotle 1103^a31 ff.); and therefore the straw act-utilitarian, who is supposed to have what are most misleadingly called 'mere rules of thumb' which are in accord with common moral opinion, but to depart from them without a twinge when his utilitarian calculations so require, possesses psychological powers which most of us lack. The rational *human* act-utilitarian will recognize that unless the principles which he selects on utilitarian grounds and adopts for his conduct are implanted in him very firmly indeed, and are far from being 'mere rules of thumb', he is unlikely in difficult and stressful situations to observe them in his acts; and that therefore (since the principles were chosen with the express purpose of giving him the greatest chance of acting for the best) he is unlikely to live as well as he could. His supposedly optimific acts will little by little erode[1] his genuinely

---

[1] My own account is designed precisely to remove this danger of erosion, and the criticism that I incur it is therefore misplaced. See H 1988, Williams's paper and my comments.

(we hope) optimific principles. And in real life utilitarians of this sort have indeed got the doctrine a bad image.

We are now in a position to return to Rescher's vicarious affects and see what is left of his objections to utilitarianism. On the foregoing account, there is every reason why a rational act-utilitarian should favour the inculcation of a tendency to experience the positive vicarious affects; for, as Rescher himself has made abundantly clear, the having of them is conducive, on the whole, to the good of all those affected by the resulting conduct. On reflection, it is difficult to see any antagonism between the truths which Rescher so ably clarifies and the utilitarian position as I have outlined it. The appearance of an antagonism is created by taking artificial situations, schematically set out in the form of games-theory matrices, in which a direct application by an archangel of the principle of utility (never mind in precisely what form) would yield precepts markedly different from those which naturally commend themselves to us non-angelic humans.

The flaws in this procedure should by now be obvious. Our ordinary moral dilemmas are different from these neat diagrams in at least two crucial respects. The first is that we do not have the knowledge of the consequences of our actions which would enable us directly to apply the principle of utility. Therefore the argument that a utilitarian in such a dilemma would be committed by his views to acting in the way that Rescher says, is too superficial. A rational act-utilitarian, conscious of his human limitations, would, as we have seen, act like any other good man, in the belief that that was, given the limitations, the best way of pursuing utility. Secondly, the idea that a utilitarian is committed in particular to suppressing his own partial positive vicarious affects is entirely mistaken. What affects he ought to encourage or suppress in himself will depend, for the act-utilitarian, on the consequences of encouraging or suppressing them. If, as Rescher rightly thinks, the positive vicarious affects are on the whole beneficial, the act-utilitarian has every reason for encouraging them in himself and others, which means, among other things, acting on them. So where is the antagonism?

Lastly, a word about the negative vicarious affects. The answer is in part the same. Rescher thinks that utilitarianism 'gives envy, jealousy and ill-will a weight they do not deserve in ethical analysis' (1975: 82). In order to determine whether this is so, we have first to distinguish between the different levels of ethical analysis, and then to ask what weight they *do* deserve at these various levels. At the meta-ethical level they hardly enter, because we are there concerned only with the form and not the content of prescriptions; in utilitarian terms, any utility is a utility. That formal ethical thinking is not able to distinguish between motives which, in the world as it is, are good or bad ones to have, is, indeed, the reason why it is thought by many that utilitarianism as a whole is unable to distinguish between them; but in its substantial parts it is well able. For the position alters entirely when we descend to the substantial levels of moral thought. To take the critical level first: it seems obvious that a rational act-utilitarian has good reasons to discourage and suppress envy, jealousy, and ill will, because their currency in society and in himself is harmful. It is true that particular cases can be found, or invented, in which to act out of jealousy or to satisfy envy will be optimific. But, first, it would be a too self-confident or self-deceiving act-utilitarian who was at all ready to believe that this was so in his own case. And, secondly, if the cases are unusual, as they are, received opinion, which condemns the encouragement and practice of these vices, is not required by the utilitarian to withdraw any of its condemnation. What he does is to give the condemnation a ground which Rescher does not provide (except where, *malgré soi*, he gives a good utilitarian ground). What received opinion is condemning is the vice, i.e. the bad *habit of mind* or disposition; and this is to be condemned if it is a bad thing *in general* to encourage, which is indeed so in the case of these dispositions.

Coming now to the intuitive level, I have already argued that the rational act-utilitarian who knows his own human limitations will carry on at this level just like any other good man. His intuitive principles no doubt, *if* he is a good man, include proscriptions of envy, jealousy, and ill will, and he has good reason to believe that the best way of acting optimifically is to abide by these principles. So long as he remains at the intuitive level this is what he will do. In fact, he will behave exactly like an intuitionist, except that he has an awareness which the intuitionist lacks of the necessity for asking, sometimes, the critical question 'Are the intuitions I have the ones I ought to have?'.

Let me therefore ask Rescher, in conclusion, to consider whether his objections to utilitarianism really extend to the form of it which I have been defending, or whether he has not been rather too easily taken in by the caricature of it put about by its less sympathetic opponents, whom, rather than him, I have been satirizing in this essay.

15

Some Reasoning about Preferences:
A Response to Essays by Persson,
Feldman, and Schueler

I TAKE the occasion of Schueler's essay (1984) to discuss, not only some points raised in it, but also other closely related points made in essays by F. Feldman (1984) and I. Persson (1983), all about an argument in *MT* chs. 5, 6. I must confess that in that book I as usual succumbed to my besetting vice of concision and failed to spell out moves and countermoves in the game which I thought would at once suggest themselves to an alert reader. Obviously there are many more of these than can be discussed in a short book, and in my long experience it is not always of much use to do so, both because, whichever of them one chooses, somebody is bound to pick on others and because, even if one does mention a point, it is often not noticed. The second sentence of the preface to *LM* still represents my considered policy. However, since even Feldman, whose essay is fuller and more careful than the other essays, misunderstands my argument, it looks as if I did not express myself clearly enough. I shall therefore explain some points which affect more than one of the three essays, leaving aside minor points or those which affect only one of them.

All three discussants use arguments which would imperil my position only if I held that, if someone has a preference that something should happen to him, he has no other preferences that could outweigh this. This is the point of Persson's example (1983: 47) about Odysseus and the Sirens, which was very much in my mind when I wrote the book but got omitted from the final draft, and of the similar example of the dentist, which also occurs in *MT* 93, 97, as well as that of the alcoholic or drug addict (Schueler 1984: 78; Persson

From *Ethics* 95 (1984).

1983: 44; cf. *FR* 174). In all these examples, somebody has a preference as to what should happen to him in a certain contingency. Odysseus prefers that, should be beseech his companions to release him, they should not do so, because if they do their ship will be wrecked (Homer, *Od.* 12); the dentist prefers that, should he be in the position of the child he is drilling, *his* dentist should go on drilling, because otherwise he would not avoid toothache in the future; the drug addict's beneficent friend prefers that, were he to be in precisely the addict's situation with the addict's preferences, his preference to be given more of the drug should be frustrated; the alcoholic (now cured) prefers that, were he himself to form a preference for having a drink, the drink should be withheld. In all these cases, a now-for-then preference is in conflict with a foreseen then-for-then preference, in the sense that if the first is satisfied the second will not be. In some of the cases the thens are hypothetical thens; but that, as we shall see later, makes no difference to the argument.

It is obvious that, if my view were that a preference on the part of *A* that, were he in *B*'s situation with *B*'s preferences, *x* should happen to him, automatically overrides all other preferences that *A* has, then these would be counter-examples to it. Although Odysseus will then prefer that his sailors should set him free, he does not now prefer overall that they then should. My argument was (put in terms of this example) that if he fully represents to himself now the situation that he will then be in, with its preferences, he will form *a* preference for what should happen to him in that situation that is identical in content and strength to that which he will actually have in that situation. And in the other examples my view is that the person who fully represents to himself another's situation with the other's preferences will form *a* preference for what should happen to him, were he in the other's situation with the other's preferences, which is identical in content and strength to that which the other has. I did not say that he would have no other preferences that might conflict with this; indeed I said a lot about what happens when he has (*MT* 93, 103 ff.).

Obviously one may have *a* preference (what Feldman calls a 'preliminary preference'—1984: 277) that, if *p*, then *q* rather than not q, but at the same time have preferences for other things whose realization would make it impossible that q, or which cannot be realized if q. Thus Odysseus, although (indeed because) he fully represents to himself the situation (with its preferences) that he will be in when he hears the Sirens, prefers *overall* that his sailors should not set him free, although he will then have, *pro tanto*, a preference that they should free him, in order that he might listen to the songs from near by. He prefers overall that they should not free him because he also knows that if they do the ship will be wrecked, which will frustrate other much stronger preferences which he now has and knows that he will later have (e.g. to see Ithaca and Penelope again).

So there is a contradiction in Odysseus' will very analogous to that which occurs in moral cases (*MT* 109). He is compelled to choose in order to resolve the contradiction; and my thesis is that he will choose on the basis of the overall strength of his preferences. No one preference has a veto. All I need for my argument in the moral case is that the person who fully represents to himself the situation of another, including the other's preferences, should inevitably form a preference that, if he were in the other's situation with the other's preferences, that should happen to him which the other now prefers should happen to *him*. He can form this preference but have it overridden by other stronger preferences, if they really are stronger. The similarity of my view to utilitarianism survives this overriding of preferences by stronger preferences; that, indeed, is precisely what a preference-utilitarian will say should happen.

In other words, the argument in *MT* ch. 5 is intended to put into our moral reasonings the ingredient supplied by the preferences of other people, which universalization, employed thereafter in ch. 6, compels us to treat as of equal weight with our own equal preferences and those of all affected parties. The argument of ch. 6 shows how these preferences are to be balanced against one another: they are to be given equal weight, strength for strength, as utilitarianism also enjoins. The claim is not made that any person's preference (whoever he is and whatever its content or weight) has to override those of other affected parties if its weight does not entitle it to. The 'veto' theory (if I may call it that) which is attributed to me by Schueler and Persson, and at one point by Feldman though he subsequently relents, is very far from what I intended, and I thought (mistakenly it turns out) that I had made this clear. The 'veto' theory is well expressed by Feldman (1984: 277) as follows: 'A fully rational critical thinker could never endorse any ought-statement that prescribed an action that anyone preferred not to occur.'

It is worth noticing that these objections are similar in form to one made by Kant, to a too-simple application of the Golden Rule (1785: § 2 n.) and advanced by some against my own views, in spite of receiving a very clear answer in *FR* 155 ff. The point made in *FR* is that, if the judge is applying the same Golden Rule to all those affected by his decision, he will punish the criminal if that produces the best consequences for their interests overall, considered impartially. If the laws and the legal system are good, and the accused is really guilty, this will be the case. If they are defective, or if he is not, it will not be the case. A utilitarian theory of punishment can deal quite easily with the vulgar objections to this claim based on bizarre examples, on the lines suggested for the handling of all such examples in *MT* ch. 8, and for the treatment of justice in ch. 9 (see also H 1986). The answers to them depend on the recognition that moral thinking takes place at more than one level, at one of which (the intuitive) we apply without question the principles of justice (as the judge should in this case) but at the other of which we justify these principles by their acceptance-utility and settle conflicts between them, and between any two moral principles, in unusual cases.

The other main move made by Feldman (1984: 278) and Schueler (1984: 79) concerns the need, if my argument is to go through, to treat hypothetical cases as if they were going to be actual. This point is discussed at length on *MT* 112-16, a discussion to which neither refers. I shall not repeat the argument here, and I cannot at present improve on it. Another way, however, of putting the same point may help: the universal principles involved in any moral prescription are nomological and not merely material conditionals, as Schueler supposes (1984: 80; see p. 75).

If that argument be accepted, then Feldman cannot legitimately make the move he makes (ibid.) when he says that (in the car-bicycle example adapted from *MT* 109) the following propositions logically both could be true and do not contradict one another because the first is categorical and the second conditional or hypothetical:

(9) *A* prefers, with strength 3, that the bicycle be moved;

(11) *A* preliminarily prefers, with strength 2, that, if he were to swap places with *B*, then the bicycle should not be moved.

A, if he is making a moral judgement, and if (9) and (11) are true, will have to find some universal prescription to accept which is consistent with the preferences described in them. But if it is a requirement of moral thinking that hypothetical cases just like the actual in their universal properties should be treated as if they were going to be actual, then he cannot do this. If the moral prescription has to be universal, and hypothetical cases count as if they were going to be actual, then he will have to say the same about the situation in which he has swapped roles with *B* as he does about the actual case. In other words, he has to prefer universally (since the prescription he is going to adopt has to be a universal one) that the same thing should be done whether he occupies the role of *A* or of *B*. So, if he sticks to the preference described in (11), he will have to abandon that described in (9), and vice versa. Both preferences, though they are of different strengths, are positive, and they are for outcomes both of which cannot be realized, if the same has to be done whichever individual occupies whichever role. I further argue in *MT* that his decision which to abandon will depend on the strength of the preferences (which is in accord with utilitarianism); but that is not immediately relevant to the move of Feldman that I am presently discussing and which I think I have now countered.

Exactly the same answer can be given to the similar objection raised by Schueler (1984: 79). He makes the further mistake (specifically warned against in *MT* 113–14) of taking together hypothetical cases different in their universal properties from the actual and cases which differ only in the roles played by individuals. His 'lethal injection' case is of the former sort and therefore has no bearing on the argument. Feldman's principle AC, which he rightly rejects (1984: 280), involves an analogous though not identical mistake: 'If A prefers, with strength S, that p occur, then A preliminarily prefers, with strength S, that if A swaps roles with B, then p occur.'

References and Bibliography

References are to the date and page-number, unless otherwise indicated. References beginning '*LM* ', '*FR* ', and '*MT* ' are to *The Language of Morals* (H 1952), *Freedom and Reason* (H 1963*a*) and *Moral Thinking* (H 1981*a*) respectively. References beginning with 'H' are to the first part of the bibliography; the rest, beginning with the author's name unless this is clear from the context, are to the second. Full bibliographies of the writings of R. M. Hare are to be found in H 1971*a* (to 1971), *MT* (1971–81), and H 1988 (1981–7).

1. Writings of R. M. Hare

1952 *The Language of Morals* (Oxford UP). Translations: Italian, *Il linguaggio della morale* (Ubaldini, 1968); German, *Die Sprache der Moral* (Suhrkamp, 1972); Spanish, *El lenguaje de la moral* (Mexico UP, 1975). Also Chinese and Japanese.

1954 Review of *What is Value?*, by E. W. Hall, *Mind* 63.

1955*a* 'Universalisability', *Ar.Soc.* 55. Repr. in H 1972*b*.

1955*b* 'Ethics and Politics' (two articles and letters), *Listener* (Oct.). First article repr. in H 1972*d*. Spanish trans. in *Revista Universidad de San Carlos* 33, 1955.

1960 '"Rien n'a d'importance": l'anéantissement des valeurs est-il pensable?', in *La Philosophie Analytique*, ed. with foreword by L. Beck (Minuit). English version in H 1972*d*.

1962 Review of *Generalization in Ethics*, by M. Singer, *Ph.Q.* 12.

1963*a Freedom and Reason* (Oxford UP). Translations: Italian, *Libertà e ragione* (Il Saggiatore, 1971); German, *Freiheit und Vernunft* (Patmos, 1973; Suhrkamp). Also Japanese.

1963*b* 'Descriptivism', *British Academy* 49. Repr. in *The 'Is–Ought' Question*, ed. W. D. Hudson (Macmillan, 1969) and in H 1972*b*. Spanish trans. in *Etica y analysis*, ed. E. Rabossi and F. Salmeron (Mexico UP).

1964 'Pain and Evil', *Ar.Soc.* suppl. 38. Repr. in *Moral Concepts*, ed. J. Feinberg (Oxford UP, 1969) and in H 1972*b*.

1967 'Some Alleged Differences between Imperatives and Indicatives', *Mind* 76. Repr. in H 1971*c*.

1968 Review of *Contemporary Moral Philosophy*, by G. J. Warnock, *Mind* 77.

1971*a* 'Wanting: Some Pitfalls', in *Agent, Action and Reason*, ed. R. Binkley *et al.*, (Toronto UP and Blackwell). Repr. in H 1971*c*.

1971*b* *Essays on Philosophical Method* (Macmillan). Italian translation: *Studi sul metodo filosofico* (Armando, 1978).

1971*c* *Practical Inferences* (Macmillan).

1972*a* *Essays on the Moral Concepts* (Macmillan).

1972*b* 'Rules of War and Moral Reasoning', *Ph. and Pub. Aff.* 1. Repr. in *War and Responsibility*, ed. M. Cohen *et al.* (Princeton UP, 1974). Repr. in H 1989.

1972*c* 'Nothing Matters' (English version of H 1960), in author's *Applications of Moral Philosophy* (Macmillan).

1977 'Justice and Equality', *Etyka* 14 (Warsaw, in Polish with English and Russian summaries). English version (revised) in *Justice and Economic Distribution*, ed. J. Arthur and W. Shaw (Prentice-Hall, 1978). Discussion in *Dialectics and Humanism* 6 (Warsaw, 1979, in English). Repr. in H 1989.

1978 'Prediction and Moral Appraisal', *Mid-West Studies* 3.

1981*a* *Moral Thinking: Its Levels, Method, and Point* (Oxford UP).

1981*b* Review of *The Expanding Circle*, by P. Singer, *New Republic* (Feb.).

1984*a* 'Utility and Rights: Comment on David Lyons' Paper', *Nomos* 24: *Ethics, Economics and the Law*. Repr. in H 1989.

1984*b* 'Arguing about Rights', *Emory Law J.* 33. Repr. in H 1989.

1984*c* 'Liberty and Equality: How Politics Masquerades as Philosophy', *Social Philosophy and Policy* 2. Repr. in H 1989.

1984*d* 'Rights, Utility and Universalization: A Reply to John Mackie', in *Utility and Rights*, ed. R. Frey (U. of Minnesota P.). Repr. in H 1989.

1985 'Philosophy and Practice: Some Issues about War and Peace', in *Philosophy and Practice*, ed. A. P. Griffiths (R. Inst. of Ph. Lectures 19, suppl. to *Philosophy* 59, Cambridge UP). Repr. in H 1989.

1986 'Punishment and Retributive Justice', in *Philosophical Topics 14*, ed. J. Adler and R. N. Lee (U. of Arkansas P.). Repr. in H 1989.

1987*a* 'An Ambiguity in Warnock', *Bioethics* 1.

1987*b* '*In Vitro* Fertilization and the Warnock Report', in *The Ethics of Human Design*, ed. R. Chadwick (Croom Helm).

1987c 'Why Moral Language?', in *Metaphysics and Morality: Essays in Honour of J. J. C. Smart*, ed. P. Pettit *et al.* (Blackwell).

1987d 'Appendix' (Comment on Putnam 1987), *Critica* 18.

1988 Replies to Critics in *Hare and Critics*, ed. N. Fotion and D. Seanor (Oxford UP).

1989a 'Philosophy of Language in Ethics', in *Sprachphilosophie*, ed. M. Dascal *et al.* (De Gruyter).

1989b *Essays on Political Morality* (Oxford UP)

2. Other Writings

ANSCOMBE, G. E. M. (1958), 'Modern Moral Philosophy', *Philosophy* 33.

ARISTOTLE, *Nicomachean Ethics* and *De Anima* (refs. to Bekker pages, and to *NE* unless otherwise stated).

AUSTIN, J. L. (1961), *Philosophical Papers* (Oxford UP).

—— (1962), *How to Do Things with Words* (Oxford UP).

BENNETT, J. (1965), ' "Whatever the Consequences" ', *Analysis* 26.

BENTHAM, J. (1825), *The Rationale of Reward*.

BLACK, M. (1964), 'The Gap between "Is" and "Should" ', *Ph.Rev.* 73.

BLACKBURN, S. (1971), 'Moral Realism', in *Morality and Moral Reasoning*, ed. J. Casey (Methuen).

—— (1981), 'Rule-Following and Moral Realism', in *Wittgenstein: To Follow a Rule*, ed. S. H. Holtzman and C. M. Leich (Routledge).

—— (1985), 'Supervenience Revisited', in *Exercises in Analysis: Essays in Honour of Casimir Lewy*, ed. I. Hacking (Cambridge UP).

—— (1984), *Spreading the Word* (Oxford UP).

BRANDT, R. B. (1952), 'The Status of Empirical Assertion Theories in Ethics', *Mind* 61.

—— and FIRTH, R. (1955), 'The Definition of an Ideal Observer Theory in Ethics', *Ph. and Phen. Res.* 15.

—— (1963), 'Towards a Credible Form of Utilitarianism', in *Morality and the Language of Conduct*, ed. H.-N. Castaneda and G. Nakhnikian (Wayne UP).

BURKE, E. (1815), *Reflections on the Revolution in France*.

BUTLER, J. (1726), *Sermons*. Part repr. in *The British Moralists*, ed. D. D. Raphael (Oxford UP, 1969).

DAVIDSON, D. (1980), *Essays on Actions and Events* (Oxford UP).

DWORKIN, R. M. (1981), 'Is there a Right to Pornography?', *Oxford J. of Legal St.* 1.

EWING, A. C. (1959), *Second Thoughts in Moral Philosophy* (Routledge).

FELDMAN, F. (1984), 'Hare's Proof ', *Ph.St.* 45.

FOOT, P. R. (1959), 'Moral Beliefs', *Ar.Soc.* 59 (1958/9). Repr. in her *Virtues and Vices* (Blackwell, 1978) and in her *Theories of Ethics* (Oxford UP, 1967).

—— (1961), 'Goodness and Choice', *Ar.Soc.* suppl. 35.

FRANKENA, W. K. (1958), 'MacIntyre on Defining Morality', *Philosophy* 33.

GAUTHIER, D. P. (1968), 'Hare's Debtors', *Mind* 77.

GRICE, H. P. (1956), see STRAWSON (1956).

GRIFFIN, J. P. (1982), 'Modern Utilitarianism', *Rev. Int. de Ph.* 36.

HASLETT, D. (1974), *Moral Rightness* (Nijhoff).

HAUGELAND, J. (1982), 'Weak Supervenience', *APQ* 19.

HODGSON, D. (1967), *The Consequences of Utilitarianism* (Oxford UP).

HUME, D. (1739), *A Treatise of Human Nature*.

KANT, I. (1785), *Groundwork of the Metaphysic of Morals* (refs. are to the Royal Prussian Academy edn., trans. H. J. Paton, *The Moral Law*, Hutchinson, 1948).

KIM, J. (1982), 'Psychophysical Supervenience as a Mind-Body Theory', *Cognition and Brain Theory* 5.

—— (1983), 'Supervenience and Supervenient Causation', *S.J. Phil.* 22, suppl.

LEWIS, C. I. (1946), *An Analysis of Knowledge and Valuation* (Open Court).

LEWIS, H. (1985), 'Content and Community' (symposium with A. Woodfield), *Ar. Soc.* suppl. 59.

LOVIBOND, S. (1983), *Realism and Imagination in Ethics* (Blackwell).

LYONS, D. (1965), *Forms and Limits of Utilitarianism* (Oxford UP).

McDOWELL, J. (1981), 'Non-Cognitivism and Rule-Following', in *Wittgenstein: To Follow a Rule*, ed. S. H. Holtzman and C. M. Leich (Routledge).

MACINTYRE, A. (1957), 'What Morality is Not', *Philosophy* 32.

—— (1959), 'Hume on "Is" and "Ought"', *Ph.Rev.* 68.

—— (1984), 'Relativism, Power and Philosophy', *Proc. of Am. Ph. Assn.* 59 (1985).

MACKIE, J. L. (1972), Review of Hodgson, *Consequences of Utilitarianism*, *Ph.Q.* 23.

—— (1977), *Ethics: Inventing Right and Wrong* (Penguin).

McLEAN, S. (1980), *Female Circumcision, Excision and Infibulation*, with contributions from Marie Assaad, Eddah Gachukia, Esther

Ogunmedede, Awatif Osman, Isabelle Tevoedfre, and Awa Thiam (London, Minority Rights Group).

MILL, J. S. (1861), *Utilitarianism.*

MOORE, G. E. (1903), *Principa Ethica* (Cambridge UP).

PERSSON, I. (1983), 'Hare on Universal Prescriptivism and Utilitarianism', *Analysis* 43.

PLATO, *Protagoras* and *Republic* (refs. to Stephanus pages).

POPPER, Sir KARL (1959), *The Logic of Scientific Discovery* (Hutchinson). Originally published as *Logik der Forschung* (Springer, 1934).

PUTNAM, H. (1987), 'Rationality in Decision Theory and in Ethics', *Critica* 18.

QUINE, W. V. (1951), 'Two Dogmas of Empiricism', *Ph.Rev.* 60. Repr. in the next item.

—— (1953), *From a Logical Point of View* (Harvard UP).

RAWLS, J. (1955), 'Two Concepts of Rules', *Ph.Rev.* 64.

—— (1971), *A Theory of Justice* (Harvard and Oxford UPs).

RESCHER, N. (1975), *Unselfishness* (U. of Pittsburgh P.).

RICHARDS, D. A. J. (1970), *A Theory of Reasons for Action* (Oxford UP).

ROSS, W. D. (1930), *The Right and the Good* (Oxford UP).

RYLE, G. (1949), *The Concept of Mind* (Hutchinson).

SCHILLER, F. C. S. (1929), *Logic for Use* (Bell).

SCHUELER, G. F. (1984), 'Some Reasoning about Preferences', *Ethics* 95.

SEARLE, J. R. (1964), 'How to Derive "Ought" from "Is" ', *Ph.Rev.* 73.

SINGER, M. (1961), *Generalization in Ethics* (Knopf).

SINGER, P. (1972), Review of Hodgson, *Consequences of Utilitarianism*, *Ph.Rev.* 81.

—— (1981), *The Expanding Circle: Ethics and Sociobiology* (Oxford UP).

SMART, J. J. C. (1973) and WILLIAMS, B. A. O., *Utilitarianism: For and Against* (Cambridge UP).

STRAWSON, Sir PETER (1950), 'Truth', *Ar.Soc.* suppl. 24.

—— and GRICE, H. P. (1956), 'In Defense of a Dogma', *Ph.Rev.* 65.

URMSON, J. O. (1950), 'On Grading', *Mind* 49.

—— (1975), 'A Defence of Intuitionism', *Ar.Soc.* 75.

VENDLER, Z. (1976), 'A Note to the Paralogisms', in *Contemporary Aspects of Philosophy*, ed. G. Ryle (Oriel P.).

WARNOCK, G. J. (1967), *Contemporary Moral Philosophy* (Macmillan).

—— (1971), *The Object of Morality* (Methuen).

WARNOCK, Baroness MARY (1984), chairman, *Report of the Committee of Inquiry into Human Fertilization and Embryology* (London, HMSO, Cmnd. 9314).

WILLIAMS, B. A. O. (1973), see SMART, J. J. C.

—— (1979), chairman, *Report of the Committee of Inquiry on Obscenity and Film Censorship* (London, HMSO, Cmnd. 7772).

WITTGENSTEIN, L. (1953), *Philosophical Investigations* (Blackwell).

—— (1956), *Remarks on the Foundations of Mathematics* (Blackwell).

Index

abortion 10, 165
acceptance-utility 64, 171 n., 224,
    228, 237, 240 f., 248
actual and logically possible cases
    197, 204, 223, 234 f., 249; *see also*
    unusual c.
affective states 40; *see also* suffering
agapē 219 n.; cf. 229
alike, no two cases ever exactly
    55 f.
amoralism 86, 186 f., 211
analyticity 9, 146, 176; cf. 79
animals, treatment of non-human
    123, 162; *see also* vegetarians
Anscombe, G. E. M. 52-9, 64 f.
anthropological statements,
    theories 137, 150
approval 20
Archangel 111 f., 188-90, 205,
    222-8, 239-42
Aristotle 6 f., 66, 99, 126, 157, 183,
    202, 219, 226, 228, 241
assent 20, 22, 184-6
attitudes 15, 82, 89-91 f., 96, 104,
    106, 122, 125, 128, 140
Austin, J. L. 21, 120
author of moral decision not
    privileged 218 f.
authority, moral 57, 106
Ayer, Sir Alfred 94, 101

benevolence 158
Bennett, J. 52
Bentham, J. 100, 232 f.
bilinguals 121
Black, M. 131
Blackburn, S. 66, 69, 72, 126
Brandt, R. 214
Burke, E. 221

Butler, J. 58, 60, 63 f., 110, 239

cannibals 115
Carnap, R. 101
causal explanation, laws 73-6
choices 35-48, 91
circumcision, female 115, 126, 128 f.
cognitivism 18, 47 f., 82, 92-7 f.,
    101, 105
colour-blindness 91, 105 f.
    communication 114-17, 121,
    127 f., 182
compassion 171 n.
conflicts, moral 2 f., 110, 223, 238-
    40; of preferences 246
conscience 58-60, 110, cf. 64
consensus 3, 6, 13; cf. 46, 147 f.
consequences, consequentialism 37,
    39, 42 f., 45, 52 f., 57, 218, 248
contraception 164
contradiction in will 187
conversational implicature 22
convictions, moral 6-8, 11, 13, 96,
    106, 109 f., 178, 180-2; *see also*
    intuitions
corrupt mind 52-4, 57 f., 64
cost-benefit analysis 4, 111, 189
covering law theory 73
'cruel' 123-5
cultures, cultural relativism 106,
    114-17, 121 f., 128 f., 236

David, King 10
Davidson, D. 68, 72, 81, 114
deontologists 3
descriptive meaning 18, 26 f.,
    47, 95-7, 116-19, 122-30, 177,
    207 f.; independent variation of

descriptive meaning (*cont.*):
123; d. properties trivially
supervenient 70 f.
descriptivists 3, 18 f., 24, 30, 47 f.,
66, 72, 82, 87, 94–7, 100–7, 113–
30, 149, 213
desires 196–201, 217–20, 233 f.; *see
also* preferences; bad d. 221;
prudent d. 217 f.
dialectic 7
disagreement 27, 29, 102–6, 114,
178
dispositions 16, 19, 40, 90, 189,
237–40, 243
Dworkin, R. M. 3, 101

education vi, 55 f., 60–2, 104–6,
109 f., 190, 221–30, 240 f.
emotivists 33, 97, 100 f.
equality 161, 172, 216
equilibrium, reflective 2, 145, cf.
172
erosion of good principles 241 f.
error theory 83
essences, essential definitions 78,
139
evaluative and descriptive words
66, 114, 128; primarily and
secondarily e. w. 116 f., 122–9;
e. meaning 116–18, 122–30
Ewing, A. C. 34
exceptions 54
excluded middle 25 f., 29
existence 84–9, 92
existentialism 58
expectable utility 63, 189
experience 7, 55, 183–5, 200
extrapolation of use of
value-words 123

facts, existence of 84, 88 f.;
institutional and brute f. 143;
moral f. 47, 88 f., 92; moral
judgements and imperatives not
equivalent to nor dependent on
subjective f. 15, 19, 23 f., 34,
46, 46–9; f. not sole object of

reasoning 99; place of f. in moral
reasoning 145 f., 148, 152, 155 f.,
167, 181–3, 186, 200, 208 f., 222,
235
factual information and
rationality 37–9, 43–5, 182 f.,
186
fanatic 219 f.
Feldman, F. 245–50
fiction 57, 61, 64, 109
Foot, P. R. 192
formal and substantial questions
9 f., 175–8; f. and s. components
of ethical theory 234, 238; f.
constraints 153 f., 192–4, cf.
206 f., 234; formality of ethical
theory 43 f., 214 f.
Frankena, W. K. 10, 224

Gauthier, D. 211
Geach, P. T. 66
'general' facts in Rawls 166
generality of principles 49–65; g.
and specificity 50, 144; 'absolute'
g. 54 f.; *see also* universality
generations, justice between 162 f.
God 58, 60, 65, 76, 110–12, 189,
240
golden rule arguments 144, 197 f.,
248; *see also* universalizability
goodness and rightness of actions
225–8
Govind Singh 127
Grice, H. P. 22, 176
Griffin, J. P. 41
Grosseteste, R. 66
guilt, sense of 64

Hägerström, A. 101
Hampshire, Sir Stuart 101
happiness 41
Harald, King 78
Haslett, D. W. 45, 214
Haugeland, J. 69
Hesiod 126
Hodgson, D. 64, 233

Homer 246
Hume, D. 76, 82, 93, 100
hypothetical cases 44, 55, 75, 158,
186 f., 197, 200, 204, 209, 216 f.,
222 f., 249; h. choice theories 151

I myself, thinking of some person
as 185
ideal observer 65, 151–5, 158–60,
215
ideals 219 f.
Ignatius, St 57, 64
imagination 42, 184, 198, 209
impartiality 153–5, 158, 188, 199,
201 n., 209, 215, 220, 234–6, 248
imperatives, imperativism 15, 20–4,
35, 45 f., 50, 119 f., 128, 182 f.; i.
distinguished from moral
judgements 29 f., 182
individual references, roles 52 f.,
74, 81, 154 f., 158, 166 f., 191–4,
201–5, 209, 250; distinguished
from rigged descriptions 52, 154,
192–4; from logically unique r.
and relations 194 f.
infanticide 165
institutions 64, 132 f., 141–4;
institutional and brute facts 143
insufficient reason 160, 167–70
insurance strategy 170
intentionality, i. contexts 23, 94
interests 39–42, 46, 110 f., 153,
164, 215–17, 229, 248
intuitions, intuitionists 2–6, 13, 64,
95 f., 100, 104–7, 109–11, 118 f.,
147 f., 172 f., 178, 189, 202,
212 f., 220, 226, 237–40

Jesus 127
justice 145–74 (esp. 160 f., 164),
216, 224, 237, 248

Kant, I., Kantians 3, 5, 15, 99,
107 f., 141 n., 187, 213, 229, 248
Kim, J. 69

knowing how 126 f.
knowledge, limited 65, 111; *see also*
uncertainty; direct k. and k. by
inference 184
Kripke, S. 196

laws of nature 74
Leibniz 203
levels of moral thinking, critical
and intuitive 64, 109–11, 156 f.,
175, 189 f., 202–5, 221–8, 237–
44, 248
Lewis, C. I. 45, 120, 159, 216
lexical ordering 157
liberty 173; priority of l. 158, 161,
171
'like' and universal properties 55
linear inference 148
linguistic intuitions, rules,
conventions, usage 47, 91, 124,
149, 208; l. research 102, 149
logic as element in rationality 43–
5, 177; l. and conceptual
analysis 97 f.; *see also* meaning;
logical truth 176 f.
Lovibond, S. 128
Lyons, D. 239

Mach, E. 75
McDowell, J. 126
MacIntyre, A. 10, 113–30, 131
Mackie, J. L. 34, 72, 82 f., 86, 90,
92, 95, 113, 233
McLean, S. 115
mathematics 149 f.
maximin strategy 170–2
meaning and logic 8, 37, 97 f., 107,
122, 129, 145, 148 f., 152 f.,
159 f., 175, 180, 183, 212; m. and
rationality 42 f.; m. and shared
beliefs 114, 127; m. rules 70
mental events 81; m. states 16 f.,
19, 33, 81, 94, 97; *see also*
affective s.
metaethics 10, 175, 237 f.

metaphysics and philosophical
  logic 85
militarism 11, 57
Mill, James 100
Mill, J. S. 108, 233
monism, anomalous 68, 80 f.
Moore, G. E. 58 f., 63 f., 71, 118,
  239
'moral' 206
moral judgements not primarily
  statements of fact 100, 107; nor
  wholly unlike them 36, 207 f.
moral majority 8, 11
moral principles, rationality of 35,
  43-8
moral reformers 127
motivation 152, 225, 232
multilateral situations 188

Nathan 10
nationalism 11
natural kinds 76 f., 81
naturalism 9, 71 f., 100-5, 108,
  143; 180 f., 208, 213, cf. 192
necessity 69-72; kinds of n. 71 f.,
  75-80
negligence 38
neutrality of ethical theory 43, 122,
  182; *see also* relevance
'nice' 67-9, 74
nomologicality 75 f., 81, 248
non-cognitivism 18
non-descriptivism 33, 74, 82, 87,
  94 f., 101, 118, 213; n.-d. and
  subjectivism distinguished 18, 20,
  24, 34; n.d. compatible with
  truth-falsity and rightness/
  wrongness of moral statements
  24-31, 34, 46; with rationalism
  101, 107, 213

non-naturalism, n.-n. qualities 66,
  71 f., 118
noumenal green-room 163
Nozick, R. 101

objectivity, objectivism 14, 33 f.,
  83, 113, 146; *see also* subjectivism;
  objective prescriptivity 95
obligation to keep promises 131-44
observance-utility 64
ontology 82 f., 87-9
original position 150-72
overridingness 44

pacifism 11, 106
pain 40 n.
paradigm case argument 127
Parfit, D. 166 n.
Paton, H. J. 15
Paul, St 3
performatives 21, 137-9
Persson, I. 245-50
Plato 5, 7, 40; cf. 59, 148, 202, 217
pluralism 17, 147
political morality vi, 59
Popper, Sir Karl 8, 12
population policy 166
possible people, interests of 164-6
possible worlds 75 n., 203
practical issues 1, 3, 5
practical syllogisms 69
pragmatic implication 22
preferences 12, 41 f., 109, 111, 158,
  184-9, 245-50
prescriptions 24, 33-7, 46, 184;
  rationality of p. 37, 93; universal
  p. 60, 109-11, 158, 163, 180,
  186 f., 196, 201, 217-19, 229
prescriptive meaning 35, 128; *see
  also* evaluative m.
prescriptivism 21, 24, 33 f., 62, 96,
  116, 130, 149, 217
prescriptivity 119; of moral
  judgements 44, 107, 125, 179-83,
  186, 194, 209, 214, 234; of
  principles 49, 206, 210
presupposition 71, 119
Prichard, H. 101
prima facie (intuitive) principles
  202 f., 206, 221, 227, 235; cf. 57-
  65
primary goods 158, 172

primary qualities 68; *see also* secondary q.
probability 63, 109, 202-5, 223 f., 227, 240; objective p. 167-72
promising 131-44
prudence 206, 215-20, 229
punishment 248
Putnam, H. 101
Pythagoras 127

Quine, W. V. 114, 146, 176

racism 209-11
rationality 12, 33-48, 64, 92 f., 99-112, 113, 129, 152, 169, 175, 182 f., 186, 213, 215-18, 241; r. and rightness 38, 63, 224 f., 227 f.
Rawls, J. 17, 49 f., 101, 145-74, 191, 206, 214-16, 221
real definitions 139
realists 66, 72, 75 n., 82-94, 105, 128
reasons, reasoning 8, 12 f., 17, 29 f., 60, 66, 91-3, 95 f., 99 f., 107 f., 112, 119, 122, 128, 175, 182 f., 212 f., 232; r. of state 59
relativism 14, 33, 90 f., 100, 102-6, 119; *see also* cultures
relevance 38 f., 191-211; not neutral but dependent on principles 193
Rescher, N. 231
Richards, D. 163, 174
rigged descriptions, principles 52, 154, 192-4
'right' and 'wrong', used of moral statements and principles 24-31, 34, 46
rights 173, 237
risk, attitudes to 169
Ross, Sir David 66, 101, 146, 221
rules of thumb 64, 156, 205, 221, 223, 241; constitutive and regulative r. 132-42; r.-following 126 f.
Ryle, G 126

sadist, 221
Schiller, F. C. S., 124
Schueler, G. F. 245-50
Searle, J. R. 131
secondary qualities 68, 76, 89-91
selection of prima facie principles 110, 223
self-defeatingness 233
Sidgwick, H. 148
simplicity and generality 51, 60-2, 157, 225
sincerity 197 f., 201
Singer, M. 50, 192
Singer, P. 65, 124, 233,
situation ethics 58
slavery 173
Smart, J. J. C. 38, 224
special pleading 65, 188, 205, 222, 239
specificity 50, 53, 63-5, 72, 221 f.
statements are truth-claims 207
Stevenson, C. L. 15, 26, 95, 101
Strawson, Sir Peter 88, 176
stress 65, 111, 156, 221 f., 240 f.
subjectivity, subjectivism 14-32, 33 f., 47 f., 82 f., 90, 146-8, 213
suffering 11, 40, 123, 183-7, 200
supervenience 66-81; strong and weak s. 69; trivial s. 70 f.
sympathy 124
synonymy 176, cf. 114
synthetic a priori 71, 139, 141 n.

Tarski, A. 118
theory, ethical and its relation to practice 1-13, 213; formality and neutrality of e. t. 43
time, limited 65
tragic dilemmas 2, 109
Truman, H. 59
truth and falsity of moral statements 10, 19, 23, 87, 96; of prescriptions 70
truth, duty to tell 207
truth-conditions and meaning 18, 95 f., 120 f., 127; cf. 30

uncertainty, choices under 172
understanding what someone says
  and u. why 125 f., 192
universality and generality 50-6,
  61, 153 n., 221; senses of 'u' 51 f.
universalizability 10 f., 28, 30 f.,
  44-6, 55 f., 68, 70, 107 f., 122;
  cf. 154, 158, 163, 179-83, 186,
  192-5, 201 n., 204, 207-11, 214,
  222, 234
unusual or fantastic cases 64,
  109 f., 157, 216, 221-3, 227-30,
  234, 240
Urmson, J. O. 17, 66, 127
utilitarians, u.-ism 3-5, 11, 41, 45
  57, 59-65, 108-11, 155, 158-60,
  164-72, 187, 202, 212-30, 231-
  44, 247 f.; act- and rule-u. 49,
  60-5, 188 f., 222-7, 238-40;
  general and specific r.-u. 62-5,
  222-4, 227; see also cost-benefit

utility, average and total 165, 168,
  215; diminishing marginal u.
  171 n., 216; see also acceptance-u.

vegetarians 8, 91, 104-6, 162
veil of ignorance 152-8, 165-9,
  206, 215, 223
Vendler, Z. 196
verificationism 95 f.
veto, nobody has 44, 247
vicarious affects 231-44

Warnock, G. J. 49, 192
Warnock, Lady 4 f.
'water' 76-9
Williams, B. A. O. 3, 101, 219 n.,
  241 n.
Wittgenstein, L. 7, 88, 126-8,
  208 n.